The Middle East

Other books in the Current Controversies series:

The Abortion Controversy
Alcoholism
Assisted Suicide
Biodiversity
Capital Punishment
Censorship
Child Abuse
Civil Liberties
Computers and Society
Conserving the Environment
Crime
Developing Nations
The Disabled
Drug Abuse
Drug Legalization
Drug Trafficking
Espionage and Intelligence Gathering
Ethics
Europe
Family Violence
Free Speech
Garbage and Waste
Gay Rights
Genetic Engineering
Guns and Violence
Hate Crimes
Homosexuality
Hunger
Illegal Drugs
Illegal Immigration
The Information Age
Interventionism
Iraq
Issues in Adoption
Marriage and Divorce
Medical Ethics
Mental Health
Minorities
Nationalism and Ethnic Conflict
Native American Rights
Police Brutality
Politicians and Ethics
Pollution
Prisons
Racism
Reproductive Technologies
The Rights of Animals
Sexual Harassment
Sexually Transmitted Diseases
Smoking
Suicide
Teen Addiction
Teen Pregnancy and Parenting
Teens and Alcohol
The Terrorist Attack on America
Urban Terrorism
Violence Against Women
Violence in the Media
Women in the Military

The Middle East

Auriana Ojeda, *Book Editor*

Daniel Leone, *President*
Bonnie Szumski, *Publisher*
Scott Barbour, *Managing Editor*
Helen Cothran, *Senior Editor*

CURRENT CONTROVERSIES

GREENHAVEN PRESS®

THOMSON
GALE™

San Diego • Detroit • New York • San Francisco • Cleveland
New Haven, Conn. • Waterville, Maine • London • Munich

THOMSON

GALE

For more information, contact
Greenhaven Press
27500 Drake Rd.
Farmington Hills, MI 48331-3535
Or you can visit our Internet site at http://www.gale.com

Cover credit: © AFP/CORBIS

LIBRARY OF CONGRESS CATALOGING-IN-PUBLICATION DATA

Middle East / Auriana Ojeda, book editor.
p. cm. — (Current controversies)
Includes bibliographical references and index.
ISBN 0-7377-1583-9 (lib. : alk. paper) — ISBN 0-7377-1584-7 (pbk. : alk. paper)
1. Middle East. I. Ojeda, Auriana, 1977- . II. Series.
DS44 .M49 2003
956.05—dc21 2002035393

Printed in the United States of America

Contents

Chapter 3: How Can the Israeli-Palestinian Conflict Be Resolved?

Foreword

By definition, controversies are "discussions of questions in which opposing opinions clash" (Webster's Twentieth Century Dictionary Unabridged). Few would deny that controversies are a pervasive part of the human condition and exist on virtually every level of human enterprise. Controversies transpire between individuals and among groups, within nations and between nations. Controversies supply the grist necessary for progress by providing challenges and challengers to the status quo. They also create atmospheres where strife and warfare can flourish. A world without controversies would be a peaceful world; but it also would be, by and large, static and prosaic.

The Series' Purpose

The purpose of the Current Controversies series is to explore many of the social, political, and economic controversies dominating the national and international scenes today. Titles selected for inclusion in the series are highly focused and specific. For example, from the larger category of criminal justice, Current Controversies deals with specific topics such as police brutality, gun control, white collar crime, and others. The debates in Current Controversies also are presented in a useful, timeless fashion. Articles and book excerpts included in each title are selected if they contribute valuable, long-range ideas to the overall debate. And wherever possible, current information is enhanced with historical documents and other relevant materials. Thus, while individual titles are current in focus, every effort is made to ensure that they will not become quickly outdated. Books in the Current Controversies series will remain important resources for librarians, teachers, and students for many years.

In addition to keeping the titles focused and specific, great care is taken in the editorial format of each book in the series. Book introductions and chapter prefaces are offered to provide background material for readers. Chapters are organized around several key questions that are answered with diverse opinions representing all points on the political spectrum. Materials in each chapter include opinions in which authors clearly disagree as well as alternative opinions in which authors may agree on a broader issue but disagree on the possible solutions. In this way, the content of each volume in Current Controversies mirrors the mosaic of opinions encountered in society. Readers will quickly realize that there are many viable answers to these complex issues. By questioning each author's conclusions, students and casual readers can begin to develop the critical thinking skills so important to evaluating opinionated material.

Current Controversies is also ideal for controlled research. Each anthology in the series is composed of primary sources taken from a wide gamut of informational categories including periodicals, newspapers, books, United States and foreign government documents, and the publications of private and public organizations. Readers will find factual support for reports, debates, and research papers covering all areas of important issues. In addition, an annotated table of contents, an index, a book and periodical bibliography, and a list of organizations to contact are included in each book to expedite further research.

Perhaps more than ever before in history, people are confronted with diverse and contradictory information. During the Persian Gulf War, for example, the public was not only treated to minute-to-minute coverage of the war, it was also inundated with critiques of the coverage and countless analyses of the factors motivating U.S. involvement. Being able to sort through the plethora of opinions accompanying today's major issues, and to draw one's own conclusions, can be a complicated and frustrating struggle. It is the editors' hope that Current Controversies will help readers with this struggle.

Greenhaven Press anthologies primarily consist of previously published material taken from a variety of sources, including periodicals, books, scholarly journals, newspapers, government documents, and position papers from private and public organizations. These original sources are often edited for length and to ensure their accessibility for a young adult audience. The anthology editors also change the original titles of these works in order to clearly present the main thesis of each viewpoint and to explicitly indicate the opinion presented in the viewpoint. These alterations are made in consideration of both the reading and comprehension levels of a young adult audience. Every effort is made to ensure that Greenhaven Press accurately reflects the original intent of the authors included in this anthology.

"[Arab] governments face the enormous challenge of protecting Islam as the official religion while subduing powerful Islamist organizations who threaten their regimes."

Introduction

Over the last century, the Middle East has been a hotbed of ethnic rivalry, political and economic instability, religious conflict, territorial dispute, and war. Much of the friction in the Middle East derives from various interpretations of Islam and how the religion should be applied to politics and society. Knowing the basic principles of Islam is the first step toward understanding how contrasting ideas about the religion cause conflict in the Middle East.

Islam is the fastest-growing religion in the world, second only to Christianity in numbers of adherents. Muslims live in all parts of the world, but the majority of Muslims are concentrated in the Middle East and Asia. Islam has two meanings: peace and submission to Allah (God). Muslims believe that Islam is the only true religion and that it was revealed by the prophet Muhammad in Arabia in the seventh century. Muslims are divided into two major groups, the Shiites and the Sunnis. The difference between these two groups is rooted in Islam's early history. Sunnis believe that the first four caliphs, or rulers, after the prophet Muhammad were legitimate leaders. Shiites believe that Muhammad's son-in-law, Ali, should have succeeded him directly, a belief that renders the first four caliphs illegitimate. Their theology differs slightly, but both groups adhere to the five pillars of Islam: acknowledging that there is no true god except God and that Muhammad is the prophet of God; praying five times a day toward Mecca; giving alms to the poor; fasting during the month of Ramadan (the ninth month of the lunar year); and making an annual pilgrimage to Mecca for those who are financially and physically able. Islam also requires belief in six articles of faith, which are belief in God, belief in the messengers and prophets of God, belief in the Revelations and the Koran (the Islamic holy book), belief in angels, belief in Judgment Day, and belief in the ultimate power of God or God's decree. Other precepts of Islam are concerned with matters such as diet, clothing, personal hygiene, business ethics, responsibilities toward parents, spouses, and children, marriage, divorce, inheritance, civil and criminal law, fighting in defense of Islam, relations with non-Muslims, and much more.

All Muslims believe in the six articles of faith and adhere to the five pillars of Islam, but they differ in how they interpret the Koran and the shari'a (Islamic law). Colonel B.S. Burmeister, in his essay "The Rise of Islamic Fundamentalism," identifies two major divisions within Islam, the modernists and the revivalists. He argues that modernists believe in the inerrancy of the Koran, but they interpret its strictures in a modern context. Modernists accept secular governments, religious diversity, and the emancipation of women. Most Muslim modernists condemn terrorism and advocate individual relationships with God. Revivalists favor a literal interpretation of the Koran and a return to traditional Islamic ideas. These Muslims are extremely pious and closely follow the teachings of the Koran and Muhammad. They regularly attend mosques, and many promote a theocratic government and enforcement of the shari'a. Revivalists are frequently referred to as Islamists or Islamic fundamentalists. Modernists and revivalists often clash over how Islamic states should be run.

The tension between modernists and revivalists is best illustrated by Egypt's political conflicts in the mid–twentieth century. In 1928, Hassan el-Banna, the oldest son of an Egyptian watchmaker, established the Muslim Brotherhood, the first modern Islamic fundamentalist organization. The Brotherhood was comprised of young men who were frustrated with Egypt's poverty and lack of opportunities. In addition, they resented Western, especially British, presence in the Middle East, and feared that their Islamic culture would be subsumed by what they perceived as Western decadence and godlessness. They also resented the growing Zionist movement in Europe, which claimed that Palestine, a region of land inhabited by Muslims in the Middle East, should belong to the Jews because it was their Holy Land. El-Banna and his followers believed that part of the reason that their society had declined was that Muslims had fallen away from the fundamental teachings of the Koran and Muhammad. They believed that if they could influence people to return to the traditional practice of Islam, they could drive out the Western enemy and resurrect the great Islamic empire of the Middle Ages, when the Middle East led the West in cultural, philosophical, and scientific achievements. To achieve this goal, they organized centers to educate people in the fundamentals of Islam and recruit them to the Brotherhood's cause to drive the Western enemy out of the Middle East.

The Muslim Brotherhood spread quickly. Within a year of its inception, the Brotherhood boasted over fifty branches within Egypt. In 1945, frustrated with what they viewed as a disorganized and ineffectual monarchy, members of the Muslim Brotherhood ran in parliamentary elections. They suffered an abysmal defeat, partly as a result of election fraud committed by King Farouk's administration, which perceived the revivalist Brotherhood as threatening to the monarchy's moderate regime. In retaliation, the Brotherhood launched a wave of political assassinations and acts of terror throughout Egypt. Judges were assassinated, ministers were shot, bombs were placed inside businesses, and Jewish citizens were attacked. In response to the violence, Prime Minister Mahmoud el-Noqrashi banned the Brotherhood in 1948. El-Noqrashi was assassinated by a Brotherhood member twenty days later. His successor, Ibrahim Abdel-Hadi, dealt severely with the Brotherhood, and by the time his administration fell, over four thousand members were imprisoned. In 1951, the Brotherhood was permitted to return to activity under limited conditions, but they were prohibited from participating in political activities.

In 1953, a group of army officers led by Lieutenant Colonel Gamal Abdel-Nasser overthrew King Farouk's monarchy and declared Egypt a socialist republic with Islam as the official religion. Nasser took over the position of prime minister in 1954 and was voted the first president of the Egyptian Republic in 1956. Nasser clashed with the Muslim Brotherhood from the start; although he declared Islam the official religion of Egypt, he was dedicated to the idea of secular rule, unlike the Brotherhood, who believed that Egypt should be ruled by the shari'a.

In 1954, Nasser banned the organization for the second time because of their insistence on Islamic law. Infuriated, one Brotherhood member attempted to assassinate Nasser. He failed and was executed along with five other members. Over four thousand more members were also arrested and thousands more fled to Syria, Saudi Arabia, Jordan, and Lebanon. In 1964, Nasser exonerated the imprisoned members, but after their release, they made three more attempts on his life. Nasser executed the top leaders of the Brotherhood in 1966, and imprisoned hundreds of others.

Following Nasser's death in 1970, his successor, Anwar Sadat, strove to improve relations between the government and the Muslim Brotherhood. He released most of the members from prison and promised them that the shari'a would be implemented as Egyptian law. Although the Brotherhood remained illegal, it was tolerated, and in some cases encouraged, by the government as a counterbalance to leftist forces whom Sadat saw as threatening to his regime. However, many Brotherhood members were impatient with Sadat's administration and lost trust in Sadat when he signed a peace agreement with Israel—which the Brotherhood considered an enemy of Islam—in 1979. Brotherhood members assassinated Sadat in 1981, and his promises to the Brotherhood went unfulfilled.

Over the last twenty years, the Muslim Brotherhood has ostensibly renounced violence as a means of achieving their goals, but numerous sister organizations, such as al-Qaeda, Egyptian Jihad, and Hamas, have perpetrated countless acts of terrorism against their own governments and Western nations. Other Arab states, such as Saudi Arabia and Libya, have also experienced a rise in the number of Islamist organizations operating within their borders. Their governments face the enormous challenge of protecting Islam as the official religion while subduing powerful Islamist organizations that threaten their regimes. Analysts agree that most Muslims prefer an Islamic government to a secular government, but few advocate the kind of Islamist regime practiced by the Taliban in Afghanistan or by the Ayatollah Khomeini in Iran in the 1980s. The Taliban, for example, which ruled Afghanistan from 1994 to 2001, banned televisions and radios, prohibited women from working and attending school, and reinstituted the shari'a, which demanded strict punishments for crimes, such as public stoning for adultery and amputation for theft. The relentless conflict in the Middle East demonstrates how difficult it is to balance modernism and revivalism.

Current Controversies: The Middle East offers various perspectives on Islam, its role in the Middle East, and how conflict in the Middle East affects the rest of the world. The articles in this anthology should give readers a thorough understanding of current problems in the Arab world and possible solutions to them.

Chapter 1

Why Is the Middle East a Conflict Area?

Chapter Preface

Over the last hundred years, the Middle East has been one of the most troubled regions in the world. According to the *Economist*, "With barely an exception, [the Arab world's] autocratic rulers, whether presidents or kings, give up their authority only when they die; its elections are a sick joke; half its people are treated as lesser legal and economic beings, and more than half its young, burdened by joblessness and stifled by conservative religious tradition, are said to want to get out of the place as soon as they can." However, at one time, the Middle East eclipsed the West in intellectual, scientific, and literary achievements. To examine what factors contribute to the Middle East's present circumstances, a team of scholars, headed by Egyptian sociologist Nader Fergany, published the Arab Human Development Report 2002, an analysis of the Arab world's strengths and weaknesses. The study found three key attributes for success in the modern world that the Arab community lacks: freedom, knowledge, and womanpower.

According to the study, the absence of freedom is most visible in the region's absolute autocracies, sham elections, and restrictions on the media and on civil society. The authors contend that "the [global] wave of democracy that transformed governance . . . in the 1980s and early 1990s has barely reached the Arab states." Most Arab countries have the trappings of democracy—elections are held—but, more often than not, they are riddled with corruption. According to the study, people are given jobs because of whom they know, not what they know. Consequently, Arab states are plagued with an unmoving, unresponsive central authority and an incompetent public administration. As stated by Haidar Abdel-Shafi, former member of the Palestinian Legislative Council, "In some Arab countries, the absence of democracy-based participation . . . and free and honest periodic elections has formed an obstacle to the development process." Moreover, freedom of expression is sharply limited; according to a study by Freedom House, an American-based monitor of political and civil rights, not one Arab country had a completely free media in 2001.

Another obstacle to development in the Middle East, according to the study, is the shameful state of the education system. The authors allege that illiteracy rates in the Middle East are higher than the international average and even higher than the average in developing countries. Sixty-five million adult Arabs are illiterate, and nearly two-thirds of them are women. Approximately 10 million Arab children receive no schooling at all, and those who do demonstrate high failure and repetition rates. The most important consequence of this crisis in education is the system's inability to provide students with the skills necessary to participate in the development of Arab societies. According to the study, the quality of education is so poor that students emerge from school unprepared for the rapidly accelerating change produced by the world's increasing reliance on technology and the emergence of a global economy. These generations of inadequately educated Arabs harm the Middle East as a whole because young people are unable to compete in the international market.

The Arab world is also harmed, according to the study, by the systematic repression of half of its population—women. According to the authors, Arab women live under the control of a patriarchal society that relegates women to maternal figures without a place in the political or economic arena. Women's participation in the region's political and economic life is the lowest in the world, evident in the low number of women in parliaments, cabinets, and the workforce. Moreover, one in two Arab women can neither read nor write. In fact, the authors contend, Arab countries place a much lower premium on female education than they place on male education. The result of this inequality is that "society as a whole suffers when a huge proportion of its productive potential is stifled, resulting in lower family incomes and standards of living," as stated by the study.

According to the *Economist*, it is unclear how the Middle East reached such a troubling state. However, the Arab Human Development Report does offer solutions to reverse the deficits of freedom, knowledge, and womanpower, such as drastic improvements in elections, schools, and the treatment of women. However, these improvements require years of social, political, and economic change and the cooperation of the Arab world. Only time will tell whether the study's suggestions will be implemented successfully. The authors in the following chapter debate what other factors contribute to conflict in the Middle East.

Islam Causes Conflict in the Middle East

by Tarek E. Masoud

About the author: *Tarek E. Masoud is executive director of the Presidential Oral History Project and a research fellow in the Program on Contemporary Political History at the University of Virginia.*

In the early morning hours of January 22, 1997, in Cairo, Egypt's crowded capital, security forces conducted a series of house-to-house raids, detaining at least seventy-eight young Egyptians. Such mass arrests are not uncommon in that country of 60 million, where the state's war on Islamic fundamentalism has resulted in the arrest of hundreds—if not thousands—since 1981, most from villages in the Egyptian hinterland or from Cairo's slums, where angry young men with little hope and few prospects often turn to Islam for comfort. Police routinely arrest individuals on the mere suspicion of Islamist activity. It is often said that a beard—the universal sign of Islamic zealotry—is all it takes to arouse such suspicion.

But the men arrested on that January morning were not typical of Islamic fundamentalists. They were not poor, bearded slum dwellers but the well-groomed children of some of Egypt's most prosperous families. In fact, they were not Islamic fundamentalists at all. Their crime was "Satan worship" and "contempt" for Islam, the state religion. The evidence against them, though not an abundance of facial hair, was equally flimsy: a taste for black clothing and heavy-metal music. Their case caused a major stir in Cairo. Egypt's state-appointed mufti, Sheikh Nasr Farid Wassil, urged the "Satanics," as they were called, to repent or face the death penalty for "apostasy" in Egypt's Islamic courts. The president of al-Azhar university—the country's top Islamic institution—declared Satan worship part of a Zionist conspiracy to corrupt Egypt's youth, and an Egyptian author published a study linking Satanism to the popular dance, the Macarena: "I noticed that each time they played the Macarena columns of smoke filled the discos and that the movements of the dance were part of Satanic rites." In the end, the suspects repented, declared their faith in Allah and His prophet, and were released.

Pretenses to Legitimacy

To the casual observer, this is both tragic and comic. One would think a state that arrests people for listening to rock music must be having some difficulty coming to terms with things Western. But if we dig deeper, a glaring contradiction becomes evident: Islam is both avowed enemy and jealously defended state religion. Police routinely arrest Muslim radicals who would overturn the political order and establish a state based on their faith; but they also arrest those who would offend that faith. This is not merely a case of the Egyptian government throwing its Islamist opponents a few bones in an attempt to quiet them down. It is part of a repressive state's attempt to make up for what it lacks in democratic legitimacy by wrapping itself in the mantle of Islamic legitimacy. The result is the strengthening of radical Islam, its anti-Western agenda given credence by the very government that is trying to eradicate it. By setting itself up as the guardian of the faith, the government invites itself to be judged by its fidelity to it. But the Egyptian state, like all states, is a classic accumulator of power; it acts in its interests, and to do so, it must be flexible, free from the shackles of religious certainty. Invariably it must act in a way that affronts the faith—making peace with Israel, aiding the United States against Iraq—and when it does, the faithful protest furiously. University students take to the streets, and groups like the New Jihad and the Gama'a Islamiya wage a terrorist war that today threatens to rend asunder Egypt's social fabric.

"Islam is both avowed enemy and jealously defended state religion."

This disturbing phenomenon is replicated throughout the Arab world: in Saudi Arabia and Jordan, in Libya and Iraq. All these regimes seek Islamic justification for their rule. Some, like Egypt, Libya, and even Iraq and Syria, do this by seeking Islamic cover for their policies. Others, like the monarchies in Jordan and Morocco, pursue a more direct relationship to the creed, ruling by dint of their claim of descent from Islam's prophet, Muhammed. In all of them, a battle is fought between the faith and the state on two fronts: on the one hand, the state tries to force Islamic radicals to respect its power and recognize its sovereignty; on the other, it contends with them to prove itself religiously purer, more Islamic—and thus more deserving of public fealty. But when the game of politics is played by the rules of Islam, governments, which by necessity must make bargains that offend the morally consistent, are ill-equipped to win.

The Right to Rule

As Francis Fukuyama has most recently noted, "All regimes capable of effective action must be based on some principle of legitimacy." This legitimacy can take many forms. In revolutionary Egypt, for example, Gamal Abdel Nasser, the fiery exponent of Arab nationalism, ruled by virtue of what author Max Weber called "charismatic legitimacy." Charismatic leaders "in times of spiritual, economic, ethical, religious or political emergency were neither appointed officials nor trained and salaried 'professionals'. . . but those who possessed specific physical and spiritual gifts which were regarded as supernatural, in the sense of not being available to everyone." But this kind of legitimacy is obviously not sustainable for long periods of time; it is a purely personal phenomenon and cannot be passed from one leader to another. Weber suggests two additional and more durable forms of legitimacy: "rational-legal" and "traditional." Writer Milton Esman, in a recent restatement of these Weberian categories, argues that these include: a democratic mandate, usually a victory at the polls in a free and fair election; the ability to meet public expectations for individual safety and the security of property, and the ability to provide the public with goods like food, shelter, health care, education, and ample opportunities to earn a decent livelihood; and identification with the society's norms and values. The most legitimate governments score well on all of these measures; the least legitimate score poorly, and thus need to rely on coercion and force to maintain power.

"The first foundation of legitimacy—namely, democracy—seems to have eluded the Arab world."

Though we live in what author Fareed Zakaria has called the "democratic age," the first foundation of legitimacy—namely, democracy—seems to have eluded the Arab world. Of the twenty-one states of the Arab League, not one could be called democratic or liberal. In fact, in its annual survey of political rights and civil liberties entitled Freedom in the World, Freedom House ranks six Arab states (Iraq, Sudan, Libya, Saudi Arabia, Somalia, and Syria) as the world's worst in terms of political freedom. And unlike in China or Russia under communism, there is no great grassroots movement for democracy in the Arab world, largely because democracy does not resonate with the average Arab. It has no basis in the Arab past and is tainted by its association with the West. Though many Arab governments hold sham elections in which the leader is swept into office with 99.99 percent of the vote and 99.99 percent voter participation, such displays are done mostly for the outside world. When Iraq's "parliament" last winter passed a resolution refusing to respect the U.S.-imposed no-fly zones over the northern and southern parts of the country, the move was recognized as a poor attempt by Saddam Hussein to paint his transgressions as a function of popular will, and thus as somehow more legitimate. One perceptive observer of the Middle East has noted that leaders like Hussein have no idea how real democracies work and do not realize that those accustomed to holding elections would find such shams offensive. Meanwhile, to the people of the region, they are an irrelevance.

Other Arab governments, such as the monarchies of the Persian Gulf, naturally find any traffic with democratic symbols distasteful, and thus try to build legitimacy by providing significant material benefits to their people. The Gulf states have been particularly successful in this regard, using their oil wealth to create massive cradle-to-grave welfare states. For example, Saudi Arabia spends billions of dollars to give its citizens free education and health care, as well as subsidized housing and utilities. But this kind of mass bribery can only go so far, and poorer states like Egypt understandably find it unfeasible. Thus Middle Eastern states turn to the third traditional measure of legitimacy—emphasizing shared values. And in the great proselytizing culture of the Arab world, the most overriding public value, that which can immediately claim sympathy from all segments of the population, is Islam.

Legitimacy Through Islam

Islam has served as the basis for political legitimacy in the Arab world ever since the death of the prophet Muhammed in the seventh century A.D. Until the early part of this century, the Islamic world was united under a series of successive caliphates, the leader of which, the caliph (or khalifah, in Arabic), was considered the prophet's temporal and spiritual successor. The first four caliphs, men who had known the prophet during his lifetime and who were each selected by learned men of the community, are referred to today as the Rightly Guided Caliphs. In the annals of Islamic history, they are considered the most legitimate of rulers, truest to the prophet's legacy, and their period is considered a kind of Islamic utopia to which the Muslim world still aspires. After these four men passed from the scene (three of them were murdered, perhaps indicative of what sort of utopia this was), the caliphate became a much more traditional monarchy, changing hands over the centuries between competing dynasties. The first of these monarchic caliphates, that of the Umayyads, was established some thirty years after Muhammed's death and was the first regime of the Arab world to face serious problems of legitimacy. According to the Islamic historian Shireen Hunter, the Umayyads "based their rule on the absolute divine will," declaring it "part of a predetermined godly plan." This justification of Umayyad legitimacy contributed to one of the most vigorous theological debates of the day in Islam, that of predeterminism versus free will. As Hunter points out, since the Umayyads argued that their reign was God's will, they came out in favor of the predeterminist school. In this way, Islamic theological speculation eventually devoted itself to explaining—or challenging—the legitimacy of the prevailing political order.

"Islam has served as the basis for political legitimacy in the Arab world ever since the death of the prophet Muhammed."

The caliphate system was not a theocratic rule of the priests. The caliph acquired his religious credentials as "guardian of the faith" and "shadow of God on Earth"—qualities essential to his legitimacy as ruler—by virtue of assuming power, not the other way around. The full force of Islamic thought was put to the service of explaining the caliph's right to preside over the community of believers, which is why some of the most vigorous periods of Islamic judicial thought occurred when the caliphate shifted from one dynasty to another, as each one needed to explain itself anew. When the last of the great caliphates of the Islamic world, that of the Ottoman sultans, crumbled in 1918, the successor regimes of the modern Middle East inherited this notion of religion as ratifier of rulers. It was natural that they too would seek Islamic sanction for their power.

"Religion can only be manipulated for so long."

Even the leaders of the so-called secular Arab nationalist movements that arose in Syria, Egypt, and Iraq in the wake of the Ottoman collapse sought a place for Islam in their ideology, realizing that without it, the project would be unable to capture the Arab imagination. One of the founders of the Baath school of Arab nationalism, a Syrian intellectual named Michel Aflaq, though a Greek Orthodox Christian, declared Islam to be the most sublime expression of Arabism, born of the genius of Arab civilization and history. Absent Islam, being an Arab meant nothing. As the late scholar Hasan Enayat put it, "The Arabs cannot promote their identity without at the same time exalting Islam, which is the most abiding source of their pride.". . .

The Bargain Gone Bad

Nowhere are the costs of manipulating Islam to legitimize the state more evident than in the kingdom of Saudi Arabia. Saudi Arabia's story involves a Faustian bargain struck by the monarchs of that country with a brand of fundamentalist Islam called Wahhabism. The bedrock of the royal family's legitimacy is a pact made over two hundred and fifty years ago by the founding father of the Saud family, Mohammed Ibn Saud, with the religious revivalist from which the sect takes its name, Mohammed bin Abdul Wahab.

Abdul Wahab was troubled by the un-Islamic practices—the veneration of saints and ancestors, and even of the prophet Muhammed—that had crept into the popular exercise of Islam over the centuries, and was determined that they be purged. In Mohammed Ibn Saud, a minor sheik in a small desert town, he saw just the man to take up his cause. A deal was struck: Saud undertook to fight all comers for the sake of God, and Abdul Wahab promised him God's help and bounty (and assured him that God would allow him to collect taxes in any lands he captured.) Regarding themselves as the only true believers and all others as apostates and infidels, Saud's hordes conquered much of the eastern half of the Arabian peninsula, then nominally under Ottoman control. His son and grandson continued the run and by 1814 reached the Iraqi and Syrian borders before being crushed by the Ottoman governor of Egypt.

In the years following, Saudi power in the peninsula ebbed and flowed, until by the beginning of this century the family had lost its lands and was living in exile in Kuwait. In 1902 a scion of the family, Abdul Aziz Ibn Saud, began a campaign to recapture his family's glory. He took the city of Riyadh, the seat of the old Saudi kingdoms, and set his sights on the entire peninsula. To do this he manipulated things to marvelous effect. He assembled Bedouin tribesmen in camps he called hijra (migration, as in migration from ignorance to enlightenment) and schooled them in Wahhabism's radically unitarian doctrine. By 1927, the ikhwan (brothers, as they were now called) had helped Abdul Aziz capture most of Arabia and were poised to take their holy war to the rest of the Muslim world. But Abdul Aziz was a realist, and he knew his limits—if the British and French had looked the other way when he took the inconsequential oases of the Arabian peninsula, they would not be so lax in defending their interests in Syria and Iraq. He wisely concluded a treaty with the British recognizing his sovereignty over the lands he controlled but binding him to go no further. The ikhwan were outraged at this betrayal of their cause. There were more infidels to crush, more lands to bring under Islam's sway. Some eight thousand of them continued to lead raids on territories outside the Saudi domain. The contract with the faith could not hold up against the contract with British power, and by 1929 Abdul Aziz was forced to crush his former disciples.

The British political resident in Arabia at the time, Sir Percy Cox, later opined that Abdul Aziz had not made a single mistake in the process of setting up his kingdom. He was wrong. Abdul Aziz did not take away the central lesson of his clash with the ikhwan, that religion can only be manipulated for so long. Instead of abandoning Wahhabism, he went on to build a state that honored Wahabi sensibilities (in rhetoric, if not always in reality.) For example, when Wahabi leaders objected to his plan to introduce radio to the kingdom, on the grounds that it could carry the influences of Satan, Abdul Aziz arranged for them to hear a radio-transmitted recitation of the Koran, arguing that nothing that could propagate the word of God could be from Satan. Abdul Aziz based the kingdom's laws on interpretations of shariah (Islamic law); thus women are denied the right to drive automobiles, the theater is banned, Islamic education in schools is compulsory, and businesses are forced to close five times daily for prayer. All of this is enforced by the muttawas—old, bearded men employed by the government's Committee for Enjoining Virtue and Preventing Vice—who patrol the streets in search of violators of God's law: women whose ankles are exposed, men who avoid prayer, couples who show too much affection. . . .

"The answers that radical Islam offered to the woes of the Sudanese have only made them worse."

The tragic story repeats itself throughout the Arab world. The bleak situation in Sudan offers a glimpse of what might come. Sudan's president from 1969 to 1985, Jaafar Nemeiri . . . began his fling with Islamist movements in order to counter the threat from the radical left. But in 1983 he went one step further, instituting shariah law with its harsh penal code mandating executions for adultery and amputation for theft. To further please the Islamists, Nemeiri relegated the country's Christians to second-class status and suspended the Christian south's limited autonomy. The civil war between the northern Arabs and the southern Christians, which Nemeiri had succeeded in ending in 1972, began anew. Moderates and Christians resigned from the government, and Nemeiri replaced them with Islamists. In 1985, with his country wracked by war, Nemeiri was overthrown by the military. But the Islamists had had their taste of power, and in 1989 they staged a coup of their own. Today Sudan is a so-called Islamic state, one that shows little remaining trace of the public euphoria that attended its founding. Islamic economics, which promised to repair the damage wrought by decades of statist economics, turned out to be nothing more than harsh "free market" reforms designed to concentrate wealth at the top. The Sudanese pound was sharply devalued, and price controls and subsidies were lifted almost overnight. This shock therapy, coupled with the civil war in the south, has caused a famine the severity of which is measured in terms of hundreds of thousands of lives. The country's human rights record is abysmal. In addition to the so-called Islamic punishments, political opposition is not tolerated, jails are filled with political detainees, and newspapers critical of the regime—even ones with Islamic coloration—are closed by the government. The answers that radical Islam offered to the woes of the Sudanese have only made them worse. The Islamic utopia was not to be, for it existed only in the rhetoric of leaders anxious to exploit the popular longing for a more ordered, prosperous society.

"The 'Islamic State'. . . is incompatible with democracy."

Unfortunately, there seem to be no forces opposing this trend toward radical Islamic ruin. There are, of course, educated, secular elements in the Arab world, but they are being squeezed from below, by Islamists with popular support and sympathy, and from above, by regimes eager to curry favor with the Islamists and equally suspicious of calls for more open government. In short, there is nowhere for these moderates to go. There would be hope for the Arabs if the lessons of Sudan would register; but the unifying motif of the Arab world's encounters with Islam seems to be lessons not learned. . . .

Seeking Solutions

What, then, is to be done? Some have suggested that the regimes of the Middle East should institute democratic reforms, that once given the right to vote, people will elect those who can deliver a better life. More likely, they will just elect fundamentalists who can woo them with their rhetoric. But even if Islamists come to power this way, it is argued, they will be forced by the necessities of democratic consensus building to moderate their stances in the hope of winning the next election. It is more likely that they will ensure that there will never be another one. The "Islamic State," as it is conceived by leading Islamists, is incompatible with democracy. After all, the Islamic utopia strives to recreate the reign of the prophet and the caliphs—and they were never elected, never had to contend with a free press, and were unfamiliar with the need for religious freedom.

"The idea of the Islamic state . . . will be proven bankrupt only after it has had its day in the sun."

And so perhaps the only solution to the Arab world's political dysfunctions, the only way to free the Arab mind of the shackles of radical Islam and cause it finally to look elsewhere for the answers to its dilemmas, is to allow the Islamists their day. Consider Iran's Islamic Revolution of 1979. That was the Thirty Years' War turned on its head: the faith won, and the princes were sent into ignominious exile. But the reign of God on Earth is coming undone, having proven itself unable to provide for the needs of its people. Unemployment and inflation are uncontrollable, and Iran's isolation from the West has cost it countless billions of dollars. The country's youthful electorate sounded a note of protest in May of 1997, when it swept the perceived moderate, Mohammed Khatami, into power. Debates have raged about whether Khatami is indeed a moderate (this writer has argued that the reputation is largely undeserved), but there is no question that Iran's people are fed up with theocratic politics. Lay intellectuals, like the scholar Hosein Dabbagh (known by his pen name, Abdol Karim Soroush), argue that theocracy contradicts Islam's basic tenets by investing power in a clerical elite, and truly moderate clerics call for the religious establishment to rescue itself from political life before the people rise up against it and force it from society altogether. This, coupled with Iranians' unmistakable desire for more traffic with the West, indicate a drift toward a post-Islamic era in that country.

The idea of the Islamic state, the dream of the pious polity, will be proven bankrupt only after it has had its day in the sun. This is not altogether surprising. Arab nationalism, too, had to reign before it was discredited. It is already happening in Sudan, and as the Islamist challenge grows stronger in Egypt and Saudi Arabia, perhaps it can be expected to happen there too. Arab countries learn not to touch the fire only by getting burned—and, as we have seen, sometimes even that is not enough to drive the message home. It is not enough that Islam is not working in Iran or Sudan; Saudi Arabia, Egypt, and other Arab countries must also have their flings with it. It is too late to pull back from the brink.

Radical Islam has already been set loose and legitimated by governments that manipulated it to give them legitimacy of their own. If the Egyptian government ceases arresting heavy-metal fans and branding them Satan worshippers, the Islamists will not be diminished; they will merely have a new platform on which to attack the regime. And so it seems Islam will not be denied the halls of power. But, just as certainly, it will not be allowed to dwell there forever.

Islam Does Not Cause Conflict in the Middle East

by A.Z. Hilali

About the author: *A.Z. Hilali is a research scholar at the Department of Security Studies at the University of Hull in England.*

Dr. Keith Suter's article 'Is Islam a Threat to International Peace and Security?' in *Contemporary Review*, December 1996, is based on an interpretation of Samuel Huntington's well-known article, 'The Clash of Civilisations' (*Foreign Affairs*, summer 1993), in which Huntington argues that Islam must inevitably clash with a western liberal civilisation bent on exporting its values and that Islam may overwhelm the West. However, Dr. Suter is not clear about the Islamic revivalism and renaissance in the post–Cold War era. He irrationally blames all Islamic groups as threats to world peace and he also confuses Muslim societies and Islamic values. In this regard, Islam as a religion is no more and no less a source of conflict or threat to the world than any other religion whether Christianity, Judaism, or Hinduism. Many of its values are applicable to all human beings, not only Muslims. So Keith Suter should actually discuss the current Islamic activities in some Muslim countries by placing them in their proper socio-political context, not in the broader concept of Islam.

My comments seek only to offer some thoughts provoked by Dr. Suter and to clarify certain aspects of the arguments which are the major sources of conflict. It needs to be recognised that the current Islamic movements are fuelled not by absolute economic disparities but by socio-political 'relative deprivation'. Islamic revivalism is in many ways the successor to failed nationalist programmes and offers an Islamic alternative or solution, a third way distinct from capitalism and communism. Islamists argue that Islam is not just a collection of beliefs and ritual actions but a comprehensive ideology embracing public as well as personal life. It is important to understand that Islamic activism is a cause of concern but not for alarm and challenge to any civilisation. Like radicals throughout history, Islamic radicals become moderate, once accommodated

A.Z. Hilali, "Islam and Peace: A Rejoinder," *Contemporary Review*, vol. 270, April 1997, pp. 184–87.

and incorporated in the socio-political mainstream. If they do not, they perish or become sociologically irrelevant cults. Therefore, extremism can best be reduced through gradual democratisation, a process and a system of governance which the West is deliberately not encouraging in the Muslim world, particularly in the Middle East.

Islamic Resurgence

In the early 1980s, Islamic resurgence became synonymous in the Western world with political extremism, terrorism, hostage crises and suicide bombings. As the decade came to a close, Islamic resurgence began a new phase; Islamic movements began to participate in the political system instead of opposing it. However, the two momentous events of 1991—the Gulf war and the break-up of the Soviet Union—are casting their shadow over relations between the West and the arc of predominantly Muslim countries ranging from Central Asia in the east to North Africa in the West. Until recently the Muslim countries were divided between the US and Soviet Union but the collapse of the Soviet Union has made the West, led by the United States, into the principal external enemy of pan-Islamism. It is interesting to note that at the time of the Cold War, most of the Muslim states were loyal allies of the West against the 'Evil Empire' of the Soviet Union. This was a time when the West was using religion as a weapon and even financed many of the fundamentalist groups to contain and to stop the flood of communism.

"Extremism can best be reduced through gradual democratisation."

So far, however, the reality is that Islamic revivalism is neither a product of the Iranian revolution nor a result of Libyan extremist policies. The depth of frustration and anger is a reaction against European colonial rule, support for unpopular regimes and the internal weaknesses of the Muslim governments. Although some scholars argue that the present awakening in the Muslim world is a response to the decline of power and the loss of divine favour, in fact, the current revolt is a product of the weak economies of the Muslim countries, illiteracy and high unemployment, especially among the younger generation. The lack of political institutions and absence of democracies in the Muslim world is also an immediate cause of extremism. In this context, the Muslim demands for change are no different from the demands in Eastern Europe. In many Muslim countries the secular nationalists and Islamists are united in the common cause of popular democracy. They are demanding the right to gain legitimate power with ballots rather than bullets. These forces are also cooperating with each other to topple monarchies, military dictators and authoritarian governments. They blamed their governments for their countries' backwardness and failure to achieve economic self-sufficiency and development. In addition to these internal reasons, there are also some external factors which push the Islamists to struggle for the rights and protection of Muslims which are under the siege of oppressive rule. Muslims are worried about the people of Palestine and they cannot ignore the inhuman massacres of Muslims in Bosnia, Chechnya and Kashmir. Such experiences tend to make Muslims think that the West is against them.

The causes of the resurgence differ from country to country, but common catalysts and concerns are identifiable. The Arab world is under the grip of socio-political mobility and mass desertion. Egypt, Saudi Arabia, Tunisia and Algeria are facing a great challenge from Islamists and [those] who have a strong hold over resources, people and organisations. They also recruit many followers and members in the army, intelligence and other governing institutions. In this context, Algeria is the best example where the Islamic Salvation Front (FIS) won the 1992 election with a clear majority but the West publicly opposed the victory of FIS and encouraged the military to suppress the Islamists. The result is obvious; Algeria is under the shadow of bloodshed and the country is in a state of collapse.

> ***"The current revolt is a product of the weak economies of the Muslim countries, illiteracy and high unemployment."***

In Egypt, the Muslim Brotherhood was born 64 years ago and it was the West, particularly the United States, who provided the blood and energy for Islamists to counter Nasser's policies and Soviet influence in Egypt. Now, Islamists have taken deep root and they are demanding a true democratic system and Islamic laws in the country. Thousands of people have been killed in clashes with government forces and the consequences are nothing except destruction. One expert, Martin Karamer, points out that every Arab ruler threatened by Islamic opposition has found a way to contain it or confront it. The Arab governments have responded in various ways to the Islamic knock at their door. Tunisia and Morocco prefer straight repression. Syria has resorted to slaughter. Saudi Arabia, which before the Gulf war financed many of the fundamentalist groups, now finds itself tormented by its own pure faction. The military regime in Sudan is also under the brutal thumb of a fundamentalist faction. In these circumstances, more repressive actions will be provoked. Muslim militancy could be rationalised if the militants were inside the system of government, as they are in Pakistan, Malaysia and Turkey. This is the way to handle the situation and by this method they can be circumscribed, whereas outside the system, they can only be spoilers.

Consequences of Blasphemy

As regards the case of Salman Rushdie's novel, *The Satanic Verses*, the Ayatollah Khomeini's condemnation and fatwa in response to Rushdie's alleged blasphemy against Islam reinforce fears of cultural confrontation. The book-burning, the riots, the death threats and the deaths of protesters are seen as odd and irrational acts. But I would argue that much of the responsibility for this situation lies with Rushdie himself, in the sense that his writing hurt millions of people and created a gulf between Islam and Christianity.

Western analysts and experts have also created a fear that the rapidly growing Muslim population in Europe and the United States is a potential threat to Western culture and civilisation. Some view Islam as the only ideological alternative to the West that can cut across national boundaries and, perceiving it as politically and culturally at odds with Western society, fear it; others consider it a more basic demographic threat. By way of contrast, there has been agreement in the West that Muslim activism is against the interests of the Christian world and fear that the history of the Crusades may be repeated. However, although religion was one of the things that drove two major communities into battle with each other, it was never the whole explanation for such clashes. Past enmities and present bad temper need not lead us to conclude that suffering and destruction are inevitable.

Dr. Suter believes that the clash between Islam and Christianity will continue, due to their cultural differences. I disagree. My request to all Western intellectuals is that they should sympathetically study Islam and they will find that Islam is not a violent doctrine. Islam, like other world religions, is a faith of peace and social justice. In fact, Islam is as universalist as Christianity, and offers as generous a consolation when it comes to finding purpose, a guide for the soul, in a confusing world. It does not turn to fundamentalist militancy, because it has always been a tolerant religion and dislikes extremism and killing. Islam does not encourage terrorism and threatening behaviour. Wherever it comes from, it is not from Islam as a faith. Those groups who practice terror under the flag of Islam are a small minority, rejected by the great majority of Muslims. The West must realise that Iran, Algeria, Libya, Sudan, Afghanistan and Saudi Arabia are not the sole representatives of the Muslim world and Islam. In relation to aggressive attitudes, the key message to Western scholars is to oppose the extremist Muslims but not blame all Islam. Islam has proved to be a dynamic and energetic force at a time when the world is awash with new political formulations, and it has become an increasingly important political idiom.

> ***"Past enmities and present bad temper need not lead us to conclude that suffering and destruction are inevitable."***

Pan-Arabism Causes Conflict in the Middle East

by Efraim Karsh

About the author: *Efraim Karsh is a professor and director of Mediterranean studies at King's College at the University of London. He is a coauthor of* Empires of the Sand: The Struggle for Mastery in the Middle East.

Since its formation in the wake of World War I, the contemporary Middle Eastern system based on territorial states has been under sustained assault. In past years, the foremost challenge to this system came from the doctrine of pan-Arabism (or qawmiya), which sought to "eliminate the traces of Western imperialism" and unify the "Arab nation," and the associated ideology of Greater Syria (or Suriya al-Kubra), which stresses the territorial and historical indivisibility of most of the Fertile Crescent. Today, the leading challenge comes from Islamist notions of a single Muslim community (the umma). Intellectuals and politicians, denouncing the current system as an artificial creation of Western imperialism at variance with yearnings for regional unity, have repeatedly urged its destruction. National leaders—from Gamal Abdel Nasser to Ayatollah Ruhollah Khomeini to Saddam Husayn [Hussein]—have justified their interference in the affairs of other states by claiming to pursue that unity. Yet the system of territorial states has proven extremely resilient.

That resilience raises questions. From what does it result? Does it suggest that the system of territorial states is more in line with Middle Eastern realities than the vision of a unified regional order? We review the role of pan-Arabism, pan-Syrianism, and pan-Islam, then consider how the rejection of the territorial state system has affected that most intractable conflict, the disposition of the Palestinians.

The Hashemite Attempt

Pan-Arabism gives short shrift to the notion of the territorial state, declaring it to be a temporary aberration destined to wither away before long. This doctrine

Efraim Karsh, "Why the Middle East Is So Volatile," *Middle East Quarterly*, vol. 7, December 2000, p. 13.

also postulates the existence of "a single nation bound by the common ties of language, religion and history. . . . behind the facade of a multiplicity of sovereign states." The territorial expanse of this supposed nation has varied among the exponents of the ideology, ranging from merely the Fertile Crescent to the entire territory "from the Atlantic Ocean to the Persian Gulf." But the unity of the Arabic-speaking populations inhabiting these vast territories is never questioned.

This doctrine was first articulated by a number of pre–World War I intellectuals, most notably the Syrian political exiles 'Abd ar-Rahman al-Kawakibi (1854–1902) and Najib Azuri (1873–1916), as well as by some of the secret Arab societies operating in the Ottoman Empire before its collapse. Yet it is highly doubtful whether these early beginnings would have ever amounted to anything more than intellectual musings had it not been for the huge ambitions of the sharif of Mecca, Husayn [Hussein] ibn 'Ali of the Hashemite family, and his two prominent sons, 'Abdullah and Faysal. Together, they perpetrated the "Great Arab Revolt" against the Ottoman Empire.

When Husayn proposed to the British that he rise against his Ottoman master, he styled himself champion of "the whole of the Arab nation without any exception." Befitting that role, he demanded the creation of a vast empire on the ruins of the Ottoman Empire, stretching from Asia Minor to the Indian Ocean and from Iraq to the Mediterranean. When this grandiose vision failed to materialize in its full scope, the Hashemites quickly complained of being "robbed" of the fruits of victory promised to them during the war. (They were, as it happens, generously rewarded in the form of vast territories several times the size of the British Isles.) Thus arose the standard grievance that Arab intellectuals and politicians leveled at the Western powers, Britain in particular, and thus emerged the "pan-" doctrine of Arab nationalism with the avowed aim of redressing this alleged grievance.

Likewise the imperial ambitions of Faysal and 'Abdullah placed the Greater Syria ideal on the Arab political agenda. Already during the revolt against the Ottoman Empire, Faysal began toying with the idea of winning his own Syrian empire independently of his father's prospective empire. He tried to gain great-power endorsement for this ambition by telling the Paris Peace Conference that "Syria claimed her unity and her independence" and that it was "sufficiently advanced politically to manage her own internal affairs" if given adequate foreign and technical assistance. When the conference planned to send a special commission of inquiry to the Middle East, Faysal quickly assembled (a highly unrepresentative) General Syrian Congress that would "make clear the wishes of the Syrian people." And by way of leaving nothing to chance, Faysal manipulated Syrian public opinion through extensive propaganda, orchestrated demonstrations, and intimidation of opponents.

"Pan-Arabism gives short shrift to the notion of the territorial state."

Planting the Notion of Greater Syria

When all these efforts came to naught, and his position in Syria was increasingly threatened by the French, Faysal allowed the General Syrian Congress to proclaim him the constitutional monarch of Syria "within its natural boundaries, including Palestine" and in political and economic union with Iraq. On March 8, 1920, he was crowned as King Faysal I at the Damascus City Hall, and France and Britain were asked to vacate the western (that is, Lebanese) and the southern (that is, Palestinian) parts of Syria. The seed of the Greater Syria ideal had been sown.

Neither did Faysal abandon the Greater Syrian dream after his expulsion from Damascus by the French in July 1920. Quite the reverse. Using his subsequent position as the first monarch of Iraq, Faysal toiled ceaselessly to bring about the unification of the Fertile Crescent under his rule. This policy was sustained, following his untimely death in September 1933, by successive Iraqi leaders. Nuri as-Sa'id, Faysal's comrade-in-arms and a perpetual prime minister, did so, as did 'Abdullah, Faysal's older brother, who articulated his own version of the Greater Syria ideal. While 'Abdullah had some success, with the occupation and annexation of some 6,000 square kilometers of western Palestine to his kingdom in the late 1940s (an area to be subsequently known as the West Bank), his coveted Syrian empire remained unattainable.

"There is not and has never existed an 'Arab nation.'"

As Hashemite ambitions faded away, following 'Abdullah's assassination in 1951 and the overthrow of the Iraqi monarchy seven years later, the championship of "pan-" movements migrated to other leaders. Cairo became the standard bearer of a wider pan-Arab ideal. Egypt's sense of pan-Arabism had already manifested itself in the 1930s but it peaked in the 1950s with the rise to power of Gamal Abdel Nasser. For a while, Abdel Nasser's hegemonic aspirations seemed to be within reach. His subversive campaign against the pro-Western states drove the Lebanese and Jordanian regimes to the verge of collapse and pushed Saudi Arabia and Iran onto the defensive. An Egyptian-Syrian union in 1958 seemed to bring the ideal of pan-Arab unity to fruition. By the early 1960s, however, Abdel Nasser's dreams were in tatters. The pro-Western regimes were weathering the Egyptian onslaught; Syria acrimoniously seceded from the bilateral union; and the Egyptian army bogged down in an unwinnable civil war in Yemen. Abdel Nasser's inter-Arab standing took a steep plunge. Then came the 1967 Six Day War, dealing his ambitions—and the pan-Arab ideal as a whole—a mortal blow. While there would never be a shortage of contenders to Abdel Nasser's role as pan-Arabism's champion, notably Saddam Husayn, the dream of the "Arab nation" would not regain its earlier vibrancy or appeal. . . .

Why, for all the sustained intellectual and political efforts behind it, did pan-

Arabism make such little headway towards its goal of unifying the "Arab nation"? Because there is not and has never existed an "Arab nation." Rather, its invocation has been a clever ploy to harness popular support to the quest for regional mastery by successive Middle Eastern dynasties, rulers, and regimes.

If a nation is a group of people sharing such attributes as common descent, language, culture, tradition, and history, then nationalism is the desire of such a group for self-determination in a specific territory that they consider to be their patrimony. The only common denominators among the widely diverse Arabic-speaking populations of the Middle East—the broad sharing of language and religion—are remnants of the early imperial Islamic epoch. But these have generated no general sense of Arab solidarity, not to speak of deeply rooted sentiments of shared history, destiny, or attachment to an ancestral homeland, for both Islam and the Arabic language have far transcended their Arabian origins. The former has become a thriving universal religion boasting a worldwide community of believers of which Arabs are but a small minority. The latter, like other imperial languages such as English, Spanish, and French, has been widely assimilated by former subject populations, often superseding their native tongues. As T.E. Lawrence ("Lawrence of Arabia"), the foremost early champion of the pan-Arab cause, admitted in his later days: "Arab unity is a madman's notion—for this century or next, probably. English-speaking unity is a fair parallel."...

"Arab rulers systematically convinced their peoples to think that the independent existence of their respective states was a temporary aberration."

Neither had the Arabic-speaking provinces of the Ottoman Empire experienced the processes of secularization and modernization that preceded the development of nationalism in western Europe in the late 1700s. When the Ottoman Empire collapsed, its Arab populations still thought only in local or imperial terms. Their intricate webs of local loyalties (to one's clan, tribe, village, town, religious sect, or localized ethnic minority) were superseded only by submission to the Ottoman sultan-caliph in his capacity as the head of the Muslim community. They were wholly unfamiliar with the idea of national self-determination and so created no pressure for states.

Into this vacuum moved ambitious political leaders, speaking the Western rhetoric "Arab nationalism," but actually aiming to create new empires for themselves. The problem with this state of affairs was that the extreme diversity and fragmentation of the Arabic-speaking world had made its disparate societies better disposed to local patriotism than to a unified regional order. But then, rather than allow this disposition to run its natural course and develop into modern-day state nationalism (or wataniya), Arab rulers systematically convinced their peoples to think that the independent existence of their respective states was a temporary aberration that would be rectified before too long. The result was a dissonance that was to haunt the Middle East for most of the twentieth century, between the reality of state nationalism and the dream of an empire packaged as a unified "Arab nation."

A New Arab Empire?

This dissonance (speaking the language of nationalism while pursuing imperial aggrandizement) was introduced into the political discourse by the Hashemites. Though styling themselves representatives of the "Arab nation," Sharif Husayn and his sons were no champions of national liberation but rather imperialist aspirants anxious to exploit a unique window of opportunity to substitute their own empire for that of the Ottomans. Husayn had demonstrated no nationalist sentiments prior to the war when he had generally been considered a loyal Ottoman apparatchik; and neither he nor his sons changed in this respect during the revolt. They did not regard themselves as part of a wider Arab nation, bound together by a shared language, religion, history, or culture. Rather, they held themselves superior to those ignorant creatures whom they were "destined" to rule and educate. David Hogarth, director of the Cairo Arab Bureau, held several conversations with Husayn in January 1918 and reported his attitude as follows: "Arabs as a whole have not asked him to be their king; but seeing how ignorant and disunited they are, how can this be expected of them until he is called?" It was the "white man's burden," Hijaz-style. . . .

What the Hashemites demanded of the post-war peace conference, therefore, was not self-determination for the Arabic-speaking subjects of the defunct Ottoman Empire but the formation of a successor empire, extending well beyond the predominantly Arabic-speaking territories and comprising such diverse ethnic and national groups as Turks, Armenians, Kurds, Greeks, Assyrians, Chechens, Circassians, and Jews, among others, apart of course from the Arabs. As Husayn told T.E. Lawrence in the summer of 1917: "If advisable, we will pursue the Turks to Constantinople and Erzurum—so why talk about Beirut, Aleppo, and Hailo?" And 'Abdullah put it in similar terms when asking British officer Sir Mark Sykes (in April 1917) that Britain abide by the vast territorial promises made to Sharif Husayn: "it was . . . up to the British government to see that the Arab kingdom is such as will make it a substitute for the Ottoman Empire." This imperial mindset was vividly illustrated by the frequent Hashemite allusion to past Arab and Islamic imperial glory, rather than to national rights, as justification of their territorial claims. . . .

> ***"[The Hashemites] held themselves superior to those ignorant creatures whom they were 'destined' to rule and educate."***

The "Palestine question" is an issue that has constituted an integral part of inter-Arab politics since the mid-1930s, with anti-Zionism forming the main common denominator of pan-Arab solidarity and its most effective rallying cry.

But the actual policies of the Arab states show they have been less motivated by concern for pan-Arabism, let alone for the protection of the Palestinians, than by their own interests. Indeed, nothing has done more to expose the hollowness of pan-Arabism than this, its most celebrated cause.

Consider, for instance, the pan-Arab invasion of the newly proclaimed State of Israel in mid-May 1948. This, on the face of it, was a shining demonstration of pan-Arab solidarity. But the invasion had less to do with concern for the Palestinian struggle to liberate a part of the Arab homeland than with ‘Abdullah’s desire to incorporate substantial parts of Mandatory Palestine into his kingdom—and the determination of other Arab players, notably Egypt, to prevent that eventuality. Had the Jewish state lost the war, its territory would have been divided among the invading forces.

During the decades of Palestinian dispersal following the 1948 war, the Arab states manipulated the Palestinian national cause to their own ends. Neither Egypt nor Jordan allowed Palestinian self-determination in the parts of Palestine they occupied during the 1948 war (respectively, the West Bank and the Gaza Strip). Palestinian refugees were kept in squalid camps for decades as a means for whipping Israel and stirring pan-Arab sentiments. Abdel Nasser cloaked his hegemonic goals by invoking the restoration of “the full rights of the Palestinian people.” Likewise, Saddam Husayn disguised his predatory designs on Kuwait by linking the crisis caused by his invasion of that country with “the immediate and unconditional withdrawal of Israel from the occupied Arab territories in Palestine.”

> ***“Nothing has done more to expose the hollowness of pan-Arabism than [the Palestine question].”***

Self-serving interventionism under the pretence of pan-Arab solidarity had the effect of transforming the bilateral Palestinian-Israeli dispute into a multilateral Arab-Israeli conflict, thereby prolonging its duration, increasing its intensity, and making its resolution far more complex and tortuous. By refusing to recognize Palestinian nationalism (or for that matter any other Arab state nationalism) and insisting on its incorporation into a wider Arab framework, Arab intellectuals, rulers, and regimes disrupted the natural national development of this community. They instilled unrealistic visions, hopes, and expectations in Palestinian political circles at key junctures. The consequence has been to deny Palestinians the right to determine their own fate. . . .

The Quest for the Empire of God

The other great challenge to state ideals was voiced by Ayatollah Ruhollah Khomeini, spiritual father of the Islamic Republic of Iran, which he created in 1979 on the ruins of the Pahlavi monarchy. Like pan-Arab ideologues, Khomeini viewed Western imperialism as the source of all evil. But while the former invoked Muslim past glory as the justification for the creation of a unified pan-Arab empire, Khomeini viewed it as a precedent for the unification of the world's Muslim community, the umma. In his understanding, having partitioned the umma into artificial separate states after World War I, the great powers did their best to keep Muslim communities in a permanent state of ignorance and fragmentation. "The imperialists, the oppressive and treacherous rulers, the Jews, Christians, and materialists are all attempting to distort the truth of Islam and lead the Muslims astray," he cautioned:

"[Ayatollah] Khomeini viewed Western imperialism as the source of all evil."

> We see today that the Jews (may God curse them) have meddled with the text of the Qur'an . . . We must protest and make the people aware that the Jews and their foreign backers are opposed to the very foundations of Islam and wish to establish Jewish domination throughout the world. Since they are a cunning and resourceful group of people, I fear that—God forbid!—they may one day achieve their goal, and that the apathy shown by some of us may allow a Jew to rule over us one day.

This meant that Middle Eastern states—indeed, the entire contemporary international system—were totally illegitimate, for they perpetuated an unjust order imposed on "oppressed" Muslims by the "oppressive" great powers. Muslims were obliged to "overthrow the oppressive governments installed by the imperialists and bring into existence an Islamic government of justice that will be in the service of the people." An Islamic world order would see the state transcended by the territorial broader entity of the umma.

As the only country where the "government of God" had been established, ran Khomeini's line of reasoning, Iran had a sacred obligation to serve as the core of the umma and the springboard for worldwide dissemination of Islam's holy message:

> The Iranian revolution is not exclusively that of Iran, because Islam does not belong to any particular people . . . We will export our revolution throughout the world because it is an Islamic revolution. The struggle will continue until the calls "there is no god but God and Muhammad is the messenger of God" are echoed all over the world.

Exporting the Revolution

Khomeini made good on his promise. In November 1979 and February 1980 widespread riots erupted in the Shi'i towns of the oil-rich Saudi province of Hasa, exacting many casualties. Similar disturbances occurred in Bahrain and Kuwait which became the target of a sustained terrorist and subversive campaign. Iraq suffered from a special subversive effort, whereby the Iranians sought to topple the ruling Ba'th regime, headed since July 1979 by Saddam Husayn at-Tikriti. They urged the Iraqi people to rise against their government;

supported the Kurdish revolt in northern Iraq and underground Shi'i movements; and they launched terrorist attacks against prominent Iraqi officials. When these pressures eventually led to the Iraqi invasion of Iran in September 1980, Khomeini wholeheartedly embraced "the imposed war" as a means of consolidating his regime and furthering its influence throughout the region. The war would continue, he vowed, "until the downfall of the regime governing Baghdad."...

Despite these efforts, Iran's pan-Islamic doctrine has had no greater success than did pan-Arabism in denting the Middle Eastern territorial state system. Not only did most Sunnis reject it as a distinctly Shi'i doctrine, but even Iraq's majority Shi'i community found it unconvincing and gave more allegiance to the Iraqi territorial state instead. And Iran's only successful export of its revolution, namely [the terrorist organization] Hizbullah [Hezbollah] in Lebanon, had more to do with the struggle against Israel than with dreams of establishing a unified community of believers.

Eliminating the "Pan-" Factor

The Middle East's experience in the twentieth century has been marked by frustration, and much of it has resulted from a gap between delusions of grandeur and the grim realities of weakness and fragmentation. Just as the challenge to the continental order by the European "pan-" movements, notably pan-Germanism and pan-Slavism, led to mass suffering and dislocation, so the rejection of the contemporary Middle Eastern state system by pan-Arabs and pan-Islamists has triggered many wars among Arabs and Jews, Arabs and Arabs, Arabs and Kurds, Arabs and Iranians, and others. . . .

Only when the "pan-" factor is banished from the Middle East's political scene and replaced by general acceptance of the region's diversity will its inhabitants look forward to a better future. Any attempt to impose a national or religious unity on the region's individual states is not only bound to fail but it will perpetuate the violence and acrimony that have for too long plagued the Middle East. Only when the political elites reconcile themselves to the reality of state nationalism (wataniya) and forswear the imperial dream of a unified "Arab nation" will regional stability be attained.

The Arab-Israeli Dispute Causes Conflict in the Middle East

by Beverley Milton-Edwards and Peter Hinchcliffe

About the authors: *Beverley Milton-Edwards is a professor of Middle Eastern politics at Queen's University in Belfast and the author of* Contemporary Politics in the Middle East. *Peter Hinchcliffe is an honorary fellow at the Department of Islamic and Middle Eastern Studies at the University of Edinburgh.*

The conflict between those regularly referred to as the Jews and the Arabs has been well under way for nearly a century. While major military confrontation between Israel and its Arab neighbours has not occurred since the Israeli invasion of Lebanon in 1982, the absence of meaningful peace and the maintenance of conflict continued to the end of the twentieth century. Within its confines the differences between these peoples, religions and attitudes has at times manifested itself in conventional wars, and led to the militarization of the entire region, where even aspiring democrats have only recently begun to discard their military uniforms. Inevitably under such a climate, economic relations, culture, history, literature, mass media and communications, international organizations, regional associations and interest groups have all been enlisted and manipulated to demonize the enemy. Rival nationalisms, the superpower conflict, the right to self-determination, anti-Semitism, control of oil, and the emergence of the Third World radicalism and anti-Western sentiment have all played their part, making up the cocktail of conflict described by Professor Emile Sahliyeh as 'the most lethal and volatile . . . and the most difficult to resolve'.

A Broad Conflict

Although the essence of the conflict is the battle between two people over one land, the territory of the Holy Land including Jerusalem, the Arab-Israeli dimension has developed over time characteristics often far-removed from the original Palestinian issue and territorial focus. One example is the bitter dispute and battle that has raged from the late 1970s between Israel and the Lebanese Islamic resistance movements, and latterly the Shi'a Hizballah [also known as Hezbollah] organization. While Israel's original motives in invading and subsequently occupying Lebanon in 1978 and 1982 were to rout the PLO [Palestine Liberation Organization], once the PLO had left the country, the Israeli Defence Force (IDF) remained as an occupying force and made themselves the principal enemies of the Lebanese Shi'a population. Hizballah was subsequently formed as a resistance movement to end Israel's illegal occupation of southern Lebanon and, until Israel's withdrawal in spring 2000, waged a major military campaign against its enemy and those perceived to be its supporters. While it may be true that there was little love lost between the PLO and Hizballah during the Lebanese civil war they ended up sharing a common antipathy to Israel as an occupying force on Arab lands. Certainly this is an instance where Israel's policies may have inadvertently created allies out of enemies, thus undermining the security of their own state.

The roots of this conflict lay in the resistance mounted by the Arabs and their leaders in the region against the initial attempt by settler Zionists, most of whom were immigrants from Europe, to build a state in Palestine. But it was the subsequent dispossession of the Palestinian Arab population, the creation of a Palestinian national identity and the emergence of new Arab nationalisms united in opposition to Zionism and to the close association it was perceived as having with the forces of imperialism and colonialism, which gave the conflict its wider dimension. The struggle to gain and retain Arab rights to self-determination over Palestine in the face of European dominance over the entire region had its roots in the First World War, when the British made contradictory commitments to the Arabs and to the Zionist Jews to enlist their support against Germany and its Ottoman (Turkish) allies. The Arab leadership was led to believe that Arabs would control much of the region following the defeat of the Ottomans. But at the same time the British and the French were planning to replace Istanbul as the dominant power in the region. The situation was complicated further by a British promise to the Zionists to support the establishment of a Jewish national home in Arab Palestine: the Balfour Declaration. The expediency of measures taken to further war aims was to be questioned in the decades that followed. It soon emerged that the British had promised more than they could deliver and had engaged in what later emerged as duplicitous behaviour described as a 'disgusting scramble for the Middle East'.

Under Colonial Rule

When the Ottoman Empire was dissolved at the end of the First World War most of the Middle East became subject to colonial rule or influence. European powers, principally Britain and France, re-drew the boundaries of the Middle East and many Arab areas came under their direct political control. This period of direct and indirect colonial control, short lived though it was, resulted in the invention and promotion of new Arab rulers and monarchs presiding over newly created states within artificial boundaries. It sowed the seeds of future conflicts—between Israel and the Arabs (involving the Iranians) and amongst the Arabs themselves—that for the most part remained unresolved throughout the last century.

> ***"The roots of [the Arab-Israeli conflict] lay in the resistance mounted by the Arabs . . . against the initial attempt by settler Zionists."***

The incipient conflict between the Jews and Arabs in the region took shape during the first three decades of the twentieth century and culminated in the first direct war in 1948 as Britain ended its mandate in Palestine, which had lasted from 1919 to 1948. During this period the British authorities were, according to the official remit of the mandate as agreed by the League of Nations, supposed to assist the mandated territory to self-government. But they were caught between conflicting pressures: Zionist attempts to establish their own state (something more than the 'National Home' envisaged in the Balfour Declaration, as incorporated into the mandate's provisions) and Arab efforts to oppose this in the pursuit of their own national aspirations. In these circumstances the British had little option but to pursue an often oppressive policy of control and public order.

The perceived grievances of the Palestinian community in Palestine at the time (particularly the large influx of Jewish immigrants) raised tension between the two communities and resulted in the 1929 riots when Jews in Jerusalem and Hebron were murdered. This event was followed by further conflict including the 1936 General Strike and the Palestinian revolt from 1936 to 1939. The British authorities, also under attack from militant Jewish organizations, appeared to be unable to develop policies or strategies to resolve the conflict, and the outbreak of the Second World War in Europe in 1939, and the Nazi-perpetrated Holocaust against 6 million Jews, had unforeseen consequences for the future of Palestine. After the Second World War Jewish immigration reached new heights, and pressure for a Jewish state in Palestine as a haven for the persecuted survivors of the Holocaust grew relentlessly. The British were increasingly unable to maintain law and order, and meanwhile the Palestinians and their national leadership demanded self-determination. Eventually the whole problem was turned over by the British to the newly established United Nations, who decided to resolve the competing claims for self-determination by promoting partition between the Jews and the Arabs, with Jerusalem falling under international authority. The Zionist movement accepted statehood as a much better deal than the 'national home' they had been offered under the Balfour Declaration. They already faced considerable hostility and incipient conflict from their Arab neighbours. There was a belief that securing statehood would promote the much-needed sense of security for the Jewish people and an end to their exile. The diaspora could be gathered in under the flag of Israel. However, the Palestinians and Arab states rejected the UN partition plan, arguing that it was inherently biased and ignored the legitimate rights of Palestinians. The Palestinians complained that their land was being given away as a means of appeasing European guilt over the Holocaust. When the British withdrew in May 1948 the battle for the land of Palestine broke out in earnest between the Israelis and the Arabs.

Fighting for Palestinian Soil

The war broke out shortly after the Israeli Declaration of Independence on 15 May 1948, as units from the Arab armies of Egypt, Jordan, and Syria (backed by forces from Lebanon and Iraq) attempted to win back the Palestinian soil that had been lost to the Israeli state. The Arab armies, poorly led and equipped, were ultimately unsuccessful and failed to defeat the small but well motivated and highly trained Israeli Defence Force. The armistice negotiations did not occur until January 1949, by which time between 700,000 and 800,000 Palestinians had fled their homes or been forced to flee. In some cases Palestinians, encouraged by their Arab leaders, left the battle-zones in the belief that after a swift Arab victory they would be able to return. In other cases Palestinians fled their villages after hearing news of the massacre by Israeli forces in the village of Deir Yassin. As author Maxime Rodinson notes, 'Many leading Jews were glad to see the departure of a population which by its very presence presented an obstacle to the realisation of the Jewish state projected by the Zionists'. The Palestinians who arrived as refugees in Lebanon, Transjordan, Syria, Egypt and the Gaza Strip quickly realized that they had lost their homes and would not be allowed to return to them. The only comfort that the leaders of the Arab world could offer was the promise that this first encounter was just one war in a major conflict that would continue on their behalf. The Palestinian community refers to this period in their history as *'al-nakbah'*—the catastrophe.

> ***"When the Ottoman Empire was dissolved at the end of the First World War most of the Middle East became subject to colonial rule."***

In terms of territory the end of the war meant the effective partition of Palestine as it was formerly known. The West Bank and East Jerusalem (including the old city) came under the control of Jordan and its monarch King Abdullah. The Egyptian government administered the Gaza Strip from Cairo. The rest of the country, which as a result of the armistice had enlarged from 14,000 to 21,000 square kilometres, came within the new Israeli state. The Arabs were thus left with one-fifth of the original territory of their land and their aspirations for an Arab Palestine battered and weakened by the war.

Thus, within hours of its birth the new Israeli state had been compelled into war with its Arab neighbours. The war lasted until armistice agreements secured in January 1949. Aware of their poor chances, the intertwined political and military leadership of Israel had no option but to engage in the fight against the six Arab armies ranged against them. One advantage that the Israelis believed they had over their enemy was referred to by Israeli Chief of Operations Yigael Yadin in May 1948 when he remarked, 'the problem is to what extent our men will be able to overcome enemy forces by virtue of their fighting spirit, of our planning and our tactics'. The new state, forged in war, emerged from that experience with a unique character and an emphasis on institutions such as the military which might not, under more peaceful circumstances of statehood, have been necessary.

> ***"The British authorities . . . appeared to be unable to develop policies or strategies to resolve the conflict."***

The repercussions of the conflict were widespread and enduring. Amongst them was an initial period of instability in the Arab countries as they came to terms with their defeat, and a backlash against British and Western influence in the region. This was most noticeable in increasing popular opposition to the British-supported Hashemite monarchies in Iraq and in Jordan. In 1951 Jordan's King Abdullah was assassinated and the new King Hussein—bowing to popular pressure—dismissed General Glubb Pasha, the British commander of the Arab Legion. The upsurge of popular nationalism elsewhere across the region in response to the Arab defeat signalled the end of the corrupt royalist regime in Egypt, where, in 1952, the Free Officer Movement led by Gamal Abdel Nasser mounted a coup, trumpeting the rhetoric of Arab nationalism and unity in the face of the Zionist enemy across the region. In the eyes of Arab nationalist radicals in Cairo, Beirut, Baghdad and Damascus, Israel was an enemy not just because of the injustice against their brethren in Palestine, but also because of its close association with what they perceived as Western imperialist aspirations towards the region, and in particular its recently exploited massive oil reserves. Thus, radical Arab nationalism and pan-Arab pretensions created a new dimension in the conflict with Israel, as was strikingly demonstrated during the 1956 Suez war.

The Suez War

The Suez conflict, which erupted over the decision by Nasser to nationalize the Suez Canal Company in July 1956, was a major escalation of anti-colonialist and, by association, anti-Zionist sentiment in the Arab world. The Suez Canal was built in the 1860s and by the late 1880s came under British and other foreign control (via a number of shareholders), maintained by British occupation of Egypt. The British saw the canal as an essential element in their control of the main sea route to India. In the 4-year period leading up to the nationalization of the Suez Canal, Nasser embarked on a programme of pan-Arab cohesion and made military pacts with Syria, Saudi Arabia and Yemen. Nasser's goal was the restoration of the Arab nation under Egyptian leadership and an end to foreign influence in the area. The nationalization of Suez was the first time that a Third World country had successfully regained one of its major foreign-owned assets.

Both the French and the British were outraged at Nasser's decision. A highly secret tripartite operation in collusion with the Israelis was organized. They hatched a plot to regain control over the Suez Canal. On 29 October 1956 the Israeli army launched Operation Kadesch; their forces crossed the border and entered the Sinai desert. Over a period of five days they routed the Egyptian army and approached the canal. In accordance with a pre-arranged plan—'Operation Musketeer'—the British and French bombed Egyptian targets and sent their troops to occupy Port Said and Port Fuad on the pretext of protecting it from hostile action, whether from Israel or Egypt. The Israelis had accepted a cease-fire as part of the secret pre-arrangement with the British and French, but the Egyptians refused to pull their troops back from the canal. Despite the military successes, the British and French were forced to accept a ceasefire and withdraw their forces as a result of US economic pressure on Britain and international public opinion as expressed through the UN. Nasser had held on to the canal and Arab nationalist feelings and anti-imperialist sentiment reached an all-time high.

The dispute between the Arabs and Israelis was exacerbated by the Arab perception of the Israeli role in the conflict as nothing more than defender of Western interests in the region. As a result tensions remained high and the deep animosity between the nations worsened. By siding with France and Britain and continuing to occupy the Gaza Strip between 1956 and 1957, the Israelis managed not only to further deepen the rift with Egypt but also to anger the USA, bringing a close relationship under severe pressure. Within Israel the involvement of their armed forces in the 1956 crisis was perceived quite differently. The Israeli political and military establishment were concerned by persistent Arab attacks on Israel mounted from Gaza and the Sinai and by the Egyptian blockade of the Red Sea; consequently, the Israeli port of Eilat took defensive steps against Egyptian belligerence. While it is true that the Israeli withdrawal from the Sinai in March 1957 was prompted by US and UN pressure, Israeli involvement in Suez, secret agreements apart, would have been considered part of the domestic security strategy and sold as such to the Israeli people. In many respects the legacy of 1956 would not be visited upon the Israelis for some ten years or more. There can be little doubt, however, that Nasser's motives in 1967 were, at least partially, rooted in the 1956 encounter and his memories of military humiliation.

"The Palestinians complained that their land was being given away as a means of appeasing European guilt over the Holocaust."

The Six-Day War

The war of 1967 was inevitable; the disputes between the Arabs and the Israelis had remained unresolved and the era of fervent and self-confident Arab nationalism was at its peak. On the eve of the war the combined Arab troop numbers were more than double those of the Israelis. The Arabs also had three times as many tanks and aircraft, yet within 6 days they were totally routed by the Israeli army. The build up to the war on the Arab side had been fraught with reckless rhetoric and strident propaganda about the military prowess of the 'Arab people' and their ability to defeat the Israelis, to sweep them into the sea and win back Palestine. Egypt was the most eager of the combatants and was in a sense a victim of its own propaganda, which grossly exaggerated its potential as a military power. The Syrians and Jordanians, with territory at stake, were somewhat less hawkish but came under pressure from Nasser and the weight of their own public opinion intoxicated by the prospect of victory. Nasser, determined to earn his place in the history books as the undisputed leader of the Arab world, pursued the liberation of Palestine as if it were a Holy Grail. At the same time he oppressed the Egyptian-administered Palestinian population of the Gaza Strip and the refugee community in Egypt, imprisoning thousands of them throughout his presidency.

"Within hours of its birth the new Israeli state had been compelled into war with its Arab neighbours."

The war was over in a matter of five or six days between 5 and 11 June. The Jordanian army was defeated and its airforce destroyed; similar Israeli victories occurred over the Egyptians in the Gaza Strip and the Syrians in the Golan Heights. By Saturday 10 June 1967 the Israeli army occupied the Sinai Peninsula, the Gaza Strip, the West Bank (including East Jerusalem and the old city) and the Golan Heights. The acquisition of territory by the end of the war had increased Israel's size by six times (almost half that formerly administered by Jordan), and this had massive logistical, military and political implications for the Israeli government.

The role of the UN during the hostilities was minimal. However, on 22 November after five months of bargaining, the UN passed SCR 242 which required a withdrawal of Israeli forces from the territories occupied in exchange for the cessation of fighting, the recognition of all states in the region, freedom of navigation in the Suez Canal and in the Gulf of Aqaba, and the creation of demilitarized zones. Once again Israel was able to prevail militarily despite the odds stacked against it. Following the appointment of Moshe Dayan as Defence Minister just days before the war, the Israeli armed forces meticulously planned their daring campaign against a belligerent Nasser and his Egyptian forces. By seizing the initiative, launching the war before the Arabs got there first, the Israelis were able to dominate the rest of the military campaign, first by air and then by land. By the end of the war, Israel, a 'country that had felt embattled and threatened only days before was now the decisive military power in the Middle East . . . Equally Israel had changed in the process, for she was now an occupying power', as stated by author T. Fraser.

The fourth conflict between Israel and the Arabs in twenty-five years since 1948 [it occurred in 1973] had a number of unique features. First, Egyptian and Syrian forces were able (albeit temporarily) to break through Israeli lines, an unprecedented military success for the Arabs. Second, although Israel was the ultimate victor, the perceived weakness of the army in initial stages of the hostilities affected national morale and self-confidence and led political leaders to re-think their position vis-à-vis their Arab neighbours. Third, the war was an Egyptian and Syrian attempt to recover their own territory, with the Palestinian issue coming a poor second in terms of strategy and objectives. Finally, it was during this war that the Gulf States started to use oil prices and boycott as major weapons against the West. For the first time the West was made aware of the significant leverage the Arab states held over the oil-dependent economies of the capitalist world. . . .

"The Suez conflict . . . was a major escalation of anti-colonialist and . . . anti-Zionist sentiment in the Arab world."

Attack on Lebanon

Throughout 1981 there was a noticeable rise in tension: a missile crisis with Syria in spring was followed on 7 June by the raid against the Iraqi nuclear centre of Tammuz. By December Israel had formally annexed the Golan Heights, which had been captured from the Syrians in the war of 1967. But, crucially, in June 1981 the IDF and PLO troops based in south Lebanon began shelling each other until the United States negotiated a ceasefire with the two parties. Against this background, it was inevitable that certain elements of the Israeli military would use their influence within government to take action against the PLO in Lebanon. Although there were splits within the military over this issue, the 'hawks' prevailed and steered Prime Minister Menachem Begin into a further course of invasion.

'Peace for Galilee' was the name given to the Israeli invasion of Lebanon in June 1982. Officially the Israelis declared that their march across the border was only a question of affirming control of a 40 km strip, from which terrorists would no longer be able to shell the north of the country. Yet, despite these apparently limited aims, the IDF soon found itself in Beirut. The city was soon under Israeli imposed blockade. Thus began the siege of mainly Muslim and Palestinian West Beirut, where Palestinians and the Lebanese National Movement fought side by side, whilst the Christian Phalangists [Lebanese Christian political party and militia] lent support to the IDF as it attempted to eradicate the PLO. There seemed no end to the phosphorous, napalm, scatter, and imploding bombs that relentlessly poured down on the starving, parched west section of the city. Apart from 6,000 PLO guerrillas in the besieged city, there were some half a million Lebanese and Palestinian civilians, and every day of the bombardment about 200 or 300 of them were killed.

As the bombardment went on, day after day, the international community looked on impotently, seemingly mesmerized by the brutal nature of the Israeli action. The European Economic Community (EEC), the UN Security Council and other bodies issued condemnations, while the United States remonstrated ineffectually with its protégé and was brusquely snubbed. Yet, it is difficult to disagree with D. Gilmour's conclusion in *Dispossessed: The Ordeal of the Palestinians* that

> the most feeble reaction came from the Arab world which seemed petrified into silence and inaction. Beirut, the ideological birthplace of Arab nationalism and for long the intellectual and commercial capital of the Arab world, was being pulverised by a brutal foreign army while the Arab states did nothing.

In this respect Israel succeeded in its greatest victory in its conflict with the Arab world, and exposed the hollow posturing of the grand slogans of 'Arab unity' in the face of the Zionist threat. If the leaders of the Arab world could not rally to the defence of its brethren in Beirut as Israeli tanks rolled into its suburbs, what did unity mean?

On 30 August 1982 the PLO admitted defeat and the leadership and guerrillas left Lebanon in shame. Arafat moved on to Tunis and the PLO network went with him. The departure of the PLO, however, was not the end of Israel's battle against the Palestinians of Lebanon. On 16 and 17 September Israeli troops moved into West Beirut, and their Phalangist allies massacred at least 2,000 children, women and elderly men in the refugee camps of Sabra and Shatilla. Israeli collusion in the massacres appalled the world.

Such was the tragic end of the first phase of the Lebanon war. A second phase now began: that of Israel's occupation of southern Lebanon, which came to a humiliating end for them in May 2000 when Hizballah resistance fighters hastened the retreat of the Israeli army, which by then had suffered heavy casualties and brought about the collapse of Israel's local ally, the South Lebanon Army (SLA). For eighteen years Israel remained in Lebanon and promoted its presence through its local ally, the Christian-led SLA. United Nations forces, mandated in 1978 to act as peacekeepers until Israel withdrew, found themselves embroiled in various battles between Lebanon's militias and the SLA and IDF. Israel's northern border remained vulnerable to attack and domestic pressure grew for an end to Israel's Lebanon experience. As Israeli casualty rates rose the country's political leaders responded. In 1999, following his election as Prime Minister, former Defence Chief Ehud Barak announced that Israeli troops would finally be withdrawn from Lebanon.

> ***"The war [of 1967] was over in a matter of five or six days."***

Chapter 1

Too Many Losers

As this viewpoint has demonstrated, there are no outright winners and far too many losers in this brief balance sheet of the Arab-Israeli conflict. During the course of these hostilities national revenues have been squandered on the purchase of weapons. Some states have further impoverished themselves in seeking loans from Western arms manufacturers and governments to purchase a technology dedicated to regional domination rather than development. In as much as the Palestinian issue has closed Arab ranks in the quest for justice it has perhaps also done as much to divide the Arab world, ordinary citizens and leaders alike.

Progress towards resolving the dispute seems to have only been achieved under two significant conditions. The first is American pressure, influence and guarantees in winning concessions from Israel and rewarding the parties involved (financially) for taking risks on peace. The second is the Israeli-preferred route of negotiation via bilateral rather than multi-lateral or international forums such as the United Nations. Washington, generally speaking, has supported this tactic and facilitated such a process at Camp David in the negotiation of a separate peace between Israel and Egypt. For those who still believe that the only way a just and comprehensive peace can be forged in the Middle East is through the participation of the international community and the UN there can be little cause for comfort in achievements so far. But, however reached, a lasting and just peace depends not on treaties forged by outside parties able to cajole and pressure leaders, but in the quality of that peace and its sustainability through popular acceptance over present and future generations in both Israel and the Arab world.

Israeli Leadership Contributes to Conflict in the Middle East

by Gershom Gorenberg

About the author: *Gershom Gorenberg is the author of* The End of Days: Fundamentalism and the Struggle for the Temple Mount.

Editor's note: At the time of publication, Ariel Sharon was the prime minister of Israel. Should Sharon be removed from office, the issues discussed in this viewpoint would still be timely. Sharon's causes are inextricably related to his office.

The ruling arrived like a letter from another era, written in strange script, waiting to be deciphered. In mid-February 2002, the Israeli supreme court upheld a lower-court decision, thereby dismissing Prime Minister Ariel Sharon's libel suit against the *Ha'aretz* newspaper and its political commentator Uzi Benziman. At issue was a column Benziman wrote a decade ago on Sharon's record as defense minister during Israel's disastrous 1982 invasion of Lebanon. Benziman wrote that Prime Minister Menachem Begin—still alive at the time—knew "full well that Sharon deceived him" on the goals and conduct of that war.

Sharon has spent years trying to erase the stain of the Lebanon War. Still, the legal defeat would seem to be the least of his troubles. After he won the premiership by promising to bring peace and security to Israel's citizens, Sharon has produced neither. The conflict with the Palestinians continues to escalate. The day of the court ruling, four Israelis died in Palestinian attacks; the following day, six soldiers died in a strike against an army roadblock. Sharon responded with a rare speech to the nation—in which he disappointed all expectations that he would announce a new policy direction. Among voters, confidence that he has a strategy is bleeding away. In one Israeli public-opinion poll, 29

Gershom Gorenberg, "A Belief in Force: Ariel Sharon's Decades-Old, Unworkable Plan for Palestine," *American Prospect*, vol. 13, April 8, 2002, pp. 10–12.

percent of respondents said that Sharon had a clear plan, while 58 percent said he was simply reacting to events.

Sharon's Goals

Since his election, Sharon has stated two policy goals. The first is an unconditional cease-fire. "Violence and peacemaking are diametrically opposed. Therefore the position of the national-unity government is that Israel will not negotiate under fire," said Dore Gold, ex-ambassador to the United Nations and a member of Sharon's inner policy circle. After quiet is achieved, Gold added, "the diplomatic strategy is to get to a long-term interim agreement" with the Palestinians, rather than a final peace accord. Sharon has said he'd offer the Palestinians a state in 42 percent of the West Bank and Gaza Strip. That's the amount of land that Israel already turned over to Palestinian administration under the Oslo Accords, in the form of a collection of jagged enclaves. It's far less than former Prime Minister Ehud Barak's offer at the July 2000 Camp David summit, which Palestinian Authority Leader Yasir Arafat rejected. So it's tempting to conclude that Sharon's proposal isn't meant seriously—and that he lacks any vision of how to conclude the conflict.

February 2002's court ruling, however, is a timely reminder that Sharon has a long, troubling history that provides a basis for understanding his moves today. Rather than reacting erratically, he almost certainly has a detailed strategy. It's likely to be ambitious—and deeply flawed.

As a general and a politician, Sharon always has acted according to a strategic vision. It includes "battalion-level calculations regarding the value of territory," noted Yossi Alpher, a leading Israeli strategic analyst. To maintain overall military control of the West Bank and Gaza Strip, Sharon believes, Israel must "control every strategic hilltop and fragment the Palestinian population," Alpher said.

As an architect of Israeli settlement policy, Sharon implemented that approach. Alpher recalls a conversation with Sharon several years ago in which Sharon took out a map and pointed to a desolate corner of the southern West Bank. In one wadi, there was a Bedouin tribe, he said, and in the next wadi there was another. So, Sharon said, explaining his method, "I plant an Israeli settlement on the hilltop between them" to keep them from uniting. In an interview soon after he became prime minister in 2001, Sharon said that even the isolated Gaza Strip settlement of Netzarim, where a few dozen Israelis live between hundreds of thousands of Palestinians, "has strategic importance" because it divides the Palestinian cities of Gaza and Khan Younis. When Sharon offers the Palestinians enclaves divided by Israeli territory, that really is his map of a long-term solution.

> ***"[Sharon] lacks any vision of how to conclude the conflict [between Israel and the Palestinians]."***

Does he expect Palestinians to accept such a map? The answer lies in another aspect of Sharon's thinking, revealed during his tenure as defense minister under Menachem Begin from 1981 to 1983: He presumed that he could use force to manipulate Arab politics and produce leaders who would bend to Israel's needs. Under Sharon in those years, Israeli government in the West Bank gave funds and guns to fatal groups known as "village leagues." The goal was to create Israeli clients in place of the pro-Palestine Liberation Organization (PLO) leadership in the territories. It was a bid to "bypass the national movement," according to Menachem Klein of Bar-Ilan University, an expert on Palestinian politics, and in the end it "failed utterly."

Heading to Lebanon

Meanwhile, Sharon began preparing to invade Lebanon as soon as he became defense minister. His plan was to drive PLO forces out of southern Lebanon and Beirut and bring the Christian Phalange Party under Bashir Gemayel to power in the country. Sharon expected Gemayel to sign a peace treaty with Israel and, it seems, to remain under Israeli hegemony.

In early June 1982, the Israeli cabinet approved what Sharon described as a brief operation that would extend 25 miles into Lebanon. Within a week, Israeli troops were besieging the PLO in West Beirut. Antiwar protests grew at home; relations with the United States turned grim. But by August, the PLO evacuated Beirut and the Lebanese parliament elected Gemayel president.

> ***"[Sharon] presumed that he could use force to manipulate Arab politics."***

Sharon was euphoric. On U.S. television, he told of meeting village-league leaders and argued that peace could now be negotiated with moderate Palestinians. In another interview, with Italian journalist Oriana Fallaci, he said that "politically, [Arafat] is crashed." And he stressed one more piece of his vision: The Palestinians, he said, already "have a homeland. It is the Palestine that is called Jordan." Palestinian refugees in Lebanon, the West Bank, and elsewhere "could transfer themselves to Transjordan."

In the words of professor Arye Naor of Ben-Gurion University, who was cabinet secretary under Begin until the spring of 1982: "It's pretty clear his intent was . . . that the Palestinians in Lebanon would go to Jordan and overthrow the government, and [Israel] would help them create a Palestinian state in Jordan. It's belief in force: We'll make the process happen."

But Sharon's design quickly unraveled. Gemayel was assassinated. Sharon sent Phalange forces to take control of the Beirut refugee camps of Sabra and Shatila, where they slaughtered hundreds of Palestinians. The Israeli inquiry commission into the massacre forced Sharon to resign as defense minister. The PLO didn't vanish. But it took Israel until 2000 to extricate its army from Lebanon.

In 2001's election campaign, Sharon tried to present himself as a mellowed statesman. But he also has insisted that the only change in his views is that he no longer regards Jordan as the Palestinian state. The lesson he has taken from the Lebanon War is to avoid a repeat of the 1982 crisis in U.S.-Israeli relations and to maintain wide support at home. That's why he brought the rival Labor Party into his coalition, and why he has sought to avoid any serious clash with the George W. Bush administration.

Manipulating Arab Leadership

Sharon's strategic thinking, though, has not changed. The most reasonable reading of his actions [in 2001 and 2002] is that he still believes Israel can "exploit territorial control to manipulate the [Arab] leadership structure," as Alpher put it. Sharon wants the Palestinians to end the uprising—and then to accept his program for a "state" in enclaves broken up by Israeli settlements. Regarding Arafat as both the cause of the violent conflict and the roadblock to Palestinian acquiescence, he seeks to push him out of power. Sharon apparently thinks that Arafat's successor will be more willing to bend. Sharon, said Menachem Klein, expects "to get a Palestinian gas-station attendant who doesn't want a state, just better pay."

To achieve his goals, Sharon has used ever increasing military force while trying to maintain domestic and American backing. In April 2001, for instance, after Palestinians fired mortar shells from the Gaza Strip into Israel, Sharon ordered the army into Palestinian-controlled territory in the strip. U.S. Secretary of State Colin Powell immediately condemned the operation and the troops withdrew that day. But each successive operation makes the next one less startling. In October 2001, after Palestinian gunmen assassinated far-right Tourism Minister Rechavam Ze'evy, Israeli troops moved into Palestinian Authority territory in six West Bank cities. Several days passed before Labor Party politicians began protesting and the United States demanded a pullout. It was two weeks before the troops began withdrawing. For much of the winter of 2001, Israeli troops held pieces of Ramallah in what has become routine reoccupation.

Sharon has stopped short of deposing Arafat. Again, he's paying attention to domestic and U.S. pressure. "Israel has a national-unity government," observed Sharon's adviser Dore Gold, one "where perhaps [Labor's Foreign Minister Shimon] Peres believes you can give Arafat another chance to change, while the prime minister is very skeptical about that happening."

"To achieve his goals, Sharon has used ever increasing military force."

Instead, Sharon has sought to undercut Arafat's position. In mid-December 2001, following a Palestinian attack at the settlement of Immanuel, the Israeli security cabinet declared the Palestinian leader "no longer relevant to Israel." After that, Sharon announced that Arafat would not be allowed to leave his Ramallah headquarters until he arrested Ze'evy's killers. The point is to show that Arafat cannot function as leader and to encourage other Palestinians to remove him.

Terror Attacks

Palestinian terror attacks on Israeli civilians have played a central role in the escalation, and Arafat has done all he can to aid in his own delegitimation. But if Arafat's regime does crumble under Israeli pressure, Palestinian nationalism won't evaporate. If men now considered moderates replace Arafat, they will need to take hard-line positions to show that they are not Israel's lackeys. Klein says that it's more likely that a coalition of Islamic fundamentalists and radical nationalists would seize power. And if Sharon continues a slow-motion reconquest of Palestinian territory, guerrilla attacks on the Israeli army won't stop. Instead, the shifting battle without front lines will become more bitter.

It still remains possible, however, that further American pressure . . . or the drop in domestic support could put the brakes on Sharon. After a year and a half of violence, Israel still faces the dilemma of how to end the conflict and reach a livable compromise with the Palestinians. But the letter from Sharon's past deserves attention: His path has been disastrous before, and it remains dangerous today.

Palestinian Leadership Contributes to Conflict in the Middle East

by James Phillips

About the author: *James Phillips is a research fellow at the Heritage Foundation, a public policy, research, and educational organization.*

Editor's note: At the time of publication, Yasser Arafat was the leader of the Palestinian Authority. Should Arafat be deposed, the issues discussed in this viewpoint would still be timely. Arafat's causes are inextricably related to his office.

In June 2002, the Bush Administration dispatched CIA Director George Tenet to the Middle East to assess how to reform Palestinian intelligence and security agencies in order to make them more effective in fighting terrorism, rather than in supporting terrorism. It also dispatched Assistant Secretary of State William Burns to the region to explore ways to create a more democratic Palestinian Authority. Both of these missions can be described as the triumph of hope over experience.

The problem is that as long as Palestinian leader Yasser Arafat holds the reins of power, no amount of tinkering with institutional reforms is likely to produce the desired results: creating a Palestinian government that is willing and able to negotiate a lasting and stable peace with Israel.

A Radical Leader

Arafat remains what he has always been: a radical leader of a revolutionary movement that uses terrorism as a fundamental instrument of power. Unfortunately, he has not made the transition to statesman, as the Israelis gambled he would when they signed the 1993 Oslo peace accord [efforts that failed to facilitate peace between Israel and Palestine]. They vainly hoped that Arafat not only would renounce terrorism, but also would crack down on the terrorist op-

James Phillips, testimony before the Terrorism Oversight Panel of the House Armed Services Committee, June 6, 2002.

erations of HAMAS, Palestine Islamic Jihad, and other radical Palestinian movements that rejected peace with Israel.

Instead, Arafat merely paid lip service to his Oslo commitments to fight terrorism. Since 1993, he half-heartedly has gone through the motions of clamping down on terrorism. From time to time, under intense international pressure, the Palestinian Authority would "arrest the usual suspects," only to turn them loose once again when international attention waned. This revolving door policy, a direct violation of the Oslo accords, greatly undermined Israeli trust in its ostensible "partner for peace" and raised serious doubts about Arafat's long term intentions.

"Arafat merely paid lip service to his Oslo commitments to fight terrorism."

Rather than prepare his people for peace, he has indoctrinated them for war. He has praised suicide bombers as "martyrs" and repeatedly has called for a jihad (holy war) to liberate Jerusalem. Arafat, the veteran terrorist, has created an environment in which terrorists flourish. The Palestinian Authority continues to educate Palestinian children to hate Israelis. Ideas have consequences.

The sad truth is that as long as Arafat remains the leader of the Palestinians, there is little chance of a genuine peace. He has a long history of terrorism, which he has used to cement his control over the Palestinians, to attack Israel, and to attack other Arabs.

Violating Commitments

Arafat also has a long history of violating his commitments to other Arab states, as well as to Israel. In 1970 Arafat led a Palestinian uprising against King Hussein's government in Jordan, despite his previous pledges to respect Jordanian sovereignty. When the Jordanian Army crushed Arafat's forces during "Black September," the defeated Palestinian leader moved his base of operations to Lebanon. Despite repeated promises to avoid involvement in Lebanon's internal politics, Arafat formed a "state within a state" in southern Lebanon and allied himself with radical Lebanese movements that helped to precipitate the 1975–1976 Lebanese civil war. Chronic cross-border Palestinian terrorism against Israel provoked two Israeli military interventions in Lebanon and resulted in the expulsion of Arafat's forces from Beirut in 1982.

Arafat was rescued from irrelevance by the Israeli government of Prime Minister Yitzhak Rabin, which began the secret negotiations that evolved into the Oslo peace process in 1993. Rabin gambled that Arafat would be a dependable negotiating partner. But neither Rabin, nor his successors as Prime Minister, have been able to hold the slippery Arafat to make good on his commitments under the Oslo negotiating framework.

After Rabin was assassinated in 1995 and more than 60 Israelis were killed in a series of bloody bombings carried out by Palestinian Islamic militants in

1996, Benjamin Netanyahu was elected Prime Minister on a platform of "peace and security." Under U.S. pressure, Netanyahu signed several interim agreements with Arafat that the Palestinians promptly violated. By the end of his term, Netanyahu refused to sign new agreements with the Palestinians until Arafat lived up to his old agreements.

Netanyahu's successor, Ehud Barak, led one of the most dovish governments in Israeli history. Yet even Barak was unable to negotiate a final settlement with Arafat. At the Camp David summit in July 2000, Arafat walked away from a deal that offered the Palestinians over 90 percent of the disputed territories and control over the Temple Mount, located in the heart of Jerusalem.

Reverting to War

Arafat then reverted to the "war process" when he could not get everything he wanted out of the "peace process." He gave a green light to the intifada (uprising) in September 2000 and used the Palestinian Authority's radio and television broadcasts to incite violence against Israelis. The Al Aqsa Martyrs brigade, an offshoot of Arafat's Fatah faction, increasingly carried out suicide bombings, which formerly had been a tactic employed by Palestinian Islamic militants.

> ***"Arafat . . . has created an environment in which terrorists flourish."***

Arafat's destruction of the Oslo accords and intensifying Palestinian terrorism led to the early 2002 election of Ariel Sharon as Prime Minister. Sharon has toughened Israel's policy toward the Palestinians, but he remains open to a deal with them. Although vilified widely in the western press as "the bulldozer," Sharon is a pragmatic leader that could deliver on any peace agreement that he is able to negotiate. It was Sharon, after all, who uprooted the Israeli settlement of Yamit in the Sinai after the 1979 Egyptian-Israeli peace treaty. Few doubt that Sharon could deliver on whatever concessions that he promised.

But Yasser Arafat is an extremely unreliable partner in peace negotiations. He has violated every agreement that he has negotiated with Israel. Arafat has never fulfilled his obligations under the 1993 Oslo Agreement to systematically and permanently clamp down on terrorism and the organizations that engage in it. In fact, members of Arafat's police force have been caught red-handed engaging in terrorist attacks against Israelis.

Lost Credibility

After a series of suicide bombings led Israel to raid Arafat's West Bank headquarters in operation "Defensive Shield," the Israeli Defense Forces discovered numerous documents that established that Arafat has been personally involved in the planning and execution of terrorist attacks. He encouraged them ideologically and ordered financial and logistical support for terrorist operations.

Arafat has lost all credibility as a negotiating partner for Israel. He has failed to make the transition from a terrorist leader to a statesman. The sad truth is that he wants a "peace process" but not peace.

The Oslo process has allowed him to consolidate his control over Palestinians and build a terrorist infrastructure in the "liberated" territories. Arafat is willing to go through the motions of negotiating but he is not willing to sign a final agreement, because that would force him to make hard concessions on the Palestinian "right of return" [Arafat maintains that Palestinian refugees of the Arab-Israeli 1967 war should have the right to return to Palestine] and other issues. Moreover, if Arafat did actually reach a final peace agreement he would be relegated to the status of the leader of the smallest Arab state and could no longer strut around the world stage as a self-appointed revolutionary and Arab champion.

Israel is settling in for a long period of conflict that will only end if a new generation of Palestinian leaders comes to the conclusion that terrorism can not gain them a Palestinian state or improve the lives of the Palestinian people. There is little that the United States can do to rescue the Palestinians from their flawed leaders as long as they continue down the road of violence.

Arafat has had ample time to prove himself as a true partner for peace, but he has failed to do so. Largely due to Arafat's cynical policies, more terrorism and violence engulf Palestinians and Israelis now than . . . in 1993 at the outset of the Oslo process. It should be clear that Arafat is part of the problem, not part of the solution to the Israeli-Palestinian conflict.

Lack of Democracy Contributes to Conflict in the Middle East

by Victor Davis Hanson

About the author: *Victor Davis Hanson is a contributor to* City Journal *and* National Journal *and the author of* An Autumn of War: What America Learned from September 11 and the War on Terrorism.

Since [the] September 11, 2001, [terrorist attacks on America] we have heard mostly slander and lies about the West from radical Islamic fundamentalists in their defense of the terrorists. But the Middle Eastern mainstream—diplomats, intellectuals, and journalists—has also bombarded the American public with an array of unflattering images and texts, suggesting that the extremists' anti-Americanism may not be an eccentricity of the ignorant but rather a representative slice of the views of millions. For example, Egyptian Nobel Prize–winning novelist Naguib Mahfouz reportedly announced from his Cairo home that America's bombing of the Taliban [in Afghanistan] was "just as despicable a crime" as the September 11 attacks—as if the terrorists' unprovoked mass murder of civilians were the moral equivalent of selected air strikes against enemy soldiers in wartime. Americans, reluctant to answer back their Middle Eastern critics for fear of charges of "Islamophobia" or "Arab smearing," have let such accusations go largely unchecked.

False Premises

Two striking themes—one overt, one implied—characterize most Arab invective: first, there is some sort of equivalence—political, cultural, and military—between the West and the Muslim world; and second, America has been exceptionally unkind toward the Middle East. Both premises are false and reveal that the temple of anti-Americanism is supported by pillars of utter ignorance. Few in the Middle East have a clue about the nature, origins, or history of democracy, a word that, along with its family ("constitution," "freedom," and "citizen"), has no history in the Arab vocabulary, or indeed any philological pedigree in any language other than Greek and Latin and their modern European offspring. Consensual government is not the norm of human politics but a rare and precious idea, not imposed or bequeathed but usually purchased with the blood of heroes and patriots, whether in classical Athens, revolutionary America, or more recently in Eastern Europe. Democracy's lifeblood is secularism and religious tolerance, coupled with free speech and economic liberty.

Afghan tribal councils, without written constitutions, are better than tyranny, surely; but they do not make consensual government. Nor do the Palestinian parliament and advisory bodies in Kuwait. None of these faux assemblies is elected by an unbound citizenry, free to criticize (much less recall, impeach, or depose) their heads of state by legal means, or even to speak openly to journalists about the failings of their own government. Plato remarked of such superficial government-by-deliberation that even thieves divvy up the loot by give-and-take, suggesting that the human tendency to parley is natural but is not the same as the formal machinery of democratic government.

Our own cultural elites, either out of timidity or sometimes ignorance of the uniqueness of our own political institutions, seldom make such distinctions. But the differences are critical, because they lie unnoticed at the heart of the crisis in the Muslim world, and they explain our own tenuous relations with the regimes in the Gulf and the Middle East. Israel does not really know to what degree the Palestinian authorities have a real constituency, because the people of the West Bank themselves do not know either—inasmuch as they cannot debate one another on domestic television or campaign on the streets for alternate policies. Palestinian Authority leader Yasser Arafat assumed power by Western fiat; when he finally was allowed to hold real and periodic elections in his homeland, he simply perpetuated autocracy—as corrupt as it is brutal.

By the same token, we are surprised at the duplicity of the Gulf States in defusing internal dissent by redirecting it against Americans, forgetting that such is the way of all dictators, who, should they lose office, do not face the golden years of Jimmy Carter's busy house-building or Bill Clinton's self-absorbed angst. Either they dodge the mob's bullets or scurry to a fortified compound on the French coast a day ahead of the posse. The royal family of Saudi Arabia cannot act out of principle because no principle other than force put and keeps them in power. All the official jets, snazzy embassies, and expensive press agents cannot hide that these illegitimate rulers are not in the political sense Western at all.

Fearing Democracy

How sad that intellectuals of the Arab world—themselves only given freedom when they emigrate to the United States or Europe—profess support for democratic reform from Berkeley or Cambridge but secretly fear that, back home, truly free elections would usher in folk like the Iranian imams, who, in the manner of the Nazis in 1933, would thereupon destroy the very machinery that elected them. The fact is that democracy does not spring fully formed from the head of Zeus but rather is an epiphenomenon—the formal icing on a preexisting cake of egalitarianism, economic opportunity, religious tolerance, and constant self-criticism. The former cannot appear in the Muslim world until gallant men and women insist upon the latter—and therein demolish the antidemocratic and medieval forces of tribalism, authoritarian traditionalism, and Islamic fundamentalism.

> ***"Few in the Middle East have a clue about the nature, origins, or history of democracy."***

How much easier for non-voters of the Arab world to vent frustration at the West, as if, in some Machiavellian plot, a democratic America, Israel, and Europe have conspired to prevent Muslims from adopting the Western invention of democracy! Democracy is hardly a Western secret to be closely guarded and kept from the mujaheddin. Islam is welcome to it, with the blessing and subsidy of the West. Yes, we must promote democracy abroad in the Muslim world; but only they, not we, can ensure its success.

The catastrophe of the Muslim world is also explicable in its failure to grasp the nature of Western success, which springs neither from luck nor resources, genes nor geography. Like third-world Marxists of the 1960s, who put blame for their own self-inflicted misery upon corporations, colonialism, and racism—anything other than the absence of real markets and a free society—the Islamic intelligentsia recognizes the Muslim world's inferiority vis-à-vis the West, but it then seeks to fault others for its own self-created fiasco. Government spokesmen in the Middle East should ignore the nonsense of the cultural relativists and discredited Marxists and have the courage to say that they are poor because their populations are nearly half illiterate, that their governments are not free, that their economies are not open, and that their fundamentalists impede scientific inquiry, unpopular expression, and cultural exchange.

Tragically, the immediate prospects for improvement are dismal, inasmuch as the war against terrorism has further isolated the Middle East. Travel, foreign education, and academic exchanges—the only sources of future hope for the Arab world—have screeched to a halt. All the conferences in Cairo about Western bias and media distortion cannot hide this self-inflicted catastrophe—and the growing ostracism and suspicion of Middle Easterners in the West.

But blaming the West, and Israel, for the unendurable reality is easier for millions of Muslims than admitting the truth. Billions of barrels of oil, large populations, the Suez Canal, the fertility of the Nile, Tigris, and Euphrates valleys, invaluable geopolitical locations, and a host of other natural advantages that helped create wealthy civilizations in the past now yield an excess of misery, rather than the riches of resource-poor Hong Kong or Switzerland. How could it be otherwise, when it takes bribes and decades to obtain a building permit in Cairo; when habeas corpus is a cruel joke in Baghdad; and when Saudi Arabia turns out more graduates in Islamic studies than in medicine or engineering?

Self-Criticism Is Crucial

To tackle illiteracy, gratuitous state-sanctioned killing, and the economic sclerosis that comes from corruption and state control would require the courage and self-examination of Eastern Europe, Russia, South America, even of China. Instead, wedded to the old bromides that the West causes their misery, that fundamentalist Islam and crackpot mullahs have had no role in their disasters, that the subjugation of women is a "different" rather than a foul (and economically foolish) custom, Muslim intellectuals have railed since the terrorist attacks of September 11 about the creation of Israel half a century ago, and they have sat either silent or amused while the mob in their streets chants in praise of a mass murderer. Meanwhile millions of Muslims tragically stay sick and hungry in silence.

Has the Muslim world gone mad in its threats and ultimatums? Throughout this war against terrorism, Muslims have saturated us with overt and with insidious warnings. If America retaliated to the mass murder of its citizens, the Arab world would turn on us; if we bombed during Ramadan, we would incur lasting hatred; if we continued in our mission to avenge our dead, not an American would be safe in the Middle East. More disturbing even than the screaming street demonstrations have been the polite admonitions of corrupt grandees like Crown Prince Abdallah of Saudi Arabia or editor Abdul Rahman al Rashed of Saudi Arabia's state-owned Al Sharq al Awsat. Don't they see the impotence and absurdity of their veiled threats, backed neither by military force nor cultural dynamism? Don't they realize that nothing is more fatal to the security of a state than the divide between what it threatens and what it can deliver?

"Democracy is hardly a Western secret to be closely guarded."

There is an abyss between such rhetoric and the world we actually live in, an abyss called power. Out of politeness, we needn't crow over the relative military capability of 1 billion Muslims and 300 million Americans; but we should remember that the lethal, 2,500-year Western way of war is the reflection of very different ideas about personal freedom, civic militarism, individuality on the battlefield, military technology, logistics, decisive battle, group discipline, civilian audit, and the dissemination and proliferation of knowledge. . . .

We are militarily strong, and the Arab world abjectly weak, not because of greater courage, superior numbers, higher IQs, more ores, or better weather, but because of our culture. When it comes to war, 1 billion people and the world's oil are not nearly as valuable military assets as MIT, West Point, the U.S. House of Representatives, C-Span, Bill O'Reilly, and the G.I. Bill. Between Xerxes on his peacock throne overlooking Salamis and Saddam Hussein on his balcony reviewing his troops, between the Greeks arguing and debating before they rowed out with Themistocles and the Americans haranguing one another on the eve of the Gulf War, lies a 2,500-year cultural tradition that explains why the rest of the world copies its weapons, uniforms, and military organization from us, not vice versa.

Charades of Arabia

Many Middle Easterners have performed a great media charade throughout this war. They publish newspapers and televise the news, and thereby give the appearance of being modern and Western. But their reporters and anchormen are by no means journalists by Western standards of free and truthful inquiry. Whereas CNN makes a point of talking to the victims of collateral damage in Kabul, al-Jazeera would never interview the mothers of Israeli teenagers blown apart by Palestinian bombs. Nor does any Egyptian or Syrian television station welcome freewheeling debates or Meet the Press–style talk shows permitting criticism of the government or the national religion. Instead, they quibble over their own degrees of anti-Americanism and obfuscate the internal contradictions of Islam. The chief dailies in Algiers, Teheran, and Kuwait City look like Pravda of old. The entire Islamic media is a simulacrum of the West, lacking the life-giving spirit of debate and self-criticism.

As a result, when Americans see a cavalcade of talking Middle Eastern heads nod and blurt out the party line—that Israel is evil, that the United States is naive and misled, that Muslims are victims, that the West may soon have to reckon with Islamic anger—they assume the talk is orchestrated and therefore worth listening to only for what it teaches about how authoritarian governments can coerce and corrupt journalists and intellectuals.

A novelist who writes whatever he pleases anywhere in the Muslim world is more likely to receive a fatwa and a mob at his courtyard than a prize for literary courage, as Naguib Mahfouz and Salman Rushdie have learned. No wonder a code of silence pervades the Islamic world. No wonder, too, that Islam is far more ignorant of us than we of it. And no wonder that the Muslims haven't a clue that, while their current furor is scripted, whipped up, and mercurial, ours is far deeper and more lasting.

The Eastern Other

Every Western intellectual knows journalist Edward Said's much-hyped theory of "Orientalism," a purely mythical construct of how Western bias has misunderstood and distorted the Eastern "Other." In truth, the real problem is "Westernism"—the fatally erroneous idea in the Middle East that its propaganda-spewing Potemkin television stations give it a genuine understanding of the nature of America, an understanding Middle Easterners believe is deepened by the presence in their midst of a few McDonald's franchises and hired U.S. public-relations firms. That error—which mistakes ignorance for insight—helps explain why Usama bin Ladin so grossly miscalculated the devastating magnitude of our response to September 11. In reality, the most parochial American knows more about the repressive nature of the Gulf States than the most sophisticated and well-traveled sheikh understands about the cultural underpinnings of this country, including the freedom of speech and inquiry that is missing in the Islamic press.

"Blaming the West, and Israel, for the unendurable reality is easier for millions of Muslims than admitting the truth."

Millions in the Middle East are obsessed with Israel, whether they live in sight of Tel Aviv or thousands of miles away. Their fury doesn't spring solely from genuine dismay over the hundreds of Muslims Israel has killed on the West Bank; after all, Saddam Hussein butchered hundreds of thousands of Shiites, Kurds, and Iranians, while few in Cairo or Damascus said a word. Syria's Assad liquidated perhaps 20,000 in sight of Israel, without a single demonstration in any Arab capital. The murder of some 100,000 Muslims in Algeria and 40,000 in Chechnya in the last decade provoked few intellectuals in the Middle East to call for a pan-Islamic protest. Clearly, the anger derives not from the tragic tally of the fallen but from Islamic rage that Israelis have defeated Muslims on the battlefield repeatedly, decisively, at will, and without modesty.

If Israel were not so successful, free, and haughty—if it were beleaguered and tottering on the verge of ruin—perhaps it would be tolerated. But in a sea of totalitarianism and government-induced poverty, a relatively successful economy and a stable culture arising out of scrub and desert clearly irks its less successful neighbors. Envy, as the historian Thucydides reminds us, is a powerful emotion and has caused not a few wars.

Culture Determines a Nation's Prosperity

If Israel did not exist, the Arab world, in its current fit of denial, would have to invent something like it to vent its frustrations. That is not to say there may not be legitimate concerns in the struggle over Palestine, but merely that for millions of Muslims the fight over such small real estate stems from a deep psychological wound. It isn't about lebensraum or some actual physical threat. Israel is a constant reminder that it is a nation's culture—not its geography or size or magnitude of its oil reserves—that determines its wealth or freedom. For the Middle East to make peace with Israel would be to declare war on itself, to admit that its own fundamental way of doing business—not the Jews—makes it poor, sick, and weak.

Throughout the Muslim world, myth and ignorance surround U.S. foreign policy toward the Middle East. Yes, we give Israel aid, but less than the combined billions that go to the Palestinians and to Egypt, Jordan, and other Muslim countries. And it is one thing to subsidize a democratic and constitutional (if cantankerous) ally but quite another to pay for slander from theocratic or autocratic enemies. Though Israel has its fair share of fundamentalists and fanatics, the country is not the creation of clerics or strongmen but of European emigres, who committed Israel from the start to democracy, free speech, and abundant self-critique.

Far from egging on Israel, the United States actually restrains the Israeli military, whose organization and discipline, along with the sophisticated Israeli arms industry, make it quite capable of annihilating nearly all its bellicose neighbors without American aid. Should the United States withdraw from active participation in the Middle East and let the contestants settle their differences on the battlefield, Israel, not the Arab world, would win. The military record of four previous conflicts does not lie. Arafat should remember who saved him in Lebanon; it was no power in the Middle East that brokered his exodus and parted the waves of Israeli planes and tanks for his safe passage to the desert.

The Muslim world suffers from political amnesia, we now have learned, and so has forgotten not only Arafat's resurrection but also American help to beleaguered Afghanis, terrified Kuwaitis, helpless Kurds and Shiites, starving Somalis, and defenseless Bosnians—direct intervention that has cost the United States much more treasure and lives than mere economic aid for Israel ever did. They forget; but we remember the Palestinians cheering in Nablus hours after thousands of our innocents were incinerated in New York, the hagiographic posters of a mass murderer in the streets of Muslim capitals, and the smug remonstrations of Saudi prince Alwaleed to Mayor Giuliani at Ground Zero.

> ***"Don't they see the . . . absurdity of their veiled threats?"***

Saudi Arabian and Kuwaiti Westernized elites find psychological comfort in their people's anti-American rhetoric, not out of real grievance but perhaps as reassurance that their own appetite for all things Western doesn't constitute rejection of their medieval religion or their thirteenth-century caliphate. Their apologists in the United States dissemble when they argue that these Gulf sheikhs are forced to master a doublespeak for foreign consumption, or that they are better than the frightening alternative, or that they are victims of unfair American anger that is ignorant of Wahhabi custom. In their present relationship with the terrorists, these old-fashioned autocrats are neutrals only in the sense that they now play the cagier role of Franco's Spain to Hitler's Germany. They aid and abet our enemies, but never overtly. If the United States prevails, the Saudis can proclaim that they were always with us; should we lose a shooting war with the terrorists, the princes can swear that their prior neutrality really constituted allegiance to radical Islam all along.

Western Migration

In matters of East-West relations, immigration has always been a one-way phenomenon. Thousands flocked to Athens and Rome; few left for Parthia or Numidia unless to colonize or exploit. People sneak into South, not North, Korea—in the same manner that few from Hong Kong once braved gunfire to reach Peking (unless to invest and profit). Few Israeli laborers are going to the West Bank to seek construction jobs. In this vein is the Muslim world's longing for the very soil of America. Even in the crucible of war, we have discovered that our worst critics love us in the concrete as much as they hate us in the abstract.

For all the frothing, it seems that millions of our purported enemies wish to visit, study, or (better yet) live in the United States—and this is true not just of Westernized professors or globe-trotting tycoons but of hijackers, terrorists, the children of the Taliban, the offspring of Iranian mullahs, and the spoiled teenage brats of our Gulf critics. The terrorists visited lap dancers, took out frequent-flier miles, spent hours on the Internet, had cell phones strapped to their hips, and hobnobbed in Las Vegas—parasitic on a culture not their own, fascinated with toys they could not make, and always ashamed that their lusts grew more than they could be satisfied. Until September 11, their ilk had been like fleas on a lazy, plump dog, gnashing their tiny proboscises to gain bloody nourishment or inflict small welts on a distracted host who found them not worth the scratch.

This dual loathing and attraction for things Western is characteristic of the highest echelon of the terrorists themselves, often Western-educated, English-speaking, and hardly poor. Emblematic is the evil genius of [the terrorist network] al-Qaida, the sinister Dr. al-Zawahiri: he grew up in Cairo affluence, his family enmeshed in all the Westernized institutions of Egypt.

> ***"Islam is far more ignorant of us than we of it."***

Americans find this Middle Eastern cultural schizophrenia maddening, especially in its inability to fathom that all the things that Muslim visitors profess to hate—equality of the sexes, cultural freedom, religious tolerance, egalitarianism, free speech, and secular rationalism—are precisely what give us the material things that they want in the first place. CDs and sexy bare midriffs are the fruits of a society that values freedom, unchecked inquiry, and individual expression more than the dictates of state or church; wild freedom and wild materialism are part of the American character. So bewildered Americans now ask themselves: Why do so many of these anti-Americans, who profess hatred of the West and reverence for the purity of an energized Islam or a fiery Palestine, enroll in Chico State or UCLA instead of madrassas in Pakistan or military academies in Iraq?

The embarrassing answer would explain nearly everything, from [terrorist] bin Ladin to the intifada. Dads and moms who watch al-Jazeera and scream in the street at the Great Satan really would prefer that their children have dollars, an annual CAT scan, a good lawyer, air conditioning, and Levis in American hell than be without toilet paper, suffer from intestinal parasites, deal with the secret police, and squint with uncorrected vision in the Islamic paradise of Cairo, Teheran, and Gaza. Such a fundamental and intolerable paradox in the very core of a man's heart—multiplied millions of times over—is not a healthy thing either for them or for us, as we have learned since September 11.

Recognizing Middle Eastern Achievement

Most Americans recognize and honor the past achievements of Islamic civilization and the contribution of Middle-Eastern immigrants to the United States and Europe, as well as the traditional hospitality shown visitors to the Muslim world. And so we have long shown patience with those who hate us, and more curiosity than real anger.

But that was then, and this is now. A two-kiloton explosion that incinerated thousands of our citizens—planned by Middle Easterners with the indirect financial support of purportedly allied governments, the applause of millions, and the snickering and smiles of millions more—has had an effect that grows not wanes.

So a neighborly bit of advice for our Islamic friends and their spokesmen abroad: topple your pillars of ignorance and the edifice of your anti-Americanism. Try to seek difficult answers from within to even more difficult questions without. Do not blame others for problems that are largely self-created or seek solutions over here when your answers are mostly at home. Please, think hard about what you are saying and writing about the deaths of thousands of Americans and your relationship with the United States. America has been a friend more often than not to you. But now you are on the verge of turning its people—who create, not follow, government—into an enemy: a very angry and powerful enemy that may be yours for a long, long time to come.

Oil Profits Cause Conflict in the Middle East

by Lawrence G. Potter

About the author: *Lawrence G. Potter is a professor of international affairs at Columbia University.*

The Persian Gulf is a 600-mile-long arm of the Indian Ocean, which separates the Arabian peninsula from Iran. (Since the 1960s some Arab states have referred to the Persian Gulf as the Arabian Gulf, in an attempt to give it a new identity and belittle Iran.) The Gulf is surrounded by Iran, the predominant state in terms of population, and seven Arab countries: Iraq, Kuwait, Saudi Arabia, Bahrain, Qatar, the UAE and Oman. The Gulf is bounded by the Shatt al-Arab waterway in the north, which forms the frontier between Iran and Iraq, and the Strait of Hormuz in the south, which connects it to the Gulf of Oman and the Indian Ocean. The strait, which is 34 miles wide at its narrowest point, is the choke point of the Gulf: some 30,000 vessels, mostly oil tankers, pass through it each year. The possibility of its closure by Iran has long been a nightmare for Western oil importers and defense planners.

The Gulf states contain some 116 million people, representing many ethnic, religious, linguistic and political communities. A major cleavage pits Arab against Persian. Arabic, a Semitic language, is spoken in Iraq and the countries of the peninsula, whereas Iran has an Aryan heritage, and its main language, Persian (Farsi), is an Indo-European tongue. Persians regard their cultural legacy as richer than that of the Arabs, although their religion, Islam, was founded by an Arab, the Prophet Muhammad.

Muslims (followers of the Islamic religion) are split into two major sects, Sunni and Shiites. The two differ over who was legitimately entitled to lead the Islamic community after the death of Muhammad in A.D. 632. The Sunnis, who predominate, believe that the community should choose its own leader. Shiites, who are a majority in Iran, believe leadership is vested in the family of the

Prophet. Sunni Islam has historically been associated with bestowing legitimacy on the power of rulers; Shiite Islam, with opposition, martyrdom and revolt.

Vast Energy Deposits

The present importance of the Gulf stems from its energy deposits. Sixty-five percent of the world's known oil reserves are located in the Gulf countries, which produce over a third of the world's daily output. (By comparison, North America holds 8.5 percent of the world's reserves.) Saudi Arabia ranks first in reserves, with 259 billion barrels, followed by Iraq (112 billion), the UAE (98 billion), Kuwait (94 billion), and Iran (93 billion). The cost of oil production in the Gulf is the lowest in the world: it currently ranges from fifty cents a barrel in Saudi Arabia to $2 in offshore wells in the UAE. The Gulf is also rich in natural gas, with Iran and Qatar holding the world's second- and third-largest reserves, respectively. . . .

> ***"The cost of oil production in the Gulf is the lowest in the world."***

The modern strategic importance of the Gulf dates from the mid-nineteenth century, when three great empires confronted each other there: British India, czarist Russia and Ottoman Turkey. The British established political control over much of the Gulf in the early 1800s and kept it for 150 years. A tradition of outside involvement persists today.

After World War I, the political map of much of the Middle East was redrawn. The Ottoman Empire was replaced by modern nations, including Turkey, Iraq and Saudi Arabia. The small Arab shaikhdoms on the western shore of the Gulf were under British protection until 1971 (in the case of Kuwait, 1961). Iran was never a colony, and for much of the nineteenth and twentieth centuries Britain competed with Russia for influence there.

The oil revenues that began to accumulate after World War II enabled the Gulf states to modernize, and, by the 1960s and 1970s, to provide generous entitlement programs for their citizens. The state became what political scientists call a "rentier" one: the income from oil accrued directly to the ruler, who provided for his citizens' economic security in return for their political loyalty. This arrangement bought time for the tribal shaikhs who had been in power before the discovery of oil. It also led to the growth of a "rentier mentality" among the citizenry, who felt a sense of entitlement to riches, whether they worked or not.

Domestic Challenges

All of the Gulf states must contend with rapidly rising populations. In 1950, their combined population was estimated to be some 24 million; today, it is around 116 million and is projected to rise to 209 million by the year 2025. In Iran, a population of 35 million at the time of the revolution in 1978 had swollen to 60 million by 1996. The rate of population growth, however, has not been accompanied by an equivalent rise in oil revenues, the main source of government income. Today, the oil monarchies can no longer afford the generous social programs they instituted in wealthier days. Unemployment is now a widespread problem, and millions of jobs must be created in the next 15 years. At the same time that countries cut benefits, they are confronted with demands for more say in government.

The holiday from reality is over in the Gulf monarchies, both politically and economically, according to oil economist Vahan Zanoyan. To survive, the governments must forge a new social contract that allows for greater political participation. The question is whether the rulers are willing to make the changes needed, especially if their monopoly of power is threatened. It is not clear that Gulf monarchies are ready to confront their problems: "Surprisingly little indigenous discussion takes place regarding the future of the area," according to scholar Anwar Gargash of the UAE. "No regionwide consensus or outlook is emerging, and no Gulf perspective is crystallizing regarding the future state of affairs."...

Oil and Social Change

The story of the Persian Gulf in the twentieth century is the story of oil—the exploration, discovery and export of petroleum—and the effect this has had on traditional societies. The vast revenues that suddenly accrued to the fortunate Gulf states led to far-reaching economic changes, but on the Arabian peninsula, few political ones. Indeed, the oil revenues, coupled with British support, enabled monarchies, which were overthrown in most other Middle Eastern states after World War II, to survive and thrive in the Gulf.

Oil was first discovered in southwest Iran in 1908. In 1914, on the eve of World War I, the British government, which needed oil for its warships, assumed control of the producers, the Anglo-Persian Oil Company. Oil was discovered in commercial quantities in Iraq in the Kurdish region in 1927, in Bahrain in 1932, and in Saudi Arabia and Kuwait in 1938. Before World War II, Iran was the leading oil exporter in the Middle East, and its refinery at Abadan was the largest in the world.

Oil operations in a country were usually controlled exclusively by a single company, often a joint venture or partnership. Such an arrangement discouraged competition and prevented overproduction, which would lower prices. Britain initially tried to prevent the Gulf shaikhs from signing agreements with non-British companies, but eventually American firms won concessions in Bahrain, Kuwait and Saudi Arabia. The British refused the United States permission to open any consulates in the area, however, until 1950, when the first one opened in Kuwait.

> ***"The rate of population growth . . . has not been accompanied by an equivalent rise in oil revenues."***

Petroleum Partnerships

The most famous petroleum partnership was the Arabian-American Oil Company, known as Aramco, which was granted a concession by King Ibn Saud in 1933. "If the first pillar of the Saudi state has been the Wahhabi religious movement," writes historian J.B. Kelly, "the second has been the Arabian-American Oil Company. . . . The company has served the house of Saud as guide, confidant, tutor, counselor, emissary, advocate, steward and factotum." Aramco aimed to be a model company, not only seeing to the training, health care and housing of its workers, but also building roads, hospitals and water pipelines for the surrounding community. Its expatriate workers were housed in enclaves that resembled suburban America.

"The oil revenues . . . enabled monarchies . . . to survive and thrive in the Gulf."

After World War II, major changes took place in the oil industry. Iran had long complained that Britain was too stingy in the compensation it paid: in 1950, the oil company paid Iran £16 million in royalties and made £100 million in profits from its Iranian operations. When Aramco agreed in 1950 to share profits with Saudi Arabia on a 50-50 basis, Iran wanted a similar agreement. The (now renamed) Anglo-Iranian Oil Company, however, would not agree to profit sharing. Matters came to a head when Iran's prime minister, Mohammad Mossadeq (1951–53), nationalized the company. For Britain, this was a great humiliation and meant the loss of a key economic asset. Mossadeq's government was overthrown in August 1953 and the shah, Mohammad Reza Pahlavi, was restored to power in a countercoup that was organized by U.S. and British intelligence.

Thereafter, although Iran retained sovereignty over its oil, it struck a new agreement with a consortium of oil companies to operate the concession. The British share was reduced to 40 percent and American companies received an equal stake. (It was not until 1973 that Iran took full control of its oil operations.) A major consequence of the Iranian crisis was that companies across the Gulf, especially in Kuwait and Saudi Arabia, stepped up production. At the same time new commercial quantities of oil were discovered—in Qatar and Abu Dhabi in 1960, in Oman in 1963, and in Dubai in 1969.

The Impact of Oil

The development of the oil industry set in motion many changes. Between World Wars I and II, it began to open up the Gulf to the outside world at the expense of British control. For the first time, local rulers struck commercial deals with oil companies and gained a secure source of income independent of any British subsidy.

The Gulf area was also becoming more important as an international communications and transportation hub, with British airlines securing landing rights to stop over on the way to India. (Traditional ties with the subcontinent, though, were becoming less important than relations with the greater Arab world.) With increased oil exploration came more pressure to delineate boundaries. This led, after World War II, to the protracted Buraimi oasis dispute between Saudi Arabia (backed by the United States) and Oman and Abu Dhabi (backed by Britain) over boundaries in the southeastern part of the Arabian peninsula, which was believed to contain oil. In 1952, Saudi troops occupied part of the oasis. Arbitration failed, and in 1955 the Saudis were evicted by forces from Abu Dhabi and Oman under British command. Not until 1974 did Saudi Arabia relinquish its claim, in return for a strip of territory giving it access to the Gulf east of Qatar.

Oil proved to be a mixed blessing. It provided salvation to Bahrain in the 1930s, when the economy collapsed along with the pearl industry. In the postwar period, it paid for the rapid modernization of Iran and the Arab monarchies, some of which enjoyed very high per capita incomes. In the 1960s and 1970s, the Arab Gulf states began providing their people free education, health care and housing. But there was also a downside. Even the shah of Iran, in a 1973 interview with the Italian journalist Oriana Fallaci, was ambivalent about the value of Iran's great resource: "So much has been written about the curse we call oil, and believe me, when you have it, on the one hand it's a blessing but on the other it's a great inconvenience. Because it represents such a danger. The world could blow up on account of this damned oil."

"Oil proved to be a mixed blessing."

The modernization process, which lasted for centuries in the West, has been compressed into decades in the Gulf countries, putting a great strain on traditional societies. Saudi Arabian novelist Abdelrahman Munif, in the first volume of a monumental trilogy in Arabic entitled *Cities of Salt*, describes a Bedouin village's tragic encounter with American oil prospectors. The author's theme is that the discovery of oil was a curse: the desire for material gain replaced old values of loyalty, honor and respect for tradition. "The tragedy is not in our having the oil," he said in an interview, "but in the way we use the wealth it has created and in the future awaiting us after it has run out." The availability of huge oil revenues, he believes, corrupted political leaders and turned Saudi Arabia into a repressive state.

Legitimacy to Rule

Governments of the states created in the Gulf in the twentieth century—Iraq, Saudi Arabia, Kuwait, Bahrain, Qatar and the UAE—keenly feel the need to create a sense of national identity. Governments of Iraq, for example, have long promoted the idea that ethnic, religious and linguistic differences are irrelevant, since all its citizens are Iraqis. (Some fear that Iraq is now undergoing a process of "retribalization," in which people are returning to primordial loyalties of clan, family and religion.) In the Arabian peninsula, governments have tried to create a historical memory and national symbols to elicit loyalty and reinforce the legitimacy of the rulers. Governments have emphasized their cultural heritage *(turath)* by carrying out archaeological excavations and building new museums in places such as Doha (Qatar) and Dubai (UAE). The challenge in all the Gulf states has been to reconcile traditional forms of rule with modern forms of political expression.

On the Arabian side of the Gulf, Islam and tribalism have traditionally provided legitimacy to the ruling families. In Saudi Arabia, their close association with Wahhabi Islam has given the Al Saud rulers a status that other Gulf monarchs lack. However, Islam and tribalism, which had previously acted as a check on the rulers, now have been adapted to serve them, according to political scientist F. Gregory Gause III. The rulers have made the clerical establishment dependent upon the state by financing it, something that never happened in Shiite Iran. The tribes are now under effective state control, although the ruler makes a public display of his fidelity to tribal institutions, such as the *majlis* [a tradition that allows anyone to approach the ruler to seek redress of his problems] and *shura* [a consultative form of government]. "What most Westerners see as a 'traditional' political culture is in fact a construction of recent decades, in which rulers employ a political language redolent of Islamic and tribal overtones to convince their citizens of the legitimacy of their political system," notes Gause.

Over the past century, the traditional way of life in the Arab Gulf states has been irrevocably changed, due in large measure to the British intervention and the rise of the oil industry. External and internal forces have served to reinforce the power and wealth of one segment of the population, the ruling shaikhs. Because of the way in which the modern states were formed and boundaries arbitrarily delimited, tribal and family loyalties and religious, linguistic and ethnic identities in many cases are more important than country citizenship. These are at the root of many of the present tensions in the region.

Water Scarcity Could Cause Conflict in the Middle East

by Christine Drake

About the author: *Christine Drake is a professor of geography in the Department of Political Science and Geography at Old Dominion University in Norfolk, Virginia.*

In the Middle East, water may be more important than either oil or politics. While the area's proven oil reserves are estimated to be sufficient for at least a hundred years, water supplies are already insufficient throughout the region, and competition for them is inevitably going to increase in the years ahead. Already there have been a number of clashes between countries over water, and several political leaders have suggested that future conflicts may well center on access to water, both surface and subsurface sources.

Water is, after all, the most basic of resources, critical to sustainable development in the Middle East and the well-being of the area's population. (The Middle East is defined here as the traditional Southwest Asian countries, including Turkey, Iran, and also Egypt but excluding the other North African countries and the former Soviet republics.)

Geography and History

At the root of the problem of limited water resources is the physical geography of the Middle East, for this region is one of the most arid in the world. Descending air (which can hold more moisture) and prevailing northeast trade winds that blow from a continental interior region to a warmer, more southerly location explain why almost all of the Middle East is dry.

Only Turkey, Iran, and Lebanon have adequate rainfall for their needs because of their more northern locations and/or mountainous topography, which intercept rain- and snow-bearing westerly winds in winter. Every other country has at least part of its territory vulnerable to water shortages or is dependent on an exogenous water source (one originating outside its boundaries).

About 35 percent of the Middle East's annual renewable water resources is provided by exogenous rivers. Certainly, the two major river systems that bring water into the region, the Nile to Sudan and Egypt, and the Tigris-Euphrates primarily to Syria and Iraq, both have sources outside the arid zone—the Nile in the heart of East Africa (the White Nile) and especially in Ethiopia (the Blue Nile), and the Tigris and Euphrates in Turkey (and to a limited extent in Iran). Other rivers, such as the Jordan, Yarmuk, Orontes, and Baniyas, are too small to be of much significance, yet in the case of the Jordan-Yarmuk are large enough to quarrel over.

"[The Middle East] is one of the most arid [regions] in the world."

Droughts are common and a natural part of the climate. In addition, rainfall is seasonal. Thus the problem concerns not only the total volume of water available but also its seasonality—the shortage of water in the dry, hot summers. In addition, most of the Middle East's rainfall is very irregular, localized, and unpredictable. Furthermore, the region suffers from high evaporation and evapotranspiration rates, a factor that diminishes the value of the water that is available.

In the past, people adapted to the seasonality of the rainfall and the periodic droughts and were able to produce enough food to meet local demand. They devised a variety of ingenious ways to store water and meet the needs of both rural and urban populations. But such measures have become inadequate since the middle of the twentieth century and a new balance has to be found among competing needs for water.

Causes of the Conflict

Escalation of the conflict over water issues in the Middle East results from the confluence of a number of factors, especially rapidly growing populations, economic development and increasing standards of living, technological developments, political fragmentation, and poor water management. The inadequacy and relative ineffectiveness of international water laws as a means of settling and regulating freshwater issues as well as the lack of any real enforcement mechanisms compound the problem.

Underlying and exacerbating the conflict over water resources is the enormous increase in population. From somewhere around 20 million in 1750, the Middle Eastern population tripled to around 60 million by 1950, then quintupled to 301 million by 1999. It is estimated that at present rates of growth, the population will double again in less than 35 years. As populations grow, per capita availability of water decreases.

Immigration has also been a significant part of the problem, particularly in the Jordan-Yarmuk watershed area, as hundreds of thousands of Jews from all over the world have moved to Israel since its establishment in 1948 and hundreds of thousands of Palestinians have relocated to Jordan from Kuwait in the wake of the Gulf War. If an independent Palestinian state comes into being, water shortages could be compounded by up to 2.2 million Palestinians currently registered worldwide as refugees who could return and settle there.

Rapid economic development and rising standards of living, spurred on by the oil boom, have raised the demand for water both by industry and domestic users. Urbanization also adds to the strain: Over half the population of the Middle East now lives in urban areas where populations consume ten to twelve times as much water per capita as village dwellers.

Technological developments now enable people to alter their environments in unprecedented ways. People's direct dependence on the natural seasons and cyclical availability of water has been lessened by their ability to build huge dams and create vast reservoirs where increased evaporation occurs; to construct large irrigation schemes, where much water is wasted through inefficient watering methods; to extract large quantities of shallow groundwater, resulting in lowered water tables; and to damage or destroy rivers and aquifers by polluting them, often irrevocably.

Political Tension

Political fragmentation poses another problem. Whereas in times past empires covered the entire area and dampened conflict among the different peoples within them, the end of World War I saw the dissolution of the Ottoman Empire, which had controlled much of the Middle East for over five hundred years. Similarly, British colonialism and administration of most of the Nile basin reduced friction over water until the 1950s. With the creation of independent states and increasing ethnic consciousness, growing disparities and rivalries have developed among the very diverse populations in the region: Arabs, Turks, Iranians, Kurds, Ethiopians, and Israelis, to name just the main protagonists. All have become more competitive and nationalistic.

Overuse and pollution of rivers and shared aquifers (underground water-bearing formations) are a source of growing tension. Water was one of the underlying causes of the 1967 Arab-Israeli war and continues to be a stumbling block in the search for peace. Forty percent of Israel's water, for example, is obtained from aquifers beneath the West Bank and Gaza. Water was a major rallying cry both for the Palestinian Intifada in the occupied territories and for conservative parties in Israel.

> ***"Underlying . . . the conflict over water resources is the enormous increase in population."***

Poor water management exacerbates the problems of both water quantity and quality. Great quantities of water are lost through inefficient irrigation systems such as flood irrigation of fields, unlined or uncovered canals, and evaporation from reservoirs behind dams. Pollution from agriculture, including fertilizer and pesticide runoff as well as increased salts, added to increasing amounts of industrial and toxic wastes and urban pollutants, combine to lower the quality of water for countries downstream (called downstream riparians), increase their costs, and provoke dissatisfaction and frustration, again creating irritations that can lead to conflict.

"Forty percent of Israel's water . . . is obtained from aquifers beneath the West Bank and Gaza."

Existing international water laws are underdeveloped and inadequate and in some respects do not seem geared to the problems of arid developing countries, having been developed in the temperate and better watered areas of Europe and North America. Various legal principles exist, but there are no legally binding international obligations for countries to share water resources. Agreements must depend upon the mutual goodwill of co-riparians (the countries bordering a specific river) in any particular drainage basin. The likelihood of conflict or cooperation depends very much upon a number of geopolitical factors. These include the relative positions of the co-riparians within the drainage basin, the degree of their national interest in the problem, and the power available to them both externally and internally to pursue their policies.

Although there are many international rivers and several important shared aquifers in the Middle East, and all have potential for water disputes, the potential for the greatest conflicts occurs in the three major international river basins: the Tigris-Euphrates, the Nile, and the Jordan-Yarmuk.

The Tigris-Euphrates Valley

In the case of the Tigris-Euphrates there are several fundamental issues. Turkey is the source area for more than 70 percent of the united Tigris-Euphrates flow and owns large portions of the drainage basins of the two rivers. It also has the upstream position and so the opportunity to use the waters of the Tigris-Euphrates as it pleases. Indeed, the creation of Turkey's Southeast Anatolia Development Project (GAP) is evidence of its felt rights. This very ambitious plan is to build twenty-two dams on the Euphrates to increase irrigation and electricity generation and to bring greater prosperity to a heretofore neglected Kurdish region of the country. Turkey argues that the GAP project will actually benefit all three riparian countries, Syria and Iraq as well as Turkey, as it will reduce damage from floods and even out the river's flow, storing excess water from the wet season and snowmelt so it can be used in the dry summer season and soften the impact of droughts.

Inevitably, however, as more of the Euphrates water is withdrawn and used in Turkey, less will be available for downstream riparians. Indeed, the GAP project, if completed, is expected to reduce the flow of the Euphrates by 30 to 50 percent within the next fifty years. Furthermore, the water will be of lower quality, as increased amounts of salts, fertilizers, pesticides, and other pollutants enter the river after having been used for irrigation in Turkey.

Syria depends on the Euphrates for over half its water supply and has a population growing at 2.8 percent a year, with almost no effort being made to reduce that high rate of growth. It also plans to expand its irrigation projects. Iraq is even more dependent than Syria on the waters of the Euphrates and Tigris and claims historic rights to the water, but its position as the lowest riparian state renders it vulnerable to decreased water supply from both Turkey and Syria. A 1987 protocol in which Turkey promised 500 cubic meters per second at its border with Syria has not been solidified into a firm agreement or treaty, nor has Syria's pledge to deliver 290 cubic meters per second to Iraq, an amount which is only about half of what Iraq claims (570 cubic meters per second) and is clearly far below its needs. Iraq's population is expected to grow from 22.5 million in 1999 to around 35 million in 2010. The only ameliorating fact here is that Iraq can compensate for lack of water in the Euphrates by taking water from the Tigris, which at present is underutilized.

A related problem is the current dispute over the actual size of the annual flow of the Euphrates. Data on average discharge vary enormously. In addition, Syria's claims that Turkey is deliberately reducing the flow of the Euphrates are countered by Turkey's claim that the region suffers from periodic droughts.

The Nile Basin

The Nile catchment is shared by ten countries, but the main disputes over water so far involve just the three giants of Ethiopia, Sudan, and Egypt. Of the three, Egypt faces the most obvious water crisis, and the situation is becoming more severe each year. Its population of about 67 million is growing annually by more than 1 million. Egypt is almost totally dependent on the Nile (while contributing virtually nothing to it) and also claims that prior usage entitles it to a disproportionate share of the river's waters. With over 95 percent of agricultural production from irrigated land, Egypt needs to expand its agricultural land and reduce the saltwater intrusion of the Mediterranean into the Nile delta, goals threatened by growing water shortages.

Since about 85 percent of the river's flow into Egypt originates on the Ethiopian plateau, Egypt is most concerned about its relationship with Ethiopia. It has repeatedly warned Ethiopia not to take any steps that would affect the Blue Nile discharges. On several occasions, however, Ethiopia has claimed that it reserves its sovereign right to use Blue Nile and Sobat River water for the benefit of its own population (increasing at 2.5 percent a year). Indeed, it has extensive plans to develop about fifty irrigation projects and expand its hydroelectric generation potential as

> ***"Egypt is almost totally dependent on the Nile."***

well. Experts believe it is highly possible that Egypt may experience a modest reduction in the amount of Nile water available to it, as Ethiopia claims a larger share of the Nile headwaters in the future.

Egypt is also concerned about its immediate upstream neighbor, Sudan. Although Sudan is incapable of expanding its water use much at present, racked as it is by civil war, economic recession, and a shortage of foreign investment, that situation could well change. Sudan has the potential to become the breadbasket of the Middle East, but that would be possible only with increased use of Nile water. Since 1929 the two countries have had an agreement allocating the Nile waters. The 1929 allocation was adjusted, however, in 1959, by an agreement that gave Sudan more water, reducing Egypt's relative share from 12:1 to 3:1.

"Water tables are being lowered at alarming rates."

What will happen when Ethiopia and Sudan begin demanding more of the Nile's water? Will Egypt accept the Helsinki and International Law Commission rules that irrefutably entitle Ethiopia and Sudan to a larger portion of Nile water? Will Egypt try to change those rules to give greater weight to the principle of prior use? Or will it be tempted to use its position as the most powerful nation in the Nile basin to assure its present allocation, even if this means the use of military force and international conflict?

The Jordan-Yarmuk Waters

It is in the Jordan-Yarmuk basin that tensions have run the highest, and it is in the Jordan River basin, perhaps more than any other, that water has become "a highly symbolic, contagious, aggregated, intense, salient, complicated zero-sum power-and-prestige-packed crisis issue, highly prone to conflict and extremely difficult to resolve" [as stated by political scientists Frederick Frey and Thomas Naff]. All the countries and territories in and around the Jordan River watershed—Israel, Syria, Jordan, and the West Bank—are currently using between 95 percent and more than 100 percent of their annual renewable freshwater supply. Shortfalls have been made up through the overpumping of limited groundwater. Water tables are being lowered at alarming rates. It is obvious that all the surface water and groundwater resources are thus overstretched and overutilized. Jordan's situation is perhaps the most serious, with only 5 percent of its land area receiving sufficient rainfall to support cultivation. Although less than 10 percent of its agricultural land is irrigated at present, irrigation in the Jordan valley consumes about 65 percent of the country's total utilizable surface water.

Scarce water resources have either precipitated or exacerbated much of the recent political conflict in the Jordan River basin. Indeed, the Jordan basin has been described as "having witnessed more severe international conflict over water than any other river system in the Middle East . . . and [it] . . . remains by far the most likely flashpoint for the future."

For Syria, Jordan, and Israel, the proportion of water derived from international sources is very high. Over 90 percent of Syria's water resources are shared with its neighbors, Turkey, Iraq, Israel, Lebanon, and Jordan. Jordan gets more than 36 percent of its water from sources shared with Syria, the West Bank, and Israel. And more than half of Israel's water resources are shared with Syria, Lebanon, Jordan, and the Palestinians. The economies and societies of the countries in the basin of the Jordan-Yarmuk are very vulnerable to any restrictions in their water supplies; hence, the situation is highly volatile.

Water conflicts among the protagonists have been long-standing, although the situation has worsened in recent years. Both overt and covert conflict has occurred over the division of the Jordan-Yarmuk waters, as both Israel and the Arab countries have tried to divert water: Israel through its National Water Carrier to expand agriculture in the Negev; and the Arabs through their attempts to divert water from the Jordan basin to Lebanon, Syria, and Jordan. Disagreement over water was a major contributing cause of the 1967 Arab-Israeli war. Through its victory Israel enhanced its water resources by capturing the Golan Heights and the West Bank aquifer. These captured sources supply as much as 25 percent of Israel's total water needs but have led to charges that Israel is stealing Arab water. On the West Bank, Israeli authorities have prevented the Palestinians from digging new wells or even finding alternative sources of water to compensate for water lost as a result of withdrawals by Jewish settlements. The disparity between the water allocations to Jewish and Arab settlements on the West Bank is enormous: The average aggregate per capita consumption for the Jewish settlements ranges between 90 and 120 cubic meters, whereas for Arab settlements the consumption is only 25–35 cubic meters per capita. . . .

The Future

Experts disagree on the likelihood for future conflict over water. Some argue that more water conflicts are inevitable because of the combination and synergistic effect of the causes already discussed: growing water scarcity, increasing populations, rising standards of living, and higher consumption levels. Many rivers and aquifers in the region are shared, and the lack of adequate treaties and international laws, added to the absence of adequate enforcement mechanisms, increases the likelihood of confrontation. There has also been a history of hostility among some of the countries and a growing nationalistic self-awareness of the differences among the varied peoples in the Middle East. One could suggest, perhaps a bit cynically, that countries "need" enemies to deflect attention from internal divisions, political corruption, and economic hardships and to help unify or in-

> ***"States have it in their power actually to decide to treat water use as a vehicle for cooperation."***

tegrate the population. Some even contend that countries also need to justify their military forces and keep them busy.

Others argue, however, that future water conflicts are not likely for a number of substantial reasons. Cooperation is cheaper than conflict. As one person put it: "Why go to war over water, when for the price of one week's fighting you could build five desalination plants?" There is considerable international pressure to avoid war over water, partly because it could escalate into war over other, even more intractable, issues. In addition, a number of external geopolitical forces are indirectly exerting pressure for peaceful cooperation on water allocation issues, such as the end of the Cold War manipulation of states in the Middle East, progress toward a peace between Israel and its neighbors, and Turkey's goal of entering the European Union. The fact that in each river basin there is one stronger military power (Turkey, Egypt, and Israel) further deters conflict. Lack of capital will probably delay and may even prohibit development of some water-using projects. Moreover, if the solutions suggested earlier are implemented, conflict will be less likely.

Furthermore, states have it in their power actually to decide to treat water use as a vehicle for cooperation. Throughout the years of hostilities in the Middle East, water issues have actually been the subject of occasional secret talks and even some negotiated agreements between the states in the region. In peace talks, cooperation on regional water planning or technology might actually help provide momentum toward negotiated political settlement. According to Frederick Frey and Thomas Naff, "Precisely because it is essential to life and so highly charged, water can—perhaps even tends to—produce cooperation even in the absence of trust between concerned actors."

In any case, water is only one of many factors at work in the Middle East—certainly an important one but only one. Israel's settlements on the West Bank and its occupation of the Golan Heights, radical groups within not only the Palestinian population and Israel but the Kurds and other disadvantaged groups, irredentist pressures, economic pressures—these and many other factors could produce bitter conflict and lead to water's use either as a weapon or as an excuse for hostility.

Much depends on leadership in the region, including the ability of governments to control radical or conservative elements wanting to exploit water issues; obtain capital for the development of industry (which will take some pressure off agriculture); obtain secure food sources from outside the area; reduce population growth; educate the public on water issues, develop an ethos of conservation, and change water pricing systems; and finally, promote cooperation and encourage the sharing of technology, data, and research. One has to hope that the benefits of cooperation in the development of river basins and the rule of law will be seen to outweigh the costs of conflict.

Chapter 2

How Does Conflict in the Middle East Affect the International Community?

Chapter Preface

On September 11, 2001, Islamic extremists hijacked four American airplanes and crashed them into the World Trade Center towers, the Pentagon, and rural Pennsylvania, killing more than three thousand people. Media coverage of the attacks emphasized that the hijackers were Muslim, a religion many Americans know little about. Indeed, after the attacks, many Americans wondered if Islam condones terrorism and violence. However, as stated by President George W. Bush in the wake of the attacks, "These acts of violence against innocents violate the fundamental tenets of the Islamic faith." The Muslims who perpetrated the attack on America belonged to a radical extremist sect of Islam—often called Islamism—that bears little resemblance to the faith practiced by nearly 2 billion people worldwide. Many people believe that Islamism poses a terrorist threat to the international community, especially the West.

As stated by Daniel Pipes, director of the Middle East Forum, "Islamism is an ideology that demands man's complete adherence to the sacred law of Islam and rejects as much as possible outside influence. . . . It is imbued with a deep antagonism towards non-Muslims and has a particular hostility towards the West. It amounts to an effort to turn Islam, a religion and civilization, into an ideology." Thus, according to Pipes, Islamism is far removed from traditional Islam.

Islamism strives to reassert traditional Islamic principles in order to revive Muslim power and control in the modern world. Islamists contend that one of the reasons for many Arab countries' poverty and political disorganization is that Muslims abandoned traditional Islamic customs and embraced sinful Western ways. In order to regain the global superiority that Muslims enjoyed in the Middle Ages, Islamists argue, Muslims must obey the strict regulations set forth in the Koran and the shari'a (Islamic law). However, many of these tenets, such as cutting off a thief's hands or the mandatory separation of the sexes, are incompatible with modern society. In order to legitimize these precepts, Islamists condemn modernity as an evil influence in Muslim society. According to Pipes, "Islamists strain to reject all aspects of Western influence—customs, philosophy, political institutions and values."

Unfortunately, Islamist rejection of Western influence is often accompanied by intense hatred and resentment of Western nations, especially the United States. Most Islamists despise American immodesty and secularism, and some Islamist regimes, such as the Taliban in Afghanistan, have banned televisions, radios, and music to restrict non-Muslim influence in their nations. This hostility, combined with anger toward Western foreign policy, erupted in more than five terrorist attacks on Americans, mainly soldiers overseas, over the last ten years. According to Pipes, "A state of war exists between [Islamists] and the

West, mainly America, not because of the American response but because radical fundamentalist Muslims see themselves in a long-term conflict with Western values."

The attacks on September 11, 2001, proved that Islamism poses a terrorist threat to the international community. The possibility of future terrorist attacks is frightening, but it is important to remember that most Muslims are not Islamists and that most espouse a peaceful interpretation of the Koran and Islamic traditions. The majority of Muslims, especially those who live in the United States, are moderate, and they accept and value secular societies. These Muslims represent a compromise between Western and Islamic customs that celebrates cultural identity and tolerance. The authors in the following chapter debate whether or not Islam is a threat to the West and discuss other Middle East issues affecting the international community.

Islam Is a Threat to the West

by Daniel Pipes

About the author: *Daniel Pipes is a political analyst whose articles have appeared in numerous publications including the* Atlantic Monthly, Foreign Affairs, Harper's, *the* National Review, *the* New Republic, *and the* Weekly Standard. *He has also written several books, such as* The Hidden Hand: Middle East Fears of Conspiracy *and* The Long Shadow: Culture and Politics in the Middle East.

In the aftermath of the [terrorist attacks] on September 11, 2001, American politicians from George W. Bush on down have tripped over themselves to affirm that the vast majority of Muslims living in the United States are just ordinary people. Here is how the President put it during a visit to a mosque on September 17, 2001: "America counts millions of Muslims among our citizens, and Muslims make an incredibly valuable contribution to our country. Muslims are doctors, lawyers, law professors, members of the military, entrepreneurs, shopkeepers, moms and dads." Two days later, he added that "there are millions of good Americans who practice the Muslim faith who love their country as much as I love the country, who salute the flag as strongly as I salute the flag."

These soothing words, echoed and amplified by many columnists and editorial writers, were obviously appropriate at a moment of high national tension and amid reports of mounting bias against Muslims living in the United States. And it is certainly true that the number of militant Islamic operatives with plans to carry out terrorist attacks on the United States is statistically tiny. But the situation is more complex than the President would have it.

The Muslim population in this country is not like any other group, for it includes within it a substantial body of people—many times more numerous than the agents of Osama bin Laden—who share with the suicide hijackers a hatred of the United States and the desire, ultimately, to transform it into a nation living under the strictures of militant Islam. Although not responsible for the

Daniel Pipes, "The Danger Within: Militant Islam in America," *Commentary*, vol. 112, November 2001, pp. 19–25.

atrocities in September 2001, they harbor designs for this country that warrant urgent and serious attention.

Granting Righteousness and Wisdom

In June 1991, Siraj Wahaj, a black convert to Islam and the recipient of some of the American Muslim community's highest honors, had the privilege of becoming the first Muslim to deliver the daily prayer in the U.S. House of Representatives. On that occasion he recited from the Qur'an and appealed to the Almighty to guide American leaders "and grant them righteousness and wisdom."

"[Islamic radicals] harbor designs for this country that warrant urgent and serious attention."

A little over a year later, addressing an audience of New Jersey Muslims, the same Wahaj articulated a rather different message from his mild and moderate invocation in the House. If only Muslims were more clever politically, he told his New Jersey listeners, they could take over the United States and replace its constitutional government with a caliphate. "If we were united and strong, we'd elect our own emir [leader] and give allegiance to him. . . . [T]ake my word, if 6–8 million Muslims unite in America, the country will come to us." In 1995, Wahaj served as a character witness for Omar Abdel Rahman in the trial that found that blind sheikh guilty of conspiracy to overthrow the government of the United States. More alarming still, the U.S. attorney for New York listed Wahaj as one of the "unindicted persons who may be alleged as co-conspirators" in the sheikh's case.

The disparity between Wahaj's good citizenship in the House and his militant forecast of a Muslim takeover—not to mention his association with violent felons—is only one example of a larger pattern common to the American Muslim scene. Another example, about which I have written recently elsewhere, involves the American Muslims for Jerusalem, an organization whose official advocacy of "a Jerusalem that symbolizes religious tolerance and dialogue" contrasts markedly with the wild conspiracy-mongering and crude anti-Jewish rhetoric in which its spokesmen indulge at closed events. At a minimum, then, anyone who would understand the real views of American Muslims must delve deeper than the surface of their public statements.

Not a New Goal

Doing so, one discovers that the ambition to take over the United States is hardly a new one. The first missionaries for militant Islam, or Islamism, who arrived here from abroad in the 1920's, unblushingly declared, "Our plan is, we are going to conquer America." The audacity of such statements hardly went unnoticed at the time, including by Christians who cherished their own missionizing hopes. As a 1922 newspaper commentary put it:

> To the millions of American Christians who have so long looked eagerly for-

> ward to the time the cross shall be supreme in every land and the people of the whole world shall have become the followers of Christ, the plan to win this continent to the path of the "infidel Turk" will seem a thing unbelievable. But there is no doubt about its being pressed with all the fanatical zeal for which the Mohammedans are noted.

But it is in recent decades, as the Muslim population in the country has increased significantly in size, social standing, and influence, and as Islamism has made its presence widely felt on the international scene, that this "fanatical zeal" has truly come into its own. A catalyzing figure in the story is the late Ismail Al-Faruqi, a Palestinian immigrant who founded the International Institute of Islamic Thought and taught for many years at Temple University in Philadelphia. Rightly called "a pioneer in the development of Islamic studies in America," he was also the first contemporary theorist of a United States made Muslim. "Nothing could be greater," Al-Faruqi wrote in the early 1980's, "than this youthful, vigorous, and rich continent [of North America] turning away from its past evil and marching forward under the banner of Allahu Akbar [God is great]."

Al-Faruqi's hopes are today widely shared among educated Muslim leaders. Zaid Shakir, formerly the Muslim chaplain at Yale University, has stated that Muslims cannot accept the legitimacy of the American secular system, which "is against the orders and ordainments of Allah." To the contrary, "The orientation of the Qur'an pushes us in the exact opposite direction." To Ahmad Nawfal, a leader of the Jordanian Muslim Brethren who speaks frequently at American Muslim rallies, the United States has "no thought, no values, and no ideals"; if militant Muslims "stand up, with the ideology that we possess, it will be very easy for us to preside over this world." Masudul Alam Choudhury, a Canadian professor of business, writes matter-of-factly and enthusiastically about the "Islamization agenda in North America."

> ***"Establishing Islamism [in America] would signal its final triumph over . . . Christianity and liberalism."***

A Concrete Plan

For a fuller exposition of this outlook, one can do no better than to turn to a 1989 book by Shamim A. Siddiqi, an influential commentator on American Muslim issues. Cryptically titled *Methodology of Dawah Ilallah in American Perspective* (more idiomatically rendered as "The Need to Convert Americans to Islam"), this 168-page study, published in Brooklyn, remains largely unavailable to general readers but is widely posted on Islamist websites, where it enjoys a faithful readership. In it, in prose that makes up in intensity and vividness for what it lacks in sophistication and polish, Siddiqi lays out both a detailed rationale and a concrete plan for Islamists to take over the United States and establish "Islamic rule" (iqamat ad-din).

Why America? In Siddiqi's judgment, the need to assume control here is even more pressing than the need to sustain the revolution of the mullahs in Iran or to destroy Israel, for doing so will have a much greater positive impact on the future of Islam. America is central not for the reasons one might expect—its large population, its wealth, or the cultural influence it wields around the world—but on three other grounds.

The first has to do with Washington's role as the premier enemy of Islamism (or, possibly, of Islam itself). In Siddiqi's colorful language, whenever and wherever Muslims have moved toward establishing an Islamic state, the "treacherous hands of the secular West are always there . . . to bring about [their] defeat." Nor are Muslim rulers of any help, for they are "all in the pockets of the Western powers." If, therefore, Islam is ever going to attain its rightful place of dominance in the world, the "ideology of Islam [must] prevail over the mental horizon of the American people." The entire future of the Muslim world, Siddiqi concludes, "depends on how soon the Muslims of America are able to build up their own indigenous movement."

"There are indeed some . . . who see the United States as . . . an 'enemy of Islam.'"

Secondly, America is central because establishing Islamism here would signal its final triumph over its only rival, that bundle of Christianity and liberalism which constitutes contemporary Western civilization. (One cannot help noting the irony that Siddiqi's tract appeared in the same year, 1989, as futurist Francis Fukuyama's famous article speculating that, with the collapse of Communism and the apparent triumph of liberal democracy, we had begun to approach the "end of history.") And thirdly, and still more grandly, the infusion of the United States with Islamism would make for so powerful a combination of material success and spiritual truth that the establishment of "God's Kingdom" on earth would no longer be "a distant dream."

But this dream will not happen by itself. To American Muslims, writes Siddiqi, falls the paramount responsibility of bringing Islam to power in their country; and to this goal, Muslims must devote "all of their energies, talents, and resources." For this is how they will be assessed on judgment day: "Every Muslim living in the West will stand in the witness box in the mightiest court of Allah . . . in Akhirah [the last day] and give evidence that he fulfilled his responsibility, . . . that he left no stone unturned to bring the message of the Qur'an to every nook and corner of the country."

How this desired end is to be achieved is a question on which opinions differ in Siddiqi's world. Basically, the disagreement centers on the role of violence.

The Role of Violence

As has been made irrefutably clear, there are indeed some, not just abroad but living among us, who see the United States as (in the phrase of Osama bin

Laden) an "enemy of Islam" that must be brought to its knees and destroyed. In its broad outlines, this judgment came to be solidified during the crisis over Iraq's seizure of Kuwait in the early 1990's, when militants like bin Laden discerned a historic parallel between the presence of American troops on the soil of Saudi Arabia and the brutal Soviet occupation of Afghanistan in the 1980's. In their dialectical view, as the *New Yorker* writer Mary Ann Weaver has explained, the United States, just like the Soviet Union before it, represented "an infidel occupation force propping up a corrupt, repressive, and un-Islamic government." And just as the Islamist mujahideen in Afghanistan had succeeded in defeating and driving out their occupiers, and thereby played a role in the collapse of the mighty Soviet Union itself, so Islamists might cause the collapse of the United States: one down, one to go, as it were.

To the blind sheikh Omar Abdel Rahman, who after bin Laden is perhaps today's most notorious enemy of the United States, bombing the World Trade Center in 1993 was part and parcel of this revolutionary strategy to "conquer the land of the infidels" by force. The idea, as one of his followers put it, was to "bring down their highest buildings and the mighty constructions they are so proud of, in order thoroughly to demoralize them." And this was a duty that Islamists saw as incumbent on all Muslims; having helped humiliate the Soviets in Afghanistan, they now, as one native-born American convert to Islam proclaimed in July 1989, must "complete the march of jihad until we reach America and liberate her."

But there are several problems with the approach of revolutionary violence, even from the perspective of those who share its goal. The most obvious has to do with its impact on American society. Although attacks like the 1993 bombing or the suicide massacres of September 11, 2001, are intended to demoralize the American people, prompt civil unrest, and weaken the country politically, what they do instead is to bring Americans together in patriotism and purpose. Those who mastermind them, in the meantime, are often caught: Abdel Rahman is sitting out a life sentence in a federal penitentiary, his campaign of violence stillborn, while Osama bin Laden is the object of a massive manhunt to get him "dead or alive." Unlike in the very different case of the Soviet Union, it is hard to see how the use of force will succeed in wearing down this country, much less lead to a change in government.

> ***"Muslims can refashion [America] into something acceptable in God's eyes."***

Besides, as a number of commentators have recently pointed out, in targeting all Americans the perpetrators of Islamic violence do not bother even to discriminate between non-Muslim and Muslim victims. According to preliminary estimates, several hundred Muslims died in the collapse of the World Trade Center. This is not exactly calculated to enlist the participation of most resident Muslims in a campaign of violent insurrection.

The Non-Violent Strategy

For all these reasons, the non-violent way would seem to have a brighter future, and it is in fact the approach adopted by most Islamists. Not only is it legal, but it allows its enthusiasts to adopt a seemingly benign view of the United States, a country they mean to rescue and make over rather than to destroy, and it dictates a strategy of working with Americans rather than against them. As a teacher at an Islamic school in Jersey City, near New York, explains, the "short-term goal is to introduce Islam. In the long term, we must save American society." Step by step, writes a Pakistan-born professor of economics, by offering "an alternative model" to Americans, Muslims can refashion what Ismail Al-Faruqi called "the unfortunate realities of North America" into something acceptable in God's eyes.

Practically speaking, there are two main prongs to the non-violent strategy. The first involves radically increasing the number of American Muslims, a project that on the face of it would not seem very promising. Islam, after all, is still an exotic growth in the United States, its adherents representing just 1 to 2 percent of the population and with exceedingly dim prospects of becoming anything like a majority. Islamists are not so unrealistic as to think that these numbers can be substantially altered any time soon by large-scale immigration (which is politically unfeasible and might anyway provoke a backlash) or by normal rates of reproduction. Hence they focus most of their efforts on conversion.

They do so not only as a matter of expediency but on principle. For Islamists, converting Americans is the central purpose of Muslim existence in the United States, the only possible justification for Muslims to live in an infidel land. In the view of Shamim Siddiqi, there is no choice in the matter—American Muslims are "ordained by Allah" to help replace evil with good, and otherwise "have no right even to breathe." "Wherever you came from," adds Siraj Wahaj, "you came . . . for one reason—for one reason only—to establish Allah's din [faith]."

This imperative, relentlessly propagated by authoritative figures and promoted by leading Islamist organizations like the Muslim Student Association, has been widely adopted by Muslim Americans at large. Many attest to the sense of responsibility that flows from being an "ambassador for Islam," and are ever mindful of the cardinal importance of winning new adherents. And, given what they hold to be the truth of their message and the depravity of American culture, Islamists are optimistic about their chances of success. "A life of taqwah [piety] will immediately attract non-Muslims toward Islam," writes Abul Hasan Ali Nadwi, an important Indian Islamist, in his "Message for Muslims in the West.". . .

> ***"Islamists seek public financial support for Islamic schools, mosques, and other institutions."***

Numbers Are Insufficient

But if increasing numbers are necessary, they are also not sufficient. After all, whole countries—Turkey, Egypt, Algeria—have overwhelmingly Muslim populations, but Islamism is suppressed by their governments. From an Islamist point of view, indeed, the situation in Turkey is far worse than in the United States, for it is a more grievous thing to reject the divine message as interpreted by Islamists than merely to be ignorant of it. Therefore, in addition to building up Muslim numbers, Islamists must prepare the United States for their own brand of ideology. This means doing everything possible toward creating an Islamist environment and applying Islamic law. Activities under this heading fall into various categories.

"By whittling away at the existing order, [Islamists] would change the country's whole way of life."

Promoting Islamic rituals and customs in the public square. Islamists want secular authorities to permit students in public institutions, for example, to recite the basmallah (the formula "In the name of God, the Merciful, the Compassionate") in classroom exercises. They also want the right to broadcast over outdoor loudspeakers the five daily Islamic calls-to-prayer. Similarly, they have agitated for publicly maintained prayer facilities in such institutions as schools and airports.

Privileges for Islam. Islamists seek public financial support for Islamic schools, mosques, and other institutions. They also lobby for special quotas for Muslim immigrants, try to compel corporations to make special allowances for Muslim employees, and demand the formal inclusion of Muslims in affirmative-action plans.

Restricting or disallowing what others may do. Islamists want law-enforcement agencies to criminalize activities like drinking and gambling that are offensive to Islam. While seeking wide latitude for themselves, for instance when it comes to expressing disrespect for American national symbols, they would penalize expressions of disrespect for religious figures whom Islam deems holy, especially the prophet Muhammad; punish criticism of Islam, Islamism, or Islamists; and close down critical analysis of Islam.

Changing the Way of Life

Some of these aims have already been achieved. Others may seem relatively minor in and of themselves, implying no drastic alterations in existing American arrangements but rather only slight adjustments in our already expansive accommodation of social "diversity." Cumulatively, however, by whittling away at the existing order, they would change the country's whole way of life—making Islam a major public presence, ensuring that both the workplace and the educational system accommodate its dictates and strictures, adapting family customs to its code of conduct, winning it a privileged position in American life, and finally imposing its system of law. Steps along the way would include more radical and intrusive actions like prohibiting conversion out of Islam, criminalizing adultery, banning the consumption of pork, formalizing enhanced rights for Muslims at the expense of non-Muslims, and doing away with equality of the sexes.

"Doing battle with [Islamists] will demand focus, determination, and sacrifice."

A Muslim majority? Islamic law the law of the land? Even the most optimistic Islamists concede the task will not be easy. Just as Muhammad confronted die-hard opponents in pagan Mecca, writes Siddiqi, so pious Muslims in America will face opponents, led by the "secular press cum media, the agents of capitalism, the champions of atheism (Godless creeds) and the [Christian] missionary zealots." Doing battle with them will demand focus, determination, and sacrifice. . . .

It hardly needs pointing out that this vision is, to say the least, farfetched, or that Islamists are deluding themselves if they think that today's newborns will be attending college in an Iranian-style United States. But neither is their effort altogether quixotic: their devotion, energy, and skill are not to be questioned, and the larger Muslim-American community for which they claim to speak is assuredly in a position, especially as its numbers grow, to affect our public life in decisive ways. Indeed, despite persistent complaints of bias against them—more voluminous than ever in the wake of the airplane hijackings on September 11, 2001—Muslim Americans have built an enviable record of socioeconomic accomplishment in this country, have won wide public acceptance of their faith, and have managed to make it particularly difficult for anyone to criticize their religion or customs.

Whether and to what degree the community as a whole subscribes to the Islamist agenda are, of course, open questions. But what is not open to question is that, whatever the majority of Muslim Americans may believe, most of the organized Muslim community agrees with the Islamist goal—the goal, to say it once again, of building an Islamic state in America. To put it another way, the major Muslim organizations in this country are in the hands of extremists. . . .

That a significant movement in this country aspires to erode its bedrock social and legal arrangements, including the separation of church and state, and has even developed a roadmap toward that end, poses a unique dilemma, especially at this moment. Every responsible public official, and every American of good faith, is bent on drawing a broad distinction between terrorists operating in the name of Islam and ordinary Muslim "moms and dads." It is a true and valid distinction, but it goes much too far, and if adhered to as a guideline for policy it will cripple the effort that must be undertaken to preserve our institutions.

What such an effort would look like is a subject unto itself, but at a minimum it would have to entail the vigilant application of social and political pressure to ensure that Islam is not accorded special status of any kind in this country, the active recruitment of moderate Muslims in the fight against Islamic extremism, a keener monitoring of Muslim organizations with documented links to Islamist activity, including the support of terrorism, and the immediate reform of immigration procedures to prevent a further influx of visitors or residents with any hint of Islamist ideology. Wherever that seditious and totalitarian ideology has gained a foothold in the world, it has wrought havoc, and some societies it has brought to utter ruin. The preservation of our existing order can no longer be taken for granted; it needs to be fought for.

Islam Is Not a Threat to the West

by Antony T. Sullivan

About the author: *Antony T. Sullivan has written some eighty book chapters, journal articles, and academic reviews focusing on Arab and Islamic history and relations between the West and the Muslim world. He has lectured at some seventy universities and public policy institutes in the United States and overseas. Since 1988, Sullivan has held an appointment as Associate for the Center for Middle Eastern and North African Studies at the University of Michigan.*

Islam—as a religion, culture and society—most emphatically is not an enemy of the West.

Those who argue the contrary slander not only the third and last of the three great Abrahamic revelations but make all too likely the outbreak of either a religious war pitting Christianity (and perhaps Judaism) against Islam or a war of civilizations pitting the West against the entire Muslim world. And be assured: Any wars of religion or civilization will not be wars that the West—or the United States—will win. . . .

Similar Origins

Years before the attack on the World Trade Center and the Pentagon, distinguished scholars such as professors Samuel Huntington of Harvard University and Bernard Lewis of Princeton University, and publicists such as Daniel Pipes and Steven Emerson, were suggesting the possibility of clashes between Islam and the West, and the likelihood that Muslims worldwide might support terrorism to destroy Western civilization. Their work, implicitly or explicitly, prepared the ground for the U.S. Anti-Terrorism Act of 1996 and the consequent jailings without charge of up to 19 Arabs or Muslims in the United States. At least one of the individuals imprisoned was held for more than three years. No evidence of culpability of any of these individuals ever was adduced publicly, and most of these Arab or Muslim detainees are fortunately now free on court

Antony T. Sullivan, "Should Policymakers See Islam as an Enemy of the West? No: Islam, Judaism, and Christianity Historically Produce Societies with Like Characteristics," *Insight on the News*, vol. 17, November 5, 2001, pp. 40–44.

order. Ideas—particularly those of distinguished scholars—do have consequences, and bad ideas may indeed have very bad consequences.

Judaism, Christianity and Islam all trace their origins back at least to the Old Testament prophet Abraham. Each of these three religions venerates him. Each of these Abrahamic faiths has similarities with the other two, and each historically has produced civilizations and societies with recognizably similar characteristics.

Not only is Islam not an enemy of the West, but it, like Judaism, is part of the larger civilizational ecumene that we in the contemporary West know—or ought to. In fact, the West stops at the Indus, not at the Dardanelles. Today, Islam is part and parcel of the West, just as the West is part and parcel of Islam.

Attacking Islam

What occurred on September 11, 2001, was first and foremost an attack on Islam itself. Specifically, that criminal operation constituted an attack on the values of compassion, beneficence and mercy that pervade the Koran and that historically have characterized the practice of Islam. The ignorant terrorists responsible for the operation of September 11 might have done well to reread the fatiha (the eight opening lines) of the Koran. There, they would have found compassion and mercy mentioned a total of four times.

And they would have done well to read Chapter 5, Verse 32 of the Koran: "We prescribed . . . that whosoever kills a person, unless it be for manslaughter or for mischief in the land, it is as though he had killed all mankind. And whosoever saves a life, it is as though he had saved the lives of all men."

Moreover, had they consulted additional portions of the Koran, they might have discovered that the planned operation only could have been undertaken by Muslim apostates. To the extent that the Koran endorses war at all, it endorses only defensive combat designed to protect the Islamic community in the most dire of circumstances. No faithful Muslim possibly could justify the operation of September 11 within that limitation.

The Koran includes passages invoking violence. But so does the Old Testament, in considerable number. To wit, Deuteronomy 32:42: "I will make my arrows drank with blood, and my sword shall devour flesh; and that with the blood of the slain and of the captives, from the long-haired heads of the enemy" (See also Deuteronomy 2:34, 3:6 and 7:2.) Evocations of violence in religious texts is one of many elements the Abrahamic religions share.

> ***"Islam is part and parcel of the West, just as the West is part and parcel of Islam."***

Contemporary terrorists who invoke Islam to justify their actions are utterly ignorant of classical Islamic law. Muslim jurisprudence is categorical: It prescribes the harshest penalties, including death, for terrorism. Crimes defined as terroristic and/or criminal in classical jurisprudence include the poisoning of wells, abduction, brigandage, night assaults and rape. Modern terrorists who proclaim themselves Muslims seem unaware that the Koran makes clear that the injustice of others in no way excuses any injustice of one's own.

For almost a decade Muslim religious leaders and public figures have been sponsoring international conferences designed to demonstrate the fallacy of any notion of Islam being an enemy of the West or the likelihood of any clash of civilizations. I know, because I have participated in several of these conferences. Those who persist in merchandising notions of Islam being an enemy of the West should know that there is an almost universal rejection of this idea in the Muslim world itself. Such writers mislead Western public opinion and alienate Muslims everywhere who otherwise might be only too glad to be friends with the West.

Denouncing Terrorism

The September 11 attack has been publicly and categorically condemned by the most important Islamist leaders and public figures in the world. On September 24, 2001, the London-based Arabic daily *al Quds al Arabi* published a statement in which more than 75 such individuals forcefully denounced the "terrorist aggression on large American installations which killed innocent victims belonging to more than 60 countries." They described the tragedy as a "crime against humanity" and called upon all believers in the sanctity of human life to "denounce and fight against terrorism wherever it is and regardless of the ethnicity or religion of those involved in it." These Islamists added that "all those proved to have committed terrorist acts against humanity . . . should be tried and punished, without any kind of allowances."

> ***"Contemporary terrorists who invoke Islam to justify their actions are utterly ignorant of classical Islamic law."***

Rather than any antipathy emanating from Islam, Americans and other Westerners should recognize that anger toward the United States in the Muslim world emanates primarily from the rage at specific American policies. U.S. partiality to Israel at the expense of Palestinians, maintenance of sanctions on Iraq that fail to weaken Saddam Hussein while resulting in the death of half-a-million Iraqi children, and consistent failure to support individual liberty and limited government in Muslim states are among their major grievances. Those who pontificate on Islam somehow being an enemy of the West almost never mention or grant any legitimacy to this list of complaints. And these grievances are fully shared by the 7 million American citizens who now are Muslim.

One of the most promising contemporary initiatives in interfaith and intercivilizational dialogue is the Circle of Tradition and Progress, which brings together distinguished Western and Muslim (Islamist) thinkers to explore and combat the worldwide challenge of radical secular modernity. The philosophic basis for this joint enterprise is the thought (from the Western tradition) of such thinkers as Thomas Aquinas, Edmund Burke, Eric Voegelin, Gerhart Niemeyer and Russell Kirk. Muslim participants adduce Islamic thinkers of similar philosophic orientations. In distinction to speculations about impending civilizational conflict, the Circle of Tradition and Progress represents a practical ecumenical endeavor whereby the West and the Islamic world may jointly address the viruses of modernity that today so threaten us all.

The statement of purpose of the Circle of Tradition and Progress offers sage advice on how to conduct international relations. The statement reads: "We favor the conduct of international relations on a basis of respect for all of the world's civilizations. We oppose all attempts to export or impose cultural systems, to support dictatorial regimes or to obstruct democratic transformation. It is our conviction that attempts to reinvent the Cold War with Muslims targeted as enemies of the West, or the West as enemies of Islam, are deplorable and should be avoided. We are united in our belief that all such Manichaean formulations will impede cooperation between Muslims and the West, and are likely over time to have a dramatically negative impact on both international stability and world peace." Bush-administration officials charged with responding to the September 11 attack might well be guided by such counsel.

Understandable Prejudices

If the contemporary tendency to depict Islam as an enemy of the West is unconscionable, it also is understandable. So is the popular receptivity to this perverse idea that characterizes Western culture.

The roots of this disposition reach back at least as far as the Crusades. The Western conviction of an alien and menacing Islamic "other" was solidified by the centuries of war between the Ottoman Empire and Western and Central Europe. It was exacerbated by European colonialism and the Christian missionary enterprise of the 19th century and the evangelical revival today, and it currently flourishes as a result of the serious challenge that the Islamic revival presents to the long-term viability of the state of Israel.

It is not by chance that those most frequently proclaiming that Islam is an enemy of the West are themselves fervent partisans of Israel or (as in the case of former Israeli prime minister Benjamin Netanyahu), Israelis themselves. Islam is in no way a challenge to the West, but in its political form it may well present a threat to Israel. If so, that is Israel's problem, not ours. Israel alone can mitigate any Islamic threat only by dealing justly with all its neighbors, and most specifically with the Palestinians.

As a Republican and a conservative, I call on my philosophical comrades in arms to reject the anti-Islamic triumphalist warmongering of neoconservative ideologues. And I urge all Americans to repudiate any belief that Islam is an enemy of the West. This idea is wrong. Worse, it is dangerous. To all of us. Especially now.

Weapons of Mass Destruction in the Middle East Threaten the International Community

by Lawrence Scheinman

About the author: *Lawrence Scheinman is a Distinguished Professor at the Center for Nonproliferation Studies in Washington, D.C., and the former assistant director for the Nonproliferation and Regional Arms Control of the U.S. Arms Control and Disarmament Agency.*

For more than 30 years, the Middle East has been a region of concern with regard to nuclear weapons and recently with regard to chemical and biological weapons. Chemical and biological weapons are seen as easier to acquire than nuclear weapons and highly lethal. Middle Eastern governments have also shown increased interest in and have acquired greater access to missile delivery systems with expanded ranges. On top of this, the Middle East continues to be the world's largest recipient of conventional weapons. As costs for these conventional weapons continue to rise exponentially, pressure to acquire WMD [weapons of mass destruction] will also mount.

Israel's Nuclear Weapons Policy

Given the massive conventional threat to its survival, Israel chose to create a nuclear infrastructure that would enable it to access nuclear weapons if security conditions dictated. At the same time it maintained a posture of nuclear ambiguity claiming that it would not be the first to introduce nuclear weapons into the region. The policy of deliberate ambiguity was almost certainly adopted out of concern for the political costs and consequences to US-Israeli relations. Israel was concerned about the complications that could result for that relation-

Lawrence Scheinman, "NBC and Missile Proliferation Issues in the Middle East," *Middle East Security Issues: In the Shadow of Weapons of Mass Destruction Proliferation*, edited by Barry R. Schneider. Maxwell AFB, AL: Air University Press, 1999.

ship, in particular US conventional arms transfers and close defense ties, given the strong and public US commitment to the NPT [Nonproliferation Treaty] and to its universal acceptance. It also reflected an Israeli assessment that an open declaration of nuclear status would not strengthen Israel's security, but might create significant pressure in neighboring states to follow Israel down the nuclear path. An unleashing of a nuclear arms race in the region would not be in Israel's interest. Israel's position on nuclear ambiguity has not altered over the years. Although in the wake of the South Asian nuclear tests and Iran's flight testing of a long-range missile, it is reported that the government apparently has begun a review of its policy of nuclear ambiguity.

> ***"Iraq's motivations . . . include asserting itself as leader and spokesman for the Arab world."***

Iraq is the other Middle East state to have made a major effort to establish a nuclear capability. Unlike Israel, it pursued this objective while a party to the NPT and under obligation not to "manufacture or otherwise acquire nuclear weapons or other nuclear explosive devices; and not to seek or receive any assistance in the manufacture" of same. Iraq's motivations reach beyond security concerns engendered by its geopolitical proximity to its larger competitive neighbor, Iran, to its political ambitions, which include asserting itself as leader and spokesman for the Arab world. This pits it against Egypt, which traditionally has seen itself in that role. Iraq also aspires to be the dominant if not hegemonic power in the energy-rich Persian Gulf. This aspiration ensures continued tension and conflict with Iran, which is the other aspirant. United Nations Special Commission (UNSCOM) and IAEA [International Atomic Energy Agency] operations inside Iraq revealed major programs to acquire not only nuclear but also chemical and biological weapons and their means of delivery in an effort to establish a formidable and potentially irresistible force that could compel the behavior of other states in the region and deny outside powers the ability to intervene effectively to prevent Iraq from achieving its goals. Reflecting on behavior like this, one Israeli scholar concluded that "in the Middle East, war is still seen as a primary instrument of policy and for many states such as Iraq, Libya or Iran, limitations and global regimes (such as NPT, CWC [Chemical Weapons Convention], BTWC [Biological and Toxic Weapon Convention]) are marginal obstacles to be overcome, or . . . simply ignored."

Against this background, one must evaluate Iranian motivations and objectives vis-á-vis WMD. In many ways what is said of Iraq can be said for Iran. As described by Shahram Chubin in "Eliminating Weapons of Mass Destruction: The Persian Gulf Case,"

> (T)he parallels . . . between these two states are important. . . . Iran and Iraq border on one another and have experienced war and defeat; they harbor resentments and grievances; they are ambitious regionally, which pits them

> against Israel; and they are hostile to the West, particularly the United States, and its presence in the Gulf. . . . In the near term, the key variables affecting the proliferation of weapons of mass destruction . . . will be the lessons drawn from recent events, . . . the availability of resources and access to suppliers, and the costs and penalties incurred by clandestine WMD programs. In the longer term, the evolution of Arab-Israeli relations, the stability and orientation of the [Gulf Cooperation Council] states, and the future of the regimes in Iran and Iraq will be important factors as well. *Even without Israel, Iraq and Iran would have each other as principal justifications for pursuit of WMD capabilities.* (Emphasis added)

This last point deserves emphasis. Having been victimized by Iraqi use of chemical weapons during one Gulf war and subjected to punishing missile attacks in the "war on the cities" phase of that conflict, Iran determined not to be caught short again and to equip itself to deter and defend against future contingencies in which WMD might play a role. This theme was underscored by Hashemi Rafsanjani prior to becoming president in asserting to the Iranian parliament that "with regard to chemical, bacteriological and radiological weapons . . . it was made very clear during the war that these weapons are very decisive. . . . We should fully equip ourselves in the defensive and offensive use of (these) weapons."

"In the Middle East, war is still seen as a primary instrument of policy."

However, while security-related experience clearly plays a significant role in Iranian thinking about WMD, broader considerations are also relevant. As Chubin also notes, "As a revolutionary state intent on spreading its values and increasing its influence, Iran may consider nuclear weapons the weapons of choice. Both as a deterrent against its enemies and as a means of amplifying its voice internationally, nuclear weapons may appear tailor-made for the regime [which] is motivated more by its view of the world and Iran's role, as opposed to the country's geopolitical context or domestic political structure.". . .

Syria, Libya, and Egypt

Syrian motivations for WMD appear to be less grandiose and more focused on security-specific concerns which include not only Israel, with whom it has territorial disputes (the Golan Heights), but, in the longer run, also Iraq and Turkey. Earlier assumptions about an allied Syrian-Egyptian military challenge to Israel disappeared two decades ago at the Camp David Accords with the shift in Egyptian policy toward Israel, and with the end of the cold war and demise of the Soviet Union. This resulted in the attrition of support Damascus had been receiving from Moscow. Syria does not at present appear to have aspirations or infrastructure to be a nuclear weapon state and does not have a program that would enable it to establish capability to go down the nuclear path. It has a significant chemical weapons capability including a large stockpile of chemical agents and weapons as well as missiles capable of delivering these weapons deep in Israeli territory. With no articulated doctrine for use of such weapons, one must surmise that they are intended as a deterrent against either an overwhelming Israeli conventional attack or a nuclear threat.

Libya is more difficult to assess. Although it has no significant nuclear infrastructure, it has a history of interest in acquiring nuclear weapons, including efforts to buy them and offering lucrative rewards to nuclear scientists and technicians to work on Libya's behalf. Its flamboyant leader, Muammar Qadhafi, has for more than a decade made declarations urging Arab states to acquire nuclear weapons. In 1987, for example, Qadhafi stated that "we should be like the Chinese—poor and riding donkeys, but respected and possessing an atom bomb." A decade later, in January 1996, he made the more pointed statement that "the Arabs who are threatened by the Israeli nuclear weapons have the right to try in any way possible to possess these weapons so that a balance is achieved and so that the region is not left at the mercy of the Israelis." The first statement appeals to the prestige of having nuclear weapons and fits in with the pan-Arabist thrust of Qadhafi's policies. The second statement addresses the security implications of not having nuclear weapons not only vis-á-vis Israel, but also in relation to the United States, with which Libya has been in confrontation due to its support for terrorist activities abroad and its efforts to acquire WMD. Libya has not made headway in developing a nuclear infrastructure or capability, and instead has placed emphasis on more easily accessible chemical weapons. There is a belief that Libya has manufactured chemical weapons in large numbers using agents produced in a domestic facility at Rabat, as well as having established a research and development program for biological agents. Its alleged use of chemical weapons against neighboring Chad in the mid-1980s suggests that for Libya such weapons have operational utility and are more than deterrents. Libya also maintains a missile development program that depends heavily on outside assistance. Progress in missile development has become difficult since the UN embargo on the transfer of missile components and technologies to Tripoli.

Egypt appears to have given up its nuclear weapons aspiration since the mid-1970s following its defeat in the 1973 war with Israel. It has focused instead on building up its conventional capabilities. It has not given up all interest in WMD which may be seen as a hedge against Israeli nuclear capability and, equally likely, as important to its claims as spokesman for an Arab world. Egypt has had chemical weapons for three decades, using them in North Yemen three times in the 1960s. It is presumed to maintain some capability to produce them if needed. Egypt has refused to sign the Chemical Weapons Convention until Israel makes concessions

> ***"Nuclear weapons may appear tailor-made for [Iran]."***

on the nuclear issue in the context of the Arms Control and Regional Security (ACRS) talks that are part of the Middle East Peace Process (MEPP).

Progress in ACRS has been nonexistent largely due to a deadlock between Egypt and Israel over how to proceed with arms control. Egypt has insisted that the process begin with Israeli concessions on the nuclear issue by acceding to the NPT or moving ahead toward establishing a nuclear-weapon-free zone (NWFZ) in the region, or some other significant concessionary move in the nuclear arena. Israel sees the resolution of nuclear-related issues as something to be achieved in the context of a just, lasting, and comprehensive peace. ACRS provides a beginning, not an end, since four states (Syria, Libya, Iraq, and Iran) are hostile to Israel and are not participants in ACRS. Egypt's frustration with its failure to move Israel on nuclear issues is compounded by its inability thus far to get any satisfaction on the resolution adopted at the 1995 NPT Review and Extension Conference. This resolution called upon states in the Middle East "to take practical steps in appropriate forums aimed at making progress towards, inter alia, the establishment of an effectively verifiable Middle East zone free of WMD, nuclear, chemical and biological, and their delivery systems." Some analysts in Cairo have questioned whether Egypt's position on the NPT ought to be reassessed in light of the stalemate on nuclear dialogue, a question, which if answered positively, could have a profoundly negative impact on regional stability, not to speak of the nonproliferation regime itself.

> ***"Qadhafi . . . has for more than a decade made declarations urging Arab states to acquire nuclear weapons."***

Arab Defiance

Against this background, what is the status of WMD in the Middle East today? . . . With the exception of Iran, none of the states in the region have joined all three treaties related to WMD. There is no common obligation or commitment against proliferation. Unlike the other five states, Israel is not a party to the NPT. Only Iran has signed and ratified the CWC. While all except Israel have signed the BTWC, Syria and Egypt have not ratified it and Iraq ratified it only because it was required to do so as part of the Gulf War cease-fire terms. Not being party to the NPT, Israel is not subject to the scrutiny of the IAEA safeguards system. The Arab states, having not signed, and Israel having signed but not ratified the CWC, are not subject to verification that they do not possess and are not producing or stockpiling prohibited or controlled chemical agents. This means in both the NPT and CWC cases that an important confidence-building measure based on monitoring, transparency, and corroboration of information through independent verification is lacking.

The risk of proliferation in the region has not abated, and in some cases activity related to WMD has intensified. All states in the region are involved in one way or another in activities related to WMD. Nuclear programs or related activities exist in Iran, Israel, and Iraq. In Iraq, the nuclear program forged in the decade before the Gulf War was uncovered and destroyed or dismantled pursuant to UN Security Council resolutions. But uncertainty persists whether all aspects of that program including nuclear weapon components relevant to triggering a nuclear explosion, have been acknowledged and accounted for, and whether the nuclear file on Iraq should be closed and efforts focused on implementing the less intrusive long-term monitoring and verification regime called for by the Security Council. The basis for reconstituting a weapons program—the human infrastructure of trained scientists and engineers—remains intact and so does the political will. In the view of two experts on the Iraqi program, "Iraq could make a nuclear device within two to twelve months after deciding to do so, assuming it acquired sufficient fissile material." Iraq continues to prevent further UNSCOM inspections. Experts believe that Iraq could reconstitute its biological, chemical, and missile capabilities in less than a year. . . .

Iran's Intentions

Significantly, Iran appears to be focused on increasing self-sufficiency by acquiring indigenous production capability. This is especially true in the case of medium-range ballistic missiles to complement its existing capacity to produce short-range missiles. [A 1999] test attested that Iran is rapidly approaching the ability to indigenously produce missiles with ranges that bring much of the region under threat. Generally, the more self-sufficient and less dependent on external sources of supply a state becomes, especially one that is politically and diplomatically isolated, the less opportunity others may have to exercise influence and restraint on the state, making the situation even more problematic than before.

> ***"There is no common obligation or commitment against proliferation."***

The same pattern (but not necessarily with the same result) seems to describe activities in Syria, Libya, and Egypt. These activities include on-going research and in some cases development programs in chemical and biological weapons, especially with regard to ballistic missiles. Egypt has a continuing relationship in the ballistic missile field with North Korea; Libya seeks the same relationship in both chemical warfare and ballistic missiles; and this is also true for Syria.

In short, all countries in the region have active development or procurement programs cutting across the different kinds of WMD and in particular with respect to delivery systems. Although the MTCR [Missile Technology and Control Regime] export control system has limited and slowed the pace of acquisition of missile capabilities, missile proliferation is moving steadily ahead in all of the countries concerned. Insofar as the acquisition of missiles serves as an added driver for acquisition of WMD, it becomes clear that missile proliferation is the single most destabilizing factor currently in play in the region.

One troubling aspect to all of this is the fact that both chemical weapons and missiles have been used (separately, not together) in regional confrontations in the past. As mentioned, Egypt, Syria, Iraq, and Iran have used chemical weapons against their adversaries. Breaking the taboo against use of such weapons sets dangerous precedents. Potential targets of such weapons may acquire comparable weapons and capabilities with increased risk of threats and counterthreats of devastating retaliation. This is particularly unwelcome in a region marked by as many tensions and confrontations as the Middle East. Middle East analyst Anthony Cordesman points out the dangers are further increased by virtue of the differences among Middle Eastern states in terms of strategy (if they have one), tactics, operations, and capabilities relating to WMD, and by the fact that these weapons are largely in the hands of political loyalists to regimes rather than in the hands of professional military personnel.

Risks to U.S. Interests

The Middle East is a very dangerous place, at risk in terms of stability and security and the intensification of competitive proliferation in WMD and delivery systems throughout the region. With the United States' extensive and long-standing interests in the Middle East, this has serious implications. As described in the April 1966 Department of Defense report, *Proliferation: Threat and Response*, those interests include

> securing a just, lasting and comprehensive peace between Israel and all Arab parties with which it is not yet at peace; maintaining our steadfast commitment to Israel's security; . . . building and maintaining security arrangements that assure the stability of the Gulf region and unimpeded commercial access to its petroleum reserves; . . . ensuring fair access for American business to commercial opportunities in the region; combating terrorism; and promoting more open political and economic systems and respect for human rights and the rule of law.

A proliferated region threatens to impose limits and constraints on the ability of the United States to protect and promote these interests, in particular where the projection of military force may be involved. A nuclear-armed adversary with ballistic missile capabilities that could threaten US forces in the field or even US territory could have a major effect on the decision to deploy military forces. To the extent that the ability to intervene militarily is constrained by such considerations, the capability to support or defend US interests in the region would be compromised. As analyst Brad Roberts noted in "From Nonproliferation to Antiproliferation," it goes beyond capability to the question of political will: "In the United States, proliferation is likely to sharpen the de-

> ***"The risk of proliferation in the [Middle East] has not abated."***

bate about vital versus peripheral national interests, undermine the political support for military intervention, or even long-term engagement, increase U.S. vulnerability to coercive diplomacy by regional actors, and narrow the room for maneuver in [the] international environment." In a region where there is no indigenous balance, if a regional power acquires the ability to impose limits and constraints on outside powers to intervene, provide balance, and protect their interests, the regional power gains flexibility to pursue its objectives. This increases the potential for the regional power to achieve a predominant if not hegemonic standing which can further reduce the capacity of an outside power to support its interests in the region.

"The Middle East is a very dangerous place."

Adversaries armed with chemical or biological weapons would likely have a limited capacity to deny the United States an ability to project force into the region if the United States has passive defense measures in place that would enable military forces to survive and fight through the conditions created by such weapons.

Israel's Weaknesses

What may hold true for the United States may not hold true for its allies such as Israel. Lacking strategic depth and having a population that is largely concentrated in a few centers, Israel sees itself as vulnerable. We have already noted the impact on Israel of the Iranian test of a medium-range ballistic missile on revisiting its own nuclear posture. A senior Israeli official recently noted that "such missiles make no military sense if armed with conventional high explosives (HE) warheads. . . . Were they to be armed, however, with chemical or biological warheads they would become immensely effective terror weapons against civilian targets. Were they to be armed with nuclear warheads they would irrevocably change the face of the Near East."

The United States shares Israeli concerns that military capabilities involving WMD in the hands of revisionist or revolutionary states like Iraq and Iran could change the regional balance of power. This could make future wars more indiscriminate and more costly and make US fulfillment of commitments to allies in the region more difficult.

The Gulf War with Iraq demonstrates the problem. To carry out the military campaign to drive Iraq out of Kuwait, the United States forged a coalition including states in the region which could provide bases, staging areas, airfields, and a logistical lifeline that could support the Desert Storm campaign. Whether the coalition could have been assembled if Iraqi president Saddam Hussein was known to have nuclear weapons is a frequently raised question, and most analysts answer no. If regional states had been unwilling to host out-of-region military forces, or to join a coalition against a state known to have nuclear weapons and the means by which to deliver them, that would have made the US ability to prosecute a decision to meet and defeat the Iraqi aggression considerably more difficult or even impossible. An inability to effectively confront the aggression would have spillover effects. In particular, it may damage the confidence of allied states in US future willingness to live up to commitments to protect them.

In sum, proliferation is a fact of life in the Middle East, driven primarily by states with strong grievances against the established order and a determination to change things to suit their vision, and responded to by those who otherwise might be victimized by the success of revisionist and revolutionary regimes. The acquisition of WMD and delivery systems, particularly by states with aggressive agendas, heightens perceptions of threat, undermines the military balance, and weakens the already precarious stability of the security environment of the Middle East. Continued proliferation has the potential to severely tax the capacity and potentially the will of the United States to act assertively in defense of its significant and long-standing interests in the region. The cost of not meeting that challenge outweighs the cost of doing so, not only in terms of US interests in the region, but also concerning the global order. An open breakout of WMD proliferation in the Middle East would have serious and perhaps irremediable consequences for the nonproliferation regimes.

Middle Eastern Oil Exporters Threaten the Global Economy

by the *Economist*

About the author: *The* Economist *is a weekly newspaper on political, literary, and business events.*

How much is a barrel of oil worth? In the Middle East, reserves can cost barely a dollar to lift out of the ground. Add a decent profit margin, and you still have an exceedingly modest price. Yet quite a bit of the world's oil comes from far more expensive places. In 2000, the price averaged $27 a barrel.

OPEC's Whims

It is not geology that determines the oil price, however, still less the free interplay of supply and demand. Mostly, it is the whims of the Organisation of Petroleum Exporting Countries (OPEC), the ill-disciplined cartel led by Saudi Arabia. Small wonder, then, that the price of oil yo-yoed from 1998 to 2001. Prices have plunged to below $17 a barrel as an anaemic world economy and a stand-off between OPEC and Russia, the biggest non-cartel exporter, pushed the oil market to the brink of short-term collapse.

Only [Islamic terrorist] Osama bin Laden, it seems, can give you a fixed price for a barrel of oil. He makes it $144. Several years ago, the leader of the al-Qaeda terrorists issued a little-noticed proclamation on energy economics. In it, he accused the United States of "the biggest theft in history" for using its military presence in Saudi Arabia to keep oil prices down. In his view, that larceny adds up to $36 trillion. America, he insisted, now owes each Muslim in the world around $30,000, and still counting. After [the terrorist attack on] September 11th, 2001, energy-security experts have Mr. bin Laden, his sympathisers and terrorists in general very much in mind. America used to assume that, if a hostile group or regime took over the Middle Eastern oilfields, it would send in its troops to quash the troublemakers and protect the oil. Now those terrorists may have nuclear weapons that they could turn either against America or against the oilfields themselves.

Yet the real cause for worry, a related one, is much longer-term. Because the world remains so dependent on oil for transport, it cannot stand any disruption in supplies. And there is a strong possibility of such a supply-shock at some time in the next few decades. How will the United States cope with this?

In Too Few Hands

Oil is not scarce. Enough lies underground to keep the world's motors humming for several decades yet. The snag is that the lion's share of it—and almost all the oil that is cheap to extract—lies under the desert sands of a handful of countries around the Persian Gulf.

Today, Saudi Arabia alone sits on a quarter of the world's proven oil reserves, and four of its neighbours can boast about a tenth each. Because the Saudis choose not to produce as much oil as they could, OPEC's share of world oil exports is only about 40%: influential, but not enough to control prices completely. As the world continues to deplete non-OPEC oil, however, that share will increase dramatically—and with it, the market power of those Middle Eastern regimes. All the more likely, then, that supplies may be disrupted. This threat is particularly acute for the United States, which is both the biggest oil-guzzler and the de facto guarantor of oil supplies for its allies.

The Saudis, unsurprisingly, deny that a shock is in prospect at all. Oil is "a global market," said Ali al-Naimi, the oil minister, in 1999. "Those who propagate the issue of supply insecurity, dangers of import dependence and perceived instability of the Arabian Gulf are ignoring realities." He pointed out that his country intentionally maintains a cushion of excess capacity against any disruption of supply. It was his country's buffer, not any non-OPEC production, he noted, that came to the rescue during the Iranian revolution, the Iran-Iraq war and the Gulf war.

All this is true, but what if the Saudi regime were overthrown by some rabidly anti-western band? Not to worry, argues John Browne, chairman of BP [British Petroleum]: "However fundamentalist, a regime still needs money to look after its people." His sentiment is echoed by many economists, who insist that oil is a "fungible" commodity that is worthless unless it gets to market. In the long term, that is doubtless true. But even short-term disruptions can wreak havoc on the world economy: when the Iranian revolutionaries booted out the shah in 1979, Iran's oil exports collapsed. And some future revolutionaries may choose to forgo oil revenues and live in poverty to punish the West.

> ***"Oil is not scarce."***

Donald Losman, in a provocative paper published by the Cato Institute, a libertarian think-tank, goes further. He argues, with some justification, that the pain associated with previous oil shocks had more to do with foolish policy responses by western governments meddling in the market than with disruptions to supply. He calculates that America wastes $30 billion–60 billion a year safeguarding Middle Eastern oil supplies even though its imports from that region totalled only about $10 billion a year during the 1990s. He also observes that semiconductors, the backbone of the digital economy, come mostly from one place (Taiwan), but American soldiers do not guard chip plants.

Oil's Uniqueness

Yet semiconductors and oil are not at all the same. The American economy could manage without new semiconductors for some time, but it would grind to a painful halt the moment oil dried up. Semiconductor plants can also be built anywhere, but oil is found only in certain spots. The petrol riots in Britain in the autumn of 2000 showed how easily a modern economy can be brought to its knees when its oil supplies are disrupted.

If oil is essential, then, why not simply boost non-OPEC supplies? President George W. Bush, extolling America's "energy independence", has been trying to push a bill through Congress that would open part of the Arctic National Wildlife Refuge in Alaska to oil-drilling. But America consumes so much that all the oil in Alaska would not dent its reliance on the imported stuff.

> ***"Short-term disruptions can wreak havoc on the world economy."***

The dramatic wave of non-OPEC discoveries in the 1960s and 1970s in the North Sea, Alaska and other places has helped to counterbalance OPEC's pricing power. But these big fields are about to enter a phase of rapid decline. Part of the explanation is simple old age. In the North Sea, for example, most large fields are now 70–90% depleted. And the dramatic techniques that have allowed big oil companies to improve oil-recovery rates have ended up draining fields all the faster.

Harry Longwell, a top manager at ExxonMobil, insists that a new wave of non-OPEC development, from the Caspian to the deep waters of the Gulf of Mexico, is technically feasible. However, he says that it will require "huge new investments". How much? The International Energy Agency reckons big oil firms will have to invest a whopping $1 trillion upstream over the next decade. Developing non-conventional hydrocarbons, such as Canada's tar sands, would prove even more expensive. Such stuff would also take much longer to bring to market, and so prove less valuable as a buffer stock. In other words, the real concern is not the scarcity of hydrocarbons, but the ever-higher cost and commercial risk of finding non-OPEC reserves—especially since price volatility discourages investment.

Now here's the rub: even accepting in full the oil industry's optimistic assessment that it can meet this challenge, the "call on OPEC" will still increase dramatically over the next 20 years. In order to meet the world's unchecked thirst for oil, forecasters are assuming (perhaps praying is a better word) that Saudi Arabia and its neighbours will invest the vast sums needed to expand output. If they do not, it will be the world's consumers who will pay the price.

Saving and Conserving

What can be done? Unfortunately, petroleum has a near-monopoly grip on transport. The best thing governments can do is to buy some insurance against politically inspired supply disruptions, and the panics and hoarding that go with them, by greatly expanding buffer stocks of oil.

> ***"The real concern is . . . the ever-higher cost and commercial risk of finding non-OPEC reserves."***

This is all the more urgent because structural changes in the oil industry (mega-mergers, cost-cutting and a move to just-in-time inventories) mean that privately held reserves have fallen steeply from their levels in the 1970s. Add to this the official neglect of government stockpiles, and you get a world that is needlessly vulnerable to the next oil shock.

Mr. Bush has now begun to rebuild America's Strategic Petroleum Reserve. Conservation, too, after years of sneers, is firmly on the American political agenda. Yet even conservation has drawbacks: it may simply mean less mobility and less trade. The better way forward is to promote energy efficiency. The United States now imports about 11 million barrels of oil per day (bpd), around a seventh of the world's total production. Philip Verleger, an energy economist, reckons that the figure would be only 5 million or 6 million bpd if America had made a serious effort to improve fuel efficiency after the previous shocks.

One efficiency measure under debate is the strengthening of the Corporate Average Fuel Economy (CAFE) laws: raising them for cars, and closing the loophole that allows light trucks and sport-utility vehicles to use more petrol. A study done by America's National Academy of Sciences (NAS) in 2001 was certain that, with technologies that are readily available, reductions in fuel use of up to 20% could be achieved comfortably. Some vehicles could achieve a 50% increase in fuel economy—and more if radical new technologies, such as fuel cells, take off.

Against Shocks, Taxes

However, a world powered largely by fuel cells (which combine hydrogen and oxygen to produce electricity) could be decades away, especially if all America does is tinker with fuel-efficiency standards. The best way to encourage the development of new transport fuels and technologies is through taxation that reflects the "energy security" risk (as well as dangers to health and the environment) of burning oil. Europe recognises this, and over the past decade has started to shift the burden of taxation from income to, for example, carbon emissions.

What are the chances that America too will start to tackle its petro-addiction? James Schlesinger, a former energy secretary, says he still bears the bruises from attempting to propose higher oil taxes in the past. An encounter on Capitol Hill suggests that times have not changed much. After the NAS panel had prepared a preliminary report, Paul Portney, its chairman, was asked to address a congressional panel. George Allen, a senator from Virginia, was plainly unhappy with the report's suggestion that fossil-fuel use could be easily curbed by tightening CAFE regulations. The visitor was asked whether there was any other way to encourage fuel efficiency without resorting to market-distorting regulations.

"Why, yes," said Mr. Portney: "you could make a significant increase in the federal petrol tax." Mr. Allen was astounded. The notion, he said, was "just flat ignorant." Senator John Kerry, the panel's chairman, retorted in frustration, "I can see the headlines tomorrow: 'Virginia senator calls Europeans ignorant', or maybe worse." Mr. Allen was unrepentant. The road away from dependence on OPEC and Middle Eastern oil could be long indeed.

Saudi Arabia Fosters International Terrorism

by Mark Steyn

About the author: *Mark Steyn is the North American correspondent for the* Spectator, *a columnist for the* Daily Telegraph *and* Sunday Telegraph *in the United Kingdom, and the theater critic for the* New Criterion.

Joanne Jacobs, formerly a columnist with the *San Jose Mercury News*, spotted a dandy headline in her old paper last week. A Muslim mob had attacked a train full of Hindus, an unfortunate development which the *Mercury News* reported to its readers thus: 'Religious Tensions Kill 57 In India'.

Ah, those religious tensions'll kill you every time. Is there a Preparation H for religious tension? Or an extra-strength Tylenol, in case you feel a sudden attack coming on? I haven't looked at the *San Jose Mercury News* for 12 September, 2001, but I'm assuming the front page read, 'Religious Tensions Kill 3,000 In New York', a particularly bad outbreak.

A Religion of Peace

If I were an Islamic fundamentalist, I'd be wondering what I had to do to get a bad press. The *New York Times* had a picture the other day of a party of Palestinian suicide bombers looking like Klansmen, all dressed up and ready to blow. They were captioned 'Hamas activists'. Take my advice and try not to be standing anywhere near an activist when he activates himself. You gotta hand it to the Islamofascists: while the usual doom-mongers are now querying whether America's up to fighting a war on two fronts (Afghanistan and Iraq), the Islamabaddies blithely open up new fronts every couple of weeks. At the World Trade Center, Muslim terrorists killed mainly Christians. In Israel, they're killing mainly Jews. In India, they're killing mainly Hindus. Let's not get into the Sudan or the Philippines. Now, OK, there are two sides to every dispute, but these days one side can pretty well be predicted: Muslims v. Jews, Muslims v. Christians, Muslims v. Hindus, Muslims v. [Your Religion Here]. If war were

Mark Steyn, "Down with Saudi Arabia," *Spectator*, vol. 288, March 9, 2002, pp. 18–20.

tennis, they'd be Grand Slam champions: they'll play on anything—lawn, clay, rubble. And yet the more they kill, the more frantically the press cranks out the 'Islam is a religion of peace' editorials.

Now it would be absurd to claim that all Muslims are terrorists. But the idea that the forces at play in New York, Palestine, Tora Bora and Kashmir are some sort of tiny unrepresentative extremist fringe of Islam is equally ludicrous. The *Boston Globe* reported from the Saudi town of Abha on the subtleties of the kingdom's education system: 'At a public high school in this provincial town in the southwest part of the country, 10th-grade classes are forced to memorise from a Ministry of Education textbook entitled "Monotheism" that is replete with anti-Christian and anti-Jewish bigotry and violent interpretations of Islamic scripture. A passage on page 64 under the title "Judgment Day" says, "The Hour will not come until Muslims will fight the Jews, and Muslims will kill all the Jews."'

"It would be absurd to claim that all Muslims are terrorists."

That's pretty straightforward, isn't it? In fact, pretty much everything about Saudi Arabia, except for the urbane evasions of their Washington ambassador, Prince Bandar, is admirably straightforward. Saudi citizens were, for the most part, responsible for the terrorist attacks on 11 September 2001. The Saudi government funds the madrassahs [religious schools] in Pakistan which are doing their best to breed a South Asian branch office of Saudi Wahhabism [a strict sect of Islam]. Admittedly, the Saudis are less directly responsible for the Israeli-Palestinian conflict, except insofar as they have a vested interest in it as a distraction from other matters. So, if we don't want to be beastly about Muslims in general, we could at least be beastly about the House of Saud in particular.

Instead, the Saudi question has become the ne plus ultra of the Islamo-euphemist approach, and a beloved staple of comment pages and cable news shows. By now, 'The Saudis Are Our Friends' may even have its own category in the Pulitzers. Usually this piece turns up after the Saudis have done something not terribly friendly—refused to let Washington use the US bases in Saudi Arabia, or even to meet with British prime minister Tony Blair. Then the apparently vast phalanx of former US ambassadors to Saudi Arabia fans out across the *New York Times*, CNN, Nightline, etc., to insist that, au contraire, the Saudis have been 'enormously helpful.' At what? Recommending a decent restaurant in Mayfair?

Abdullah's Peace Plan

Charles Freeman, a former ambassador to the kingdom and now president of something called the Middle East Policy Council, offered a fine example of the genre the other day when he revealed that Crown Prince Abdullah, the head honcho since King Fahd had his stroke, was 'personally anguished' by developments in the Middle East and that that was why he had proposed his 'peace plan'. If, indeed, he has proposed it—to anyone other than journalist Thomas

Friedman of the *New York Times*, that is. And, come to think of it, it was Friedman who proposed it to the Prince—Israel withdraws to the 4 June 1967 [borders], Palestinian state, full normalised relations with the Arab League, etc. 'After I laid out this idea,' wrote Friedman, 'the Crown Prince looked at me with mock astonishment and said, "Have you broken into my desk?"

'"No," I said, wondering what he was talking about.'

'"The reason I ask is that this is exactly the idea I had in mind . . ."'

What a coincidence! Apparently, the Prince had 'drafted a speech along those lines' and 'it is in my desk'. It's just that he hadn't got around to delivering the speech. Still hasn't, in fact. Seems an awful waste of a good speech. Unless—perish the thought—it's just something he keeps in his desk to flatter visiting American correspondents. In any case, it's the same peace plan the Saudis dust off every ten years—they proposed it in 1991, and before that in 1981. It's just a couple of months late this time round. But book a meeting around October 2011 with King Abdullah (as he plans on being by then) and he'll gladly propose it to you one mo' time. Prince Abdullah has no interest in Palestinians: it's easier for a Palestinian to emigrate to Tipton in England and become a subject of the Queen than to emigrate to Riyadh and become a subject of King Fahd. But the Prince's peace plan usefully changes the subject from more embarrassing matters—such as the kingdom's role in the events of 11 September 2001.

There are only two convincing positions on the House of Saud and what happened that grim day: a) They're indirectly responsible for it; b) They're directly responsible for it. There's a lot of evidence for the former—the Saudi funding of the madrassahs, etc.—and a certain amount of not yet totally compelling evidence for the latter—a Saudi 'humanitarian aid' office in the Balkans set up by a member of the royal family which appears to be a front for terrorism. Reasonable people can disagree on whether it's (a) or (b) but for Americans to argue that the Saudis are our allies in the war on terrorism is like Ron Goldman's dad joining ex-football player O.J. Simpson [Simpson was acquitted of murdering his ex-wife Nicole Brown Simpson and her friend Ronald Goldman in 1994] in his search for the real killers. The advantage of this thesis to fellows like Charles Freeman is that it places a premium on their nuance-interpretation skills. Because everything the kingdom does seems to be self-evidently inimical to the West, any old four-year-old can point out that the King is in the altogether hostile mode. It takes an old Saudi hand like Mr. Freeman to draw attention to the subtler shades of meaning, to explain the ancient ways of Araby, by which, say, an adamant refusal to arrest associates of the 11 September hijackers is, in fact, a clear sign of the Saudis' remarkable support for Washington. If the Saudis nuked Delaware, the massed ranks of former ambassadors would be telling television host Larry King that, obviously, even the

"The Saudi question has become . . . a beloved staple of comment pages."

best allies have their difficulties from time to time, but this is essentially a little hiccup that can be smoothed over by closer consultation. . . .

Realistic Peace Proposals

Instead of presenting Prince Abdullah with Israeli-Palestinian peace proposals, Americans ought to be handing him US-Saudi peace proposals: clean up your own education system and stop destabilising Asian Muslim culture, for starters. Washington (and London, too) needs to figure out what it wants from Saudi Arabia and whether it's likely to get it from King Fahd and his bloated clan. We already know one thing we're not going to get: the Taliban [former ruling body of Afghanistan] had two major allies before 11 September, Pakistan and Saudi Arabia, and it's clear the royal house has no inclination to do a Pervez Musharraf [president of Pakistan]. If the West has a medium-term aim in the Middle East, it ought to be the evolution of Arabic Islam into something closer to the more moderate Muslim temperament of Turkey or Bangladesh. I know, I know, all these things are relative, but even that modest goal is unattainable under the House of Saud.

The royal family derives such legitimacy as it has from its role as the guardian and promoter of Wahhabism. It is, therefore, the ideological font of militant Islamism in the way that Saddam Hussein, president of Iraq, and Syrian president Bashar Assad and Egyptian president Hosni Mubarak and the other Arab thugs aren't. Saddam is as Islamic as the wind is blowing: say what you like about the old mass murderer, but his malign activities are not, in that sense, defined by his religion. One cannot say the same for the House of Saud. If the issue is 'religious tensions', who's fomenting them, from Pakistan to the Balkans to America itself? Saudi Arabia should be a 'root cause' we can all agree on.

But sadly not. John O'Sullivan, former editor of *National Review*, wrote recently that 'reforming the House of Saud will be a formidable and subtle task. But it offers a great deal more hope for everyone than blithely burning it down.' I disagree. Reforming the House of Saud is all but impossible. Lavish economic engagement with the West has only entrenched it more firmly in its barbarism. 'Stability' means letting layabout princes use Western oil revenues to seduce their people into anti-Western nihilism. On the other hand, blithely burning it down offers quite a bit of hope, given that no likely replacement would provide the ideological succour to the Islamakazis that Saud-endorsed Wahhabism does. My own view is that the Muslim holy sites and most of the interior should go to the Hashemites of Jordan, and what's left should be divided between the less wacky Gulf emirs. That should be the policy goal, even if for the moment it's pursued covertly rather than by daisy cutters.

Borders are not sacrosanct. The House of Saud is not royal; they are merely nomads who found a sugar daddy. There's no good reason why every time a soccer mom fills her Chevy Suburban she should be helping fund some toxic madrassah. In this instance, destabilisation is our friend.

Chapter 3

How Can the Israeli-Palestinian Conflict Be Resolved?

Chapter Preface

The Israeli-Palestinian conflict has been one of the most divisive contests in the history of the Middle East. Unfortunately, Israel has been a hub of violence since its inception in 1948. At that time, the area was primarily inhabited by Arab Muslims and Christians, but Jews comprised about 10 percent of the population. The Jewish population in Palestine increased after the Nazi Holocaust in World War II, which bolstered Zionist efforts to create a Jewish national homeland in Palestine, which the Jewish people consider their Holy Land. In 1947, the United Nations (UN) voted to divide Palestine into Jewish and Arab states—a decision that was bitterly rejected by neighboring Arab nations, who resented giving what they considered Arab lands to non-Arab people. In 1948, Jewish nationalists proclaimed the state of Israel according to the boundaries decided by the UN. The armies of Egypt, Jordan, Lebanon, and Iraq immediately attacked Israel, but they were defeated by the Israelis in 1949.

After 1948, large numbers of Palestinians fled the region—some uprooted by war and some fearing for their safety in a new Jewish state. Many of these refugees and their descendants are currently living in camps in the Israeli-occupied areas of the West Bank, the Golan Heights, and the Gaza Strip (territories that Israel won during subsequent wars). There are an estimated 991,577 Palestinian refugees living in refugee camps, and approximately 3,172,641 Palestinian refugees scattered throughout the Middle East. Palestinian demands for Israel to release this land to Palestinian authority, and Israeli efforts to maintain control of land that they won in their many wars are a continuing source of friction in the region.

Israel fought numerous wars with its neighbors in 1956, 1967, 1973, and 1982. In 1987, widespread violence, known as the first Palestinian Intifada (uprising), broke out in Israel. On December 8, 1987, an Israeli army truck ran into a group of Palestinians near the Jabalya refugee camp in Gaza, killing four and wounding seven. Palestinians suspected that the collision had not been an accident, and exploded with pent-up rage throughout the region the next day. At first a spontaneous outburst, the Intifada developed into a well-organized rebellion. Mobs of civilians attacked Israeli troops with stones, axes, Molotov cocktails, hand grenades, and firearms, killing and wounding soldiers and nearby civilians. Israelis responded to the violence with brutal military strategies known as "iron fist" and "broken bones" policies.

The Palestinian Intifada continued until 1993, when Israeli prime minister Yitzhak Rabin and Palestine Liberation Organization (PLO) leader Yasser Arafat signed the Declaration of Principles on Interim Self-Government Arrangements, also known as the Oslo accords. The Oslo accords—a series of compromises that emerged from secret meetings held by Rabin and Arafat in Oslo, Norway—intended to resolve the decades-old antagonism between the Israelis and the Palestinians. Oslo stipulated that during a five-year interim period, steps would be taken to build trust and partnership between the Palestinians and the Israelis. For example, Palestinians would police the areas that they controlled, cooperate with Israel in the fight against terrorism, and amend the sections of the PLO charter that called for Israel's destruction. Israel would withdraw almost entirely from Gaza and in stages from parts of the West Bank. An elected Palestinian Authority (PA) would take over governance of the territories from which Israel withdrew. After this five-year interim period, negotiators would then determine a final peace agreement to resolve the most contentious issues, such as Jewish settlements in Gaza and the West Bank, and whether the Palestinians would have an independent state. Arafat's and Rabin's efforts toward peace earned them the Nobel Peace Prize in 1994.

Unfortunately, the uneasy peace that the Oslo accords created did not last long. Israel did not withdraw from the designated territories, and Palestinians continued to engage in random acts of violence against Israelis. In 2000, the second Palestinian Intifada, known as the Al-Aqsa Intifada, officially put an end to the Oslo peace process. Palestinians claimed that their most sacred site, the Haram al-Sharif in Jerusalem, had been desecrated by Israelis on September 28, 2000. This event sparked another cycle of Palestinian attacks and Israeli reprisals that continue to this day. Rather than full-scale riots, Al-Aqsa Intifada resistors have engaged in suicide bombings of Israeli shopping centers, schools, city buses, restaurants, and nightclubs. In response to these attacks, the Israeli military has bombed PA official buildings, assassinated leading Palestinian figures, invaded Palestinian territories, and razed civilian houses. In the first two years of the Al-Aqsa Intifada, around three hundred Israelis and over a thousand Palestinians have been killed.

The pattern of Palestinian attacks followed by Israeli reprisals has earned neither the Palestinians their freedom nor the Israelis their safety. Palestinians and Israelis continue to grieve the loss of family members killed by suicide bombings and military incursions. Moreover, the Israeli-Palestinian conflict continues to cause unrest in other parts of the Middle East. As many commentators in the region and worldwide have attested, the Israelis and the Palestinians must reach an agreement that is acceptable to both sides to avoid further bitterness and bloodshed. The authors in the following chapter debate how best to resolve the Israeli-Palestinian conflict.

Israel Should Withdraw from Palestinian Territories

by Osama Shabaneh

About the author: *Osama Shabaneh is a Palestinian-American who works and lives in Redmond, Washington.*

During a recent trip to the West Bank, I happened to share a taxi ride from Bethlehem to my hometown of Hebron with a few Palestinian laborers. Throughout the hour-long trip, the laborers discussed their day at work and their plans for the next day. As I understood from the discussion, these men were construction workers who had just finished their day shift in the Israeli settlement of Har Homa, or Jabal Abu Ghneim in Arabic.

When the Israeli government in 1997 approved building in this settlement, there was not only a Palestinian but also an international outcry since the settlement was construed as changing the status quo of the boundaries of Jerusalem. Three years later, the Palestinians themselves are helping build the settlement.

Can these men be branded as traitors for helping Israel expand by usurping more Palestinian land? Or are they more victims of the Israeli-Palestinian peace process that appears to be on the edge of collapse?

The Oslo Peace Accord

The 1987–93 Palestinian uprising against the Israeli military occupation of Palestine ended with the signing of the Oslo peace accord between the two sides. I was very much in support of the peace moves that halted, for a while, the bloodshed that characterized the Israeli-Palestinian conflict for so many years. As a Palestinian, I had experienced the Israeli occupation firsthand, and I hoped that the peace accord was the beginning of giving the Palestinians their rights and freedom they had sought for a long time. I wanted my family, still back in the town of Hebron, to feel safe in their home, to have hope of a better future, and to live in peace with no Israeli soldiers around.

I grew up in Hebron accustomed to the sight of those soldiers, in their military

Osama Shabaneh, "The Fallacy of Peace in the Middle East," *Seattle Times*, October 18, 2000, p. B7.

jeeps or on foot, patrolling the streets of the West Bank, sometimes enforcing curfews on Palestinian residents and occasionally stopping and slapping or arresting Palestinians who had forgotten their identity cards, which were issued by the Israeli military authorities. Every Palestinian over 16 years of age had to obtain these orange-colored identity cards, and had to have it on them at all times.

I remember having to skip school the day I turned 16 in order to go to the Israeli military headquarters in Hebron to obtain my card. It was 1971, and it was the first time I had to undergo questioning by the Israelis about my political beliefs. I was too young to have any of those beliefs. I always took the Israeli presence for granted, and I had never imagined what freedom felt like. For many years following my 16th birthday and, in fact, until now, I have a recurring dream of me leaving my house in Hebron without my orange identity card, and being stopped by the Israeli soldiers. No peace can wipe out the scars of occupation.

"No peace can wipe out the scars of occupation."

The Peace Process Was a Ploy

Since 1993, the Israeli-Palestinian peace process has had its ups and downs. My family and friends in the region were euphoric when the prospects of peace were first offered to them. But as the years passed, they became more gloomy and dejected, and I could see why during my visits. As a consequence of the peace process, the Israeli army redeployed its forces away from heavily Palestinian-populated areas, but its presence was felt as strongly as ever.

The Palestinians came to the realization that the peace process was just a ploy by the Israelis to convince the world that Israel was granting the Palestinians self-determination, while at the same time maintaining their presence in and around every village, every town, every city, and every refugee camp in the West Bank and Gaza. Israel, during the so-called peace process years, continued killing more Palestinian civilians, confiscating more Palestinian land, arresting more people for their political beliefs, controlling every thoroughfare in Palestine, and overseeing every aspect of Palestinian life, except the mundane.

The Palestinian passport that Israel allowed the Palestinian Authority to issue to Palestinians includes, on the first page, the same ID number that is found on the Israeli-issued orange identity card. Now occupation had a new face and a new color, green instead of orange. Yet, freedom for the Palestinians remained a dream.

Take the inflammatory issue of Jerusalem. Israel has been claiming that it grants freedom of worship to all Palestinians. For 13 years now, Jerusalem, which includes one of the holiest places for Muslims, has been sealed off to most Palestinians. Israeli checkpoints at every junction around Jerusalem prevent Muslims and Christians from entering the city to worship without a special permit. The Israelis do a detailed security check on every applicant, and usually reject, without justification, issuing any permits.

Chapter 3

Media Bias

I called my family in Hebron a few days after an outbreak of violence in the West Bank. With the echo of bullets in the background, my mother told me to worry about myself and not to worry about them. She said that only God could help them in their current situation. I could not agree more. Watching TV that night, and every night, I flip through the news channels of the American media, and all I see are reports, analyses, politicians and experts—all but very few blaming the Palestinians for driving the region to the brink of war, and portraying Israel as the peace-seeker.

The utter denial of the Palestinians' humanity has characterized the media for a long time, and now it is no different. It took a peace process littered with suffering and death for the Palestinians to realize that the world just doesn't care about their struggle for freedom and self-determination.

The Palestinian laborers wanted to feed their children, and building a settlement for Israelis was the only way they found before them. This is a tragic consequence of an unjust peace. As long as Israel insists on controlling the will of another nation, as long as it keeps looking down at Palestinians as unequal peace partners, as long as it keeps confiscating Palestinian land and holding political prisoners, peace will remain a fallacy. There is only one way out, and that is not by more summits and meaningless discussions. The only way out is for Israel to set the Palestinians free, and let them be.

Israel Must Reoccupy Palestinian Territories

by Robert Tracinski

About the author: *Robert Tracinski is a writer, teacher, fellow, and analyst at the Ayn Rand Institute.*

A few days after the last tanks rolled out of Jenin and other cities across the West Bank (though they remain in Ramallah and Bethlehem), Israelis flooded back to streetside cafés to enjoy the spring weather and the security won by their army's assault on Palestinian terrorists.

This lull in anti-Israeli terrorism is likely to be short lived, however, because Israel has not committed to the one policy that can achieve a lasting peace in the Middle East: a permanent Israeli occupation and colonization of Palestinian territory.

Palestinian Terrorism Is Not New

The conventional wisdom is that the Israeli occupation and resulting Palestinian "resentment" is the cause of the current conflict. In reality, Palestinian terrorism began before Israel acquired a single acre of land in Gaza or the West Bank. Yasser Arafat's Palestinian Liberation Organization (PLO), for example, was formed in 1964, three years before the 1967 war in which Israel occupied those territories. The "Palestine" that Arafat sought to "liberate" was Israel itself.

The massive escalation of the Palestinians' terrorist war actually coincides with the *withdrawal* of Israel's occupation. Under the 1993 Oslo accords, Israel has spent most of the last decade removing its troops from Palestinian territories and transferring control to police and security forces controlled by Arafat. The result was not peace, but the creation of a Palestinian regime based on anti-Jewish terrorism.

The creation of this terror regime began during the "first intifada," the wave of Palestinian riots and terror attacks that began in 1987 and nominally ended with the Oslo accords in 1993. Of the roughly 1100 people killed by Palestinian militants during this uprising, about 800 were fellow Palestinians accused of "collaborating" with Israel. In other words, the Palestinians systematically exterminated anyone who might want to live peacefully with the Jews. (It is a process that continues today. While the press was focusing its attention on the non-existent "massacre of Jenin," in April 2002, Palestinian thugs dragged three alleged "collaborators" from their cars and shot them, to the cheers of a large crowd.)

Betraying Friendly Palestinians

Rather than seeking to protect friendly Palestinians, Israeli doves and American diplomats betrayed them by installing a terrorist thug as their new political master. Michael Kelley, a columnist who covered the event as a reporter, describes Arafat's triumphant homecoming to Gaza in 1994, a few months after the Oslo agreement:

> Arafat's entry into Gaza was an object lesson: a purposely uncaring display of brute power. He arrived from the Sinai in a long caravan of Chevrolet Blazers and Mercedes-Benzes and BMWs, 70 or 80 cars packed to the rooflines with men with guns. The caravan roared up the thronged roads and down the mobbed streets, with the overfed, leather-jacketed, sunglassed thugs of Arafat's bodyguard detail all the time screaming and shooting off their Kalashnikovs to make their beloved people scurry out of their beloved leader's way.
>
> This was the whole of the Palestinian Authority from the beginning, an ugly little cartoon of Middle East despotism. . . .
>
> That summer, I saw only three serious efforts at establishing functioning government: the imprisoning of free-speakers and potential democrats, which began immediately, the likewise prompt establishment of daily anti-Israel broadcasts, and a British-run program to train handpicked members of Arafat's Fatah group in riot control.

Any potential friends of Israel got the message and joined the thugs. No civilized Palestinian voices have dared to speak up since.

Palestinian society has been shaped by an opposite influence: an educational system in which children are showered with anti-Jewish propaganda and praise for suicide bombers; Palestinian "summer camps" in which teenagers are taught how to murder Israelis; an anarchic society in which prestige goes to young men who join armed militias and terror brigades. Terror, in this Palestinian culture, is the primary form of political currency. Arafat lieutenant Marwan Bhargouti has openly boasted that terror bombings by the Arafat-sponsored al-Aqsa Martyrs Brigade are what restored the political influence of Arafat's Fatah political faction.

> ***"Palestinian terrorism began before Israel acquired a single acre of land in Gaza or the West Bank."***

All of this has increasingly fused with the outlook of Islamic fundamentalism, which glorifies mass-murder martyrdom as a moral ideal. Israeli raids have found evidence that Arafat provided direct financial support for terrorism, but the most important form of that support is the least expensive: money for posters proclaiming the heroism of the latest suicide bomber.

Military operations of the kind that concluded in May 2002—arresting militants, destroying bomb factories, seizing weapons caches—are a necessary first step, but they are only a first step. These operations eliminate, for the moment, the products of a terrorist culture. But if Israelis want to be able to live in peace, the terrorist culture itself must be uprooted. Only an Israeli occupation can achieve that goal.

"Palestinian society has been shaped by . . . anti-Jewish propaganda and praise for suicide bombers."

President George W. Bush has referred to the "legitimate aspirations" of the Palestinian people for an independent state. But people who embrace suicide bombings and choose career killers as their leaders—as the Palestinians have done—have no legitimate political aspirations. Writer William F. Buckley, for all of his many faults, is credited with a turn of phrase that eloquently captures this fact. Speaking about an African country's desire for independence, he quipped, "They'll be ready for democracy when they stop eating each other." Although he was referring to the practice of literal cannibalism, the same thing applies metaphorically to the Palestinians. They can be trusted with a representative government only when they stop worshipping murderers.

A permanent Israeli occupation would entail the creation of a colonial administration charged with the task of civilizing a people made barbarous by decades of terrorist leadership. The goals of this occupation should be: to remove terrorist indoctrination from Palestinian schools and to remove incitement to murder from Palestinian airwaves and from Palestinian mosques; to make life safer for civilized Palestinians; to establish a vigorous and efficient police force that will make terrorism a road to prison or death, not popular adulation.

The Real Instigators of Terrorism

Most important, a new occupation is desperately needed to seal off Palestinian territories from the real instigators of terrorism. Palestinian terrorism is fed and driven, not by Israeli "provocation," but by the sponsorship of neighboring governments: by Iran, whose theocrats provide money, weapons, and training; by Iraq, whose dictator offers bounties to the families of suicide bombers; by Syria, the base for terror groups like Hezbollah; by Saudi Arabia, which raises money for Islamic terrorist groups. Whenever Israel withdraws from Palestinian territories, these forces will flow back in to rebuild the culture of terrorism.

Occupation is also necessary to keep out one of the most important world sponsors of terrorism: the United Nations. At the moment, there are several proposals to send UN "peacekeeping" troops into Palestinian territories. Such troops would merely serve as a screen to protect Palestinian terrorists; they would do nothing to prevent new Palestinian terror attacks, but they would prevent Israel from engaging in even the slightest effort to strike back.

There is only one legitimate obstacle to this solution: Israel's identity as a "Jewish state." Only universal values, the kind of values America was founded on, can be inculcated in an ethnically and religiously diverse population. But this is a problem that can be solved; after all, the majority of Israelis are essentially secular and Western in their outlook.

The primary obstacle to a new Israeli occupation, however, is the intellectual trend that has swept the secular West: the philosophy of multiculturalism, which is founded on a condemnation of "colonialism." The multiculturalists attack the very idea that there is a difference between "civilization" and "savagery," declaring that there is no way to judge one as superior to the other.

But in the current conflict, the Palestinian reign of terror has demonstrated that, as Ayn Rand once wrote, to ask "Who am I to judge?" is to ask "Who am I to live?"

Creating a Palestinian State Could Resolve the Israeli-Palestinian Conflict

by Yasser Arafat

About the author: *Yasser Arafat is the leader of the Palestinian Authority, the ruling body of Palestine.*

[Since 2002], Israelis and Palestinians have been locked in a catastrophic cycle of violence, a cycle which only promises more bloodshed and fear. The cycle has led many to conclude that peace is impossible, a myth borne out of ignorance of the Palestinian position. Now is the time for the Palestinians to state clearly, and for the world to hear clearly, the Palestinian vision.

But first, let me be very clear. I condemn the attacks carried out by terrorist groups against Israeli civilians. These groups do not represent the Palestinian people or their legitimate aspirations for freedom. They are terrorist organizations, and I am determined to put an end to their activities.

The Palestinian Vision of Peace

The Palestinian vision of peace is an independent and viable Palestinian state on the territories occupied by Israel in 1967, living as an equal neighbor alongside Israel with peace and security for both the Israeli and Palestinian peoples. In 1988, the Palestine National Council adopted a historic resolution calling for the implementation of applicable United Nations resolutions, particularly, Resolutions 242 and 338. The Palestinians recognized Israel's right to exist on 78 percent of historical Palestine with the understanding that we would be allowed to live in freedom on the remaining 22 percent, which has been under Israeli occupation since 1967. Our commitment to that two-state solution remains unchanged, but unfortunately, also remains unreciprocated.

We seek true independence and full sovereignty: the right to control our own airspace, water resources, and borders; to develop our own economy, to have nor-

Yasser Arafat, "The Palestinian Vision of Peace," *Ramallah*, February 3, 2002.

mal commercial relations with our neighbors, and to travel freely. In short, we seek only what the free world now enjoys and only what Israel insists on for itself: the right to control our own destiny and to take our place among free nations.

In addition, we seek a fair and just solution to the plight of Palestinian refugees who for fifty-four years have not been permitted to return to their homes. We understand Israel's demographic concerns and understand that the right of return of Palestinian refugees, a right guaranteed under international law and United Nations Resolution 194, must be implemented in a way that takes into account such concerns. However, just as we Palestinians must be realistic with respect to Israel's demographic desires, Israelis too must be realistic in understanding that there can be no solution to the Israeli-Palestinian conflict if the legitimate rights of these innocent civilians continue to be ignored. Left unresolved, the refugee issue has the potential to undermine any permanent peace agreement between Palestinians and Israelis. How is a Palestinian refugee to understand that his or her right of return will not be honored but those of Kosovar Albanians, Afghans, and East Timorese have been?

> ***"[The Palestinians] seek true independence and full sovereignty."***

Palestinians for Peace

There are those who claim that I am not a partner in peace. In response, I say Israel's peace partner is, and always has been, the Palestinian people. Peace is not a signed agreement between individuals—it is reconciliation between peoples. Two peoples cannot reconcile when one demands control over the other, when one refuses to treat the other as a partner in peace, when one uses the logic of power rather than the power of logic. Israel has yet to understand that it cannot have peace while denying justice. As long as the occupation of Palestinian lands continues, as long as Palestinians are denied freedom, then the path to the "peace of the brave" that I embarked upon with my late partner Yitzhak Rabin will be littered with obstacles.

The Palestinian people have been denied their freedom for far too long and are the only people in the world still living under foreign occupation. How is it possible that the entire world can tolerate this oppression, discrimination and humiliation? The 1993 Oslo Accord, signed on the White House lawn, promised the Palestinians freedom by May 1999. Instead, since 1993, the Palestinian people have endured a doubling of Israeli settlers, expansion of illegal Israeli settlements on Palestinian land, and increased restrictions on freedom of movement. How do I convince my people that Israel is serious about peace while over the past decade Israel intensified the colonization of Palestinian land from which it was ostensibly negotiating a withdrawal?

But no degree of oppression and no level of desperation can ever justify the killing of innocent civilians. I condemn terrorism. I condemn the killing of innocent civilians, whether they are Israeli, American, or Palestinian; whether they are killed by Palestinian extremists, Israeli settlers, or by the Israeli government. But condemnations do not stop terrorism. To stop terrorism, we must understand that terrorism is simply the symptom, not the disease.

The personal attacks on me currently in vogue may be highly effective in giving Israelis an excuse to ignore their own role in creating the current situation. But these attacks do little to move the peace process forward and, in fact, are not designed to. Many believe that Ariel Sharon, Israel's prime minister, given his opposition to every peace treaty Israel has ever signed, is fanning the flames of unrest in an effort to delay indefinitely a return to negotiations. Regrettably, he has done little to prove them wrong. Israeli government practices of settlement construction, home demolitions, political assassinations, closures, and shameful silence in the face of Israeli settler violence and other daily humiliations are clearly not aimed at calming the situation.

Ending the Occupation

The Palestinians have a vision of peace: it is a peace based on the complete end of the occupation and a return to Israel's 1967 borders, the sharing of all Jerusalem as one open city and as the capital of two states, Palestine and Israel. It is a warm peace between two equals enjoying mutually beneficial economic and social cooperation. Despite the brutal repression of Palestinians over the last four decades, I believe when Israel sees Palestinians as equals, and not as a subjugated people upon whom it can impose its will, such a vision can come true. Indeed it must.

Palestinians are ready to end the conflict. We are ready to sit down now with any Israeli leader, regardless of his history, to negotiate freedom for the Palestinians, a complete end of the occupation, security for Israel, and creative solutions to the plight of the refugees while respecting Israel's demographic concerns. But we will only sit down as equals, not as supplicants; as partners, not as subjects; as seekers of a just and peaceful solution, not as a defeated nation grateful for whatever scraps are thrown our way. For despite Israel's overwhelming military advantage, we possess something even greater: the power of justice.

Creating a Palestinian State Would Not Resolve the Israeli-Palestinian Conflict

by Neill Lochery

About the author: *Neill Lochery is the director of the Center for Israeli Studies at the University College in London, England.*

Ever since Palestinian Authority Leader Yasser Arafat appeared to embrace the idea of the State of Israel alongside a Palestinian state in 1988, and the Israeli government accepted the notion of a Palestinian state by signing the Oslo Accords in 1993, it was presumed that the peace process was moving toward a two-state solution. Commentators such as myself have embraced this concept for years. Sadly, however, I now sense we were wrong. Put simply, the Palestinians are not ready for statehood.

I say this with the deeply held belief that in a perfect world there would already exist a Palestinian state—one that was politically stable and economically viable. But to create a Palestinian state will not solve the problems of the Middle East as Egyptian President Hosni Mubarak suggested to President George W. Bush at Camp David in June 2002. Instead, such a move would make it even harder to bring stability to the region.

A Monopoly over Violence

The key to creating any state is a monopoly over the means of violence by the legitimate leadership of the proposed state. This is clearly absent in Palestinian Authority areas. There is mounting evidence that Mr. Arafat has lost control over the various Palestinian paramilitary groups and is afraid of challenging the freedom of radical Islamic groups, such as Hamas and Islamic Jihad, to launch attacks in Israel.

At present, the Islamic groups, and some groups closer to Mr. Arafat, reject the two-state solution to the conflict. As a result, even if a Palestinian state were created the violence would not end, Hamas and others would continue to launch attacks against Israeli citizens. Israel would be forced to retaliate, leading to increased Palestinian support for more attacks against Israeli targets. In short, statehood would not end the violence, but would more likely fan its flames.

> ***"The Palestinians are not ready for statehood."***

The question of political reform within the Palestinian Authority has become so important that to proceed with the creation of a state before this has taken place would be foolhardy for all parties. We need to see a more mature leadership emerge from the ruins and chaos. Values such as accountability and democracy need to be instilled in new leaders who must serve their people in a less selfish manner than have Mr. Arafat and his cronies. Without this, a Palestinian state would resemble Iraq under Saddam Hussein.

Relying on International Aid

Economically speaking, a Palestinian state is not viable either. There would be an over-reliance on international aid from Arab and European Union countries—dangerous given that much of what was promised in the past never arrived. The business sector has not developed as was hoped back in 1993. The majority of successful Palestinian entrepreneurs live outside the boundaries of the proposed state and have shown little inclination to invest in the Palestinian Authority, preferring markets where there is a stronger chance of financial return. Put simply, they continue to invest in global markets for business and not nationalist reasons, and there is little sign this would change with the creation of a state. Consequently, many Palestinian families would become increasingly reliant on one or more members of the family working in Israel or in Kuwait. In these circumstances, it is difficult to see how a state could raise enough taxes to pay for even the most basic services for its citizens.

So, the absence of control over armed groups, the lack of legitimate and credible political leadership and a weak economic sector suggest the only criteria for creating a state today would be to satisfy the nationalist aspirations of Palestinians.

This, however, is sheer folly. Creating such a state would only increase nationalism as the state struggled to survive. The land of milk and honey across the border would likely become a target of frustration, with increased calls to destroy Israel in order to form a more viable state of Palestine from the Mediterranean to the River Jordan.

World leaders need to understand that creating a Palestinian state today will not end the violence. President Mubarak admits this in private, as does King Abdullah of Jordan. From their perspective, however, the creation of a weak Palestinian state poses little short-term political threat to the strategic balance of the Arab world and satisfies the increasingly strong pro-Palestinian sentiment of their respective populations. What they fail to see is that a failed Palestinian state—for that is what it would eventually be—is as much a long-term danger to their own positions as to Israel. Israeli prime minister Ariel Sharon will no doubt have to remind President Bush of this point.

At present, a two-state solution represents no solution at all.

Palestinians Must Fight for Equal Rights

by Edward Said

About the author: *Edward Said is a professor of English and comparative literature at Columbia University. He is the author of* Peace and Its Discontents.

In the United States, celebrations of Israel's 50 years as a state have tried to project an image of the country that went out of fashion since the Palestinian *intifada* [uprising] (1987–92): a pioneering state, full of hope and promise for the survivors of the Nazi Holocaust, a haven of enlightened liberalism in a sea of Arab fanaticism and reaction.

On 15 April 1998, for instance, CBS broadcast a two-hour prime-time programme from Hollywood hosted by Michael Douglas and Kevin Costner, featuring movie stars such as Arnold Schwarzenegger, Kathy Bates—who recited passages from Golda Meir minus, of course, her most celebrated remark that there were no Palestinians—and Winona Ryder. None of these luminaries are particularly known for their Middle Eastern expertise or enthusiasm, although all of them in one way or another praised Israel's greatness and enduring achievements. There was even time for a cameo appearance by Bill Clinton, who provided perhaps the least edifying, most atavistic note of the evening by complimenting Israel, 'a small oasis', for 'making a once barren desert bloom', and for 'building a thriving democracy in hostile terrain.'

Ironically enough, no such encomia were intoned on Israeli television, which has been broadcasting a 22-part series, 'Tkuma', on the country's history. This series has a decidedly more complicated and, indeed, more critical content. Episodes on the 1948 war, for instance, made use of archival sources unearthed by the so-called revisionist historians (Benny Morris, Ilan Pappe, Avi Schlaim, Tom Segev, et al) to demonstrate that the indigenous Palestinians were forcibly expelled, their villages destroyed, their land taken, their society eradicated. It was as if Israeli audiences had no need of all the palliatives provided for diasporic and international viewers, who still needed to be told that Israel was a

Edward Said, "Fifty Years of Dispossession," *Index On Censorship*, May/June 1998, pp. 76–82.

cause for uncomplicated rejoicing and not, as it has been for Palestinians, the cause of a protracted, and still continuing, dispossession of the country's indigenous people.

If They're Not Mentioned, They Don't Exist

That the US celebration simply omitted any mention of the Palestinians indicated also how remorselessly an ideological mind-set can hold on, despite the facts, despite years of news and headlines, despite an extraordinary, if ultimately unsuccessful, effort to keep effacing Palestinians from the picture of Israel's untroubled sublimity. If they're not mentioned, they don't exist. Even after 50 years of living the Palestinian exile I still find myself astonished at the lengths to which official Israel and its supporters will go to suppress the fact that a half century has gone by without Israeli restitution, recognition or acknowledgement of Palestinian human rights and without, as the facts undoubtedly show, connecting that suspension of rights to Israel's official policies.

Even when there is a vague buried awareness of the facts, as is the case with a front-page *New York Times* story on 23 April 1998 by one Ethan Bronner, the Palestinian *nakba* [cataclysm] is characterized as a semi-fictional event (dutiful inverted commas around the word 'catastrophe' for instance) caused by no-one in particular. When Bronner quotes an uprooted Palestinian who describes his miseries, the man's testimony is qualified by 'for most Israelis, the idea of Mr Shikaki staking claim to victimhood is chilling', a reaction made plausible as Bronner blithely leapfrogs over the man's uprooting and systematic deprivations and immediately tells us how his 'rage' (for years the approved word for dealing with Palestinian history) has impelled his sons into joining Hamas and Islamic Jihad. Ergo, Palestinians are violent terrorists, whereas Israel can go on being a 'vibrant and democratic regional superpower established on the ashes of Nazi genocide.' But not on the ashes of Palestine, an obliteration that lingers on in measures taken by Israel to block Palestinian rights, domestically as well as in territories occupied in 1967.

Take land and citizenship for instance. Approximately 750,000 Palestinians were expelled in 1948: they are now four million. Left behind were 120,000 (now one million) who subsequently became Israelis, a minority constituting about 18 per cent of the state's population, but not fully-fledged citizens in anything more than name. In addition there are 2.5 million Palestinians without sovereignty on the West Bank and in Gaza. Israel is the only state in the world which is not the state of its actual citizens, but of the whole Jewish people who consequently have rights that non-Jews do not. Without a constitution, Israel is governed by Basic Laws of which one in particular, the Law of Return, makes it possible for any Jew anywhere to emigrate to Israel and become a citizen, at the same time that

"A half century has gone by without Israeli restitution."

native-born Palestinians do not have the same right. Ninety-three per cent of the land of the state is characterised as Jewish land, meaning that no non-Jew is allowed to lease, sell or buy it.

Before the Catastrophe

Before 1948, the Jewish community in Palestine owned a little over 6 per cent of the land. A recent case in which a Palestinian Israeli, Adel Kaadan, wished to buy land but was refused because he was a non-Jew has become something of a *cause célèbre* in Israel, and has even made it to the Supreme Court which is supposed to, but would prefer not, to rule on it. Kaadan's lawyer has said that 'as a Jew in Israel, I think that if a Jew somewhere else in the world was prohibited from buying state land, public land owned by the federal government, because they're Jews, I believe there would have been an outcry in Israel.' This anomaly about Israeli democracy, not well known and rarely cited, is compounded by the fact that, as I said above, Israel's land in the first place was owned by Palestinians expelled in 1948; since their forced exodus their property was legally turned into Jewish land by The Absentees' Property Law, the Law of the State's Property and the Land Ordinance (the Acquisition of Land for Public Purposes). Now only Jewish citizens have access to that land, a fact that does not corroborate *The Economist*'s extraordinarily sweeping statement on 'Israel at 50' that since the state's founding Palestinians 'have enjoyed full political rights'.

> ***"Israel is the only state in the world which is not the state of its actual citizens."***

What makes it specially galling for Palestinians is that they have been forced to watch the transformation of their own homeland into a western state, one of whose express purposes is to provide for Jews and not for non-Jews. Between 1948 and 1966 Palestinian Israelis were ruled by military ordinance. After that, as the state regularised its policies on education, legal practice, religion, social, economic and political participation, a regime evolved to keep the Palestinian minority disadvantaged, segregated and constantly discriminated against. There is an eye-opening account of this shabby history that is rarely cited and, when it is, elided or explained away by the euphemism (familiar from South African apartheid) that 'they' have their own system: it is the March 1998 report, *Legal Violations of Arab Minority Rights in Israel*, published by Adalah (the Arabic word for justice), an Arab-Jewish organization within Israel. Especially telling is the section on the 'discriminatory approach of Israeli courts,' routinely praised by supporters of Israel for their impartiality and fairness. In fact, the report notes that the courts having delivered progressive and decent-minded decisions on the rights of women, homosexuals, the disabled etc. have 'since 1948 dismissed all cases dealing with equal rights for Arab citizens, and have never included a declaratory statement in decisions regarding the protection of Arab group rights'. This is borne out by a survey of criminal and civil cases in which Arabs get no help from the courts and are far more likely to be indicted than Jews in similar circumstances.

It is only in the past few years that investigations of Israel's political makeup, hitherto assumed to be socialist, egalitarian, pioneering, forward-looking, have turned up a rather unattractive picture. Zeev Sternhell's book *The Founding Myths of Israel* is the work of an Israeli historian of twentieth-century right-wing European mass movements who finds a disturbing congruence between those movements and Israel's own brand of what Sternhell rightly calls 'nationalist socialism'. Far from being socialist, Israel's founders, and subsequently the polity they established, were profoundly anti-socialist, bent almost entirely upon 'conquest of the land' and the creation of 'self-realisation' and a new sense of organic peoplehood that moved steadily to the right during the pre-1948 years. 'Neither the Zionist movement abroad,' Sternhell says, 'nor the pioneers who were beginning to settle the country could frame a policy toward the Palestinian national movement. The real reason for this was not a lack of understanding of the problem but a clear recognition of the insurmountable contradiction between the basic objectives of the two sides.' After 1948, policy towards the Palestinians clearly envisioned that community's disappearance or its political nullity, since it was clear that the contradiction between the two sides would always remain insurmountable. Israel, in short, could not become a secular liberal state, despite the efforts of two generations of publicists to make it so.

"It is only in the past few years that investigations of Israel's political makeup . . . have turned up a rather unattractive picture."

Palestinian Submission and Israeli Dominance

After 1967, the occupation of the West Bank and Gaza produced a military and civil regime for Palestinians whose aim was Palestinian submission and Israeli dominance, an extension of the model on which Israel proper functioned. Settlements were established in the late summer of 1967 (and Jerusalem annexed) not by right-wing parties but by the Labour Party, a member, interestingly enough, of the Socialist International. The promulgation of literally hundreds of 'occupiers' laws' directly contravened not only the tenets of the Universal Declaration of Human Rights but the Geneva Conventions as well. These violations ran the gamut from administrative detention, to mass land expropriations, house demolitions, forced movement of populations, torture, uprooting of trees, assassination, book banning, closure of schools and universities. Always, however, the illegal settlements were being expanded as more and more Arab land was ethnically cleansed so that Jewish populations from Russia, Ethiopia, Canada and the USA, among other places, could be accommodated.

After the Oslo Accords [peace agreements between Israel and Palestine] were signed in September 1993, conditions for Palestinians steadily worsened. It became impossible for Palestinians to travel freely between one place and another, Jerusalem was declared off limits and massive building projects transformed the country's geography. In everything, the distinction between Jew and non-Jew is scrupulously preserved. The most perspicacious analysis of the legal situation obtaining after Oslo is Raja Shehadeh's in his book *From Occupation to Interim Accords: Israel and the Palestinian Territories*, an important work that demonstrates the carefully preserved continuity between Israeli negotiating strategy during the Oslo process and its land-occupation policy established in the occupied territories from the early 1970s. In addition, Shehadeh demonstrates the tragic lack of preparation and understanding in the PLO's [Palestine Liberation Organization] strategy during the peace process, with the result that much of the sympathy gained internationally for the Palestinians against Israeli settlement policy and its dismal human rights record was frittered away, unused and unexploited. 'All the support and sympathy,' he says, 'which it took years for Palestinians to rally, returned home, so to speak, with the mistaken belief that the struggle was over. The Palestinians, as much as the Israelis, helped in giving the false impression through, among other things, the highly publicised media image of the Arafat-Rabin handshake, that the Israeli-Palestinian conflict was resolved. No serious attempt was made to remind the world that one of the main causes of the conflict after 1967, the Israeli settlements in occupied Palestinian territory, remained intact. This is not to speak of the other basic unresolved questions of the return of refugees, compensation, and the issue of Jerusalem.'

Unquestionably the moral dilemma faced by anyone trying to come to terms with the Palestinian-Israeli conflict is a deep one. Israeli Jews are not white settlers of the stripe that colonised Algeria or South Africa, though similar methods have been used. They are correctly seen as victims of a long history of western, largely Christian anti-semitic persecution that culminated in the scarcely comprehensible horrors of the Nazi Holocaust. To Palestinians, however, their role is that of victims of the victims. This is why western liberals who openly espoused the anti-apartheid movement, or that of the Nicaraguan Sandanistas, or Bosnia, or East Timor, or US civil rights, or Armenian commemoration of the Turkish genocide, or many other political causes of that kind, have shied away from openly endorsing Palestinian self-determination. As for Israel's nuclear policy, or its legally underwritten campaign of torture, or of using civilians as hostages, or of refusing to give Palestinians permits to build on their own land in the West Bank—the case is never made in the liberal public sphere, partly out of fear, partly out of guilt.

"After the Oslo Accords were signed in September 1993, conditions for Palestinians steadily worsened."

An even greater challenge is the difficulty of separating Palestinian and Israeli-Jewish populations who are now inextricably linked in all sorts of ways, despite the immense chasm that divides them. Those of us who for years have argued for a Palestinian state have come to the realisation that if such a 'state' (the inverted commas here are definitely required) is going to appear out of the shambles of Oslo it will be weak, economically dependent on Israel, without real sovereignty or power. Above all, as the present map of the West Bank amply shows, the Palestinian autonomy zones will be non-contiguous (they now account for only 3 per cent of the West Bank; former Israeli prime minister Benjamin Netanyahu's government balked at giving up an additional 13 per cent) and effectively divided into Bantustans controlled from the outside by Israel. The only reasonable course therefore is to recommend that Palestinians and their supporters renew the struggle against the fundamental principle that relegates 'non-Jews' to subservience on the land of historical Palestine. This, it seems to me, is what is entailed by any principled campaign on behalf of justice for Palestinians, and certainly not the enfeebled separatism that movements like Peace Now have fitfully embraced and quickly abandoned. There can be no concept of human rights, no matter how elastic, that accommodates the strictures of Israeli state practice against 'non-Jewish' Palestinians in favour of Jewish citizens. Only if the inherent contradiction is faced between what in effect is a theocratic and ethnic exclusivism on the one hand and genuine democracy on the other, can there be any hope for reconciliation and peace in Israel/Palestine. Fudging, waffling, looking the other way, avoiding the issue entirely, or accepting pabulum definitions of 'peace' will bring Palestinians and, in the long run Israelis, nothing but hardship and insecurity.

> ***"[Israeli Jews] are correctly seen as victims of a long history of . . . persecution."***

Palestinians Must Reject Terrorism as a Weapon of War

by Gal Luft

About the author: *Gal Luft is a former lieutenant colonel in the Israel Defense Forces and the author of* The Palestinian Security Forces: Between Police and Army.

Never in Israel's history, to paraphrase former British prime minister Winston Churchill, has so much harm been inflicted on so many by so few. Since the onset of the second intifada [Palestinian uprising] in late September 2000, dozens of exploding humans—Palestinian H-bombs—have rocked the Jewish state and transformed the lives of its people. As little as a year ago, suicide bombings were seen as a gruesome aberration in the Israeli-Palestinian conflict, an expression of religious fanaticism that most Palestinians rejected. But a new, unsettling reality has emerged: the acceptance and legitimation of the practice among all Palestinian political and military factions.

Increasingly, Palestinians are coming to see suicide attacks as a strategic weapon, a poor man's "smart bomb" that can miraculously balance Israel's technological prowess and conventional military dominance. Palestinians appear to have decided that, used systematically in the context of a political struggle, suicide bombings give them something no other weapon could: the ability to cause Israel devastating and unprecedented pain. The dream of achieving such strategic parity is more powerful than any pressure to cease and desist. It is therefore unlikely that the strategy will be abandoned, even as its continued use pushes the Middle East ever closer to the abyss.

From Mortars to Martyrs

The Palestinian endorsement of suicide bombings as a legitimate tool of war was not hasty. At the start of the second intifada, the Palestinians' preferred

Gal Luft, "The Palestinian H-Bomb: Terror's Winning Strategy," *Foreign Affairs*, July/August 2002, p. 2.

method of fighting was based on the strategy that [the terrorist group] Hezbollah used to drive the Israel Defense Forces (IDF) out of southern Lebanon after 15 years of occupation—a mix of guerrilla tactics such as ambushes, drive-by shootings, and attacks on IDF outposts. It was thought that the "Lebanonization" of the West Bank and the Gaza Strip would cause the Israeli public to view these territories as security liabilities (as they had with southern Lebanon), and to pressure the government to withdraw once more.

Palestinian leader Yasir Arafat's division of labor was clear. His political wing, Fatah, authorized its paramilitary units, spearheaded by the Tanzim militias along with segments of the security services of the Palestinian Authority (PA), to carry out a guerrilla campaign against Israeli settlements and military targets in the West Bank and Gaza. The militant groups Hamas and Islamic Jihad, meanwhile, were given the liberty to carry out attacks against civilian targets inside Israel.

From the Palestinian perspective, however, the results of the guerrilla campaign in the first year were poor, especially considering the duration of the fighting and the volume of fire. Palestinian forces launched more than 1,500 shooting attacks on Israeli vehicles in the territories but killed 75 people. They attacked IDF outposts more than 6,000 times but killed only 20 soldiers. They fired more than 300 antitank grenades at Israeli targets but failed to kill anyone. To demoralize the settlers, the Palestinians launched more than 500 mortar and rocket attacks at Jewish communities in the territories and, at times, inside Israel, but the artillery proved to be primitive and inaccurate, and only one Israeli was killed.

Israel's response to the guerrilla campaign, moreover, was decisive. Using good intelligence, the Israeli security services targeted individual Palestinian militants and destroyed most of the PA's military infrastructure. Israeli soldiers also moved back into "Area A," the territory that had been turned over as a result of the Oslo peace negotiations to exclusive Palestinian control, to raze suspected mortar activity sites. At first these incursions met with international rebuke, even from the United States. Secretary of State Colin Powell, for example, denounced the first foray into Gaza in April 2001 as "excessive and disproportionate." But over time the temporary incursions became such a common practice that the international community stopped paying attention. Stung by the lack of progress in the struggle, at the end of 2001 Arafat tried a final gambit, attempting to smuggle in a cache of Iranian weapons on board the *Karine-A*. But Israeli naval commandos seized the ship and turned his ploy into a shameful diplomatic disaster. Thus ended Palestinian emulation of the "Hezbollah model."

> ***"Palestinians are coming to see suicide attacks as a strategic weapon."***

Unlike the guerrilla strategy, meanwhile, the terror campaign carried out by

Hamas and Islamic Jihad was showing results. The Islamic movements managed to kill or maim more Israelis in 350 stabbings, shootings, and bombings inside Israel than the mainstream Palestinian organizations had in more than 8,000 armed attacks in the West Bank and Gaza. The strongest impact came from 39 suicide attacks that killed 70 Israelis and wounded more than 1,000 others. If one compares this bloodshed with the limited damage caused by the 39 Scud missiles Iraqi president Saddam Hussein launched at Israel in 1991—74 fatalities, most of them caused by heart attacks—it is not hard to understand why the new methods caused such intoxication.

> ***"[Palestinians] derive comfort and satisfaction from the fact that the Jews are also suffering."***

Palestinians are fully aware of what they have suffered at the hands of the Israeli military in response to the terror campaign, but most view it as a great success nevertheless. They derive comfort and satisfaction from the fact that the Jews are also suffering. The Palestinians view the campaign's greatest achievement as not just the killing of so many Israelis but the decline of Israel's economy, the destruction of its tourism industry, and the demoralization of its people. According to a mid-May 2002 poll, two-thirds of Palestinians say that the second intifada's violence has achieved more for them than did the previous years of negotiations.

Legitimizing Terror

Before the outbreak of the second intifada, Palestinians distinguished among attacks on settlers, on Israeli military targets, and on civilians inside Israel. Now, however, those distinctions are disappearing. Although after the Israeli incursions in Spring 2002 support for attacks against civilians inside Israel dropped 6 points to 52 percent, opposition to arresting those carrying out such attacks rose 10 points to 86 percent—a figure close to the 89 percent and 92 percent support for attacks on Israeli settlers and soldiers in the territories, respectively.

In the post-September 11, 2001 era, however, when deliberate attacks against innocent civilians are anathema to most people, embracing terrorism as a strategy has required the Palestinians to persuade themselves, and others, that what they are doing is legitimate. They have therefore created what they see as a moral equivalence between Israel's harm to the Palestinian civilian population and Palestinian attacks against Israeli civilians, including children.

They have also developed a creative interpretation of what terrorism is, one that stresses ends rather than means. Thus, in December 2001, more than 94 percent of Palestinians told pollsters that they viewed Israeli incursions into Area A as acts of terror, while 82 percent refused to characterize the killing of 21 Israeli youths outside a Tel Aviv disco six months earlier that way. And 94 percent reported that they would characterize a hypothetical Israeli use of chemical or biological weapons against Palestinians as terrorism, whereas only 26 percent would say the same about Palestinian use of those weapons against Israel. Interestingly, the new definition extends beyond the conflict with Israel. Only 41 percent of Palestinians, for example, viewed the September 11, 2001, attacks as terrorism, and only 46 percent saw the Lockerbie bombing [in 1988, an American plane was blown up over Lockerbie, Scotland] that way.

Espousing Martyrdom

The more enchanted Palestinians have become with the achievements of their "martyrs," the more Fatah has found itself under pressure to adopt the suicide weapon. In 2001, fearing a loss of popular support if the "street" perceived the Islamists' methods as more effective than Fatah's tack, Fatah leaders decided they had to follow suit. The part of Arafat that wanted to show solidarity with the United States and that was determined to avoid any association with terror against civilians, in other words, succumbed to the anti-Israel rage and political calculations of his lieutenants and the members of what Palestinian pollster Khalil Shikaki has called the "young guard" of Palestinian nationalism.

Fatah's official espousal of "martyrdom" operations took place on November 29, 2001, when two terrorists blew themselves up together on a bus near the Israeli city of Hadera. One, Mustafa Abu Srieh, was from Islamic Jihad; the other, Abdel Karim Abu Nafa, served with the Palestinian police in Jericho. But the bond of blood with the Islamists did not last long, and soon Fatah's al Aqsa Martyrs Brigades and the Islamists found themselves engaged in a diabolical contest over which group could perfect the use of the suicide weapon and be viewed as most valuable to the war effort. Al Aqsa has capitalized on the Islamists' opposition to the participation of women and established squads of willing female suicide bombers named after Wafa Idris, the Palestinian woman who blew up herself and an Israeli man in Jerusalem in January 2002. Islamic Jihad, for its part, has recruited children as young as 13 for suicide missions.

> ***"[Palestinians] have . . . developed a creative interpretation of what terrorism is."***

Both Islamists and secular Palestinians have come to see suicide bombing as a weapon against which Israel has no comprehensive defense. To counter the Iraqi Scuds, Israel developed and deployed the Arrow, a $2 billion ballistic missile defense system. Against Palestinian H-bombs, Israel can at best build a fence. The suicide bombers are smarter than Scuds, and Palestinians know that even though in Israel today there are more security guards than teachers or doctors, the bomber will always get through.

If history is any guide, Israel's military campaign to eradicate the phenomenon of suicide bombing is unlikely to succeed. Other nations that have faced opponents willing to die have learned the hard way that, short of complete annihilation of the enemy, no military solution will solve the problem.

But the Israeli authorities are deeply reluctant to accept this reality. Israeli society seeks absolute security and adheres to the notion that military power can resolve almost any security problem. If the Palestinians put their faith in Allah, Israelis put theirs in a tank. Whether consciously or not, their belief in the utility of force—evident in the popular "Let the IDF Win" campaign, which advocated a freer hand for the army—reflects a strategic choice to militarize the conflict rather than politicize it. The IDF's senior leaders repeatedly claim that the smart application of military force can create a new reality on the ground that, in turn, will allow the government to negotiate political agreements under more favorable terms.

It is true that when the IDF was finally allowed to "win," Israel achieved impressive tactical results. Operation Defensive Shield in April 2002 eliminated an entire echelon of terrorist leaders in the West Bank, crippled the PA's financial and operational infrastructure, and reduced PA arsenals. But as at other times in its history, Israel failed to convert its tactical achievements into strategic gains. Its intensive use of military instruments earned it international condemnation, further radicalized Palestinian society, and created an environment of anger conducive to more terrorist activities. By May, unsurprisingly, the suicide bombings had started again.

"Israel's military campaign to eradicate the phenomenon of suicide bombing is unlikely to succeed."

IDF simulations before the second intifada had predicted that a military reentry into major Palestinian cities would lead to hundreds of Israeli casualties. In fact, however, the incursions into territories under Palestinian control proved to be almost painless. Following the assassination of Israel's tourism minister, Rehavam Ze'evi, in October 2001, the IDF launched a broad assault on the PA, entering all six major West Bank cities. Palestinian resistance was negligible, and only six Israeli soldiers were wounded. Operation Defensive Shield, the second big incursion into Area A, also met relatively weak resistance. Aside from the struggle in the Jenin refugee camp, in which 23 Israeli soldiers were killed, Israeli forces conquered six Palestinian cities and dozens of smaller towns and villages while suffering only three fatalities.

The IDF has interpreted the Palestinian lack of resistance in the cities as a sign of weakness rather than a strategic choice. Israelis view with disdain the Palestinian "victory" celebrations after each incursion comes to an end. They are puzzled by the fact that their enemy fires more bullets into the air than at Israeli troops. What Israel fails to comprehend is the paradigm by which the Palestinians are choosing to conduct their war.

Acknowledging their perpetual conventional inferiority, Arafat's people feel no need to demonstrate strong resistance to Israeli forces. They simply wait for the storm to pass while preparing another batch of "martyrs." Families of suicide bombers now receive more than double the financial compensation than do the families of those killed by other means. Nurturing an ethos of heroism fundamentally opposed to that of the Israelis, the Palestinian war of liberation has elevated the suicide bomber to the highest throne of courage and devotion to the national cause.

Fencing Lessons

Israelis' misunderstanding of the new Palestinian way of war may come back to haunt them. Their perception of their enemy's weakness is likely to embolden them and encourage more broad punitive operations in response to future attacks. But Israel's military responses will eventually exhaust themselves, whereas the Palestinians will still have legions of willing "martyrs."

In fact, despite defiant Israeli rhetoric insisting that there will be no surrender to terrorism, one can already see the opposite happening. Israelis are willing to pay an increasingly high economic and diplomatic price for increasingly short periods of calm. As a result, more and more people support panaceas such as unilateral separation—the building of walls, fences, and buffer zones to protect Israel's population centers from Palestinian wrath.

Unilateral separation would no doubt make the infiltration of suicide bombers into Israel more difficult, but it would also increase their prestige in the eyes of many in the region. The bombers would be viewed, correctly, as the catalyst that drove the Israelis out of an occupied territory yet again, and the years of agony Palestinians have endured would be sweetened by a genuine sense of victory. Israel's wall policy, perceived as withdrawal, would reassure the Palestinians that war succeeded where diplomacy failed.

As currently conceived, moreover, walling off the territories would not do much to reduce Palestinian grievances. No matter how long the fence, for example, dozens of Jewish settlements scattered on the hills of the West Bank would necessarily remain beyond it. Two-thirds of Israelis, according to recent polls, support the removal of such isolated and indefensible settlements to make the separation more feasible. But despite such views, Israeli Prime Minister Ariel Sharon has reiterated his refusal to dismantle a single settlement. "The fate of Netzarim is the fate of Tel Aviv," he said recently, referring to the tiny, isolated, and fortified Gaza Strip settlement that has been the target of repeated Palestinian attacks.

> ***"The Palestinian war of liberation has elevated the suicide bomber to the highest throne of courage and devotion to the national cause."***

Israel finds itself, therefore, at a crucial turning point in its history, but one from which no path seems particularly attractive. It must find some way of defending itself against an enemy so eager to inflict pain that it is willing to bring suffering and death on itself in the process. Retaliation is unlikely to work, but retreat is likely only to bring more of the same.

If there is any way out of this dilemma, it may lie in convincing the Palestinian public that its constructive goals can be achieved only by relinquishing its destructive strategy. Israel should therefore embark on a policy that rewards the Palestinians for genuinely fighting terrorism and avoid any policy that feeds the perception that terrorism works.

The rewards will have to be tangible and meaningful. Israel could, for example, offer the PA the removal of a number of small hilltop settlements in exchange for a period of non-belligerency and unequivocal renunciation of suicide bombing. This cooling-off period could then set the stage for renewed talks on a final-status agreement. Such an approach would indicate to the Palestinian population that Israel is serious about peace and ready to pay the necessary price for it, not only in words but in deeds. Most important, showing that Israel is prepared to confront and rein in its own radical rejectionists would put the onus on the Palestinian leadership to do the same.

Before this intifada, a large majority of Palestinians opposed attacks against civilians inside Israel. They hoped to achieve their aspirations for independence without resort to terror. Figuring out how to make that happen is not only the right thing to do, but it is also the best way to ensure Israel's security. Unless that hope can be revived, the fate of Tel Aviv could indeed become that of Netzarim—which would be a tragedy for all.

Economic Development Can Facilitate Peace Between Israelis and Palestinians

by Daniel Doron

About the author: *Daniel Doron is the president of the Israel Center for Social and Economic Progress, a private think tank in Jerusalem.*

The latest mission impossible embraced by those who would resolve the Middle East conflict is the effort to "democratize" the Palestinian Authority, an organization that has thrived on repression, violence, and aggressive irredentism. Meanwhile, a far more promising route to peace—the path of economic cooperation and development—is being neglected or given mere lip service. It's as if the only form of economic life possible for Palestinians, [is] the one that has prevailed in the last ten years—the provision of foreign billions to huge bureaucracies that squandered or stole much of it, while lawlessness and corruption suppressed private initiatives. There was a time, however, when the slow growth of a Palestinian middle class with a real stake in peace was helping mitigate the conflict and make it manageable.

A Quiet Peace

During the quarter century from the Six-Day War till the Oslo Accords [1993 agreement that intended to facilitate peace between Israel and Palestine], from 1967 to 1993, political stalemate actually enabled a quiet peace. In those years, Israel maintained a modicum of law and order in Palestinian areas, and the Palestinian economy flourished, its gross national product (GNP) more than quadrupling. The Palestinian standard of living rose dramatically, infant mortality fell, seven new colleges and universities were established (where none had

Daniel Doron, "The Way Forward for the Palestinians: It's Economic Development, Not Peace Processing," *Weekly Standard*, vol. 7, July 1, 2002, p. 29.

existed under Jordanian rule), and the welfare of the people, especially of women and children, improved so much that the birth rate soared. Most Palestinians seemed to prefer this slowly evolving peace to the political ambitions of their leaders. Thus, shortly after Oslo but before Palestine Liberation Organization (PLO) incitement had infected their minds and provoked bloody clashes with Israel, the Palestinian inhabitants of East Jerusalem were asked to choose to receive either Palestinian Authority or Israeli identity papers. Over 95 percent chose Israeli. They did so despite disliking Israeli occupation and loathing Israeli bureaucracy (which drives even Israelis up the wall). They cared more about feeding their families and advancing their personal interests than grabbing for instant political gratification.

Already they were wary of Yasser Arafat's nascent Palestinian Authority. Real estate prices plummeted in Arab sections rumored to be destined for transfer to the Palestinian Authority. More recently, most "experts" predicted that an Israeli move to occupy the Orient House, the PLO's illegal stronghold in Jerusalem, would see the city's large Arab population erupt in bloody riots. The State Department sternly warned Israel not to take this step. Yet the takeover in 2001 elicited only feeble protests by a few dozen employees of the Palestinian Authority and some peace activists and Quaker volunteers displaying signs in English for the benefit of CNN.

During the quarter century of relative peace, hundreds of thousands of Palestinians worked in Israel. Crossing through border checkpoints was infuriatingly slow and humiliating, but once inside Israel they had total freedom of movement. Had they been committed to the PLO struggle against Israel, they could have inflicted enormous damage. Yet only a very few of them, generally PLO hirelings, engaged in acts of terrorism.

Most Arabs were reluctant to join in Yasser Arafat's war. Most, after the occupation of the disputed territories in 1967, constituted a silent majority who preferred accommodation with Israel. Even now, when Arabs feel great anger about Israeli military incursions, few express their fury in violent actions. In Jerusalem, Arabs have remained moderate in the face of numerous PLO provocations because they benefit greatly from the commerce generated by tourism, which depends on peace. And in Gaza, the hotbed of radicalism, Palestinian workers in June 2002 showed their priorities when tens of thousands mounted an unprecedented "Hunger March" against the Palestinian Authority, demanding that it stop violence against Israel so they could go back to work there and earn money to support their families.

> ***"There was a time . . . when the slow growth of a Palestinian middle class . . . was helping mitigate the conflict."***

The radicals have never extinguished this normal human wish to work and provide. During the first intifada [uprising], in the late 1980s, Palestinians opened informal markets on the demarcation lines between Arab and Jewish areas catering to Israelis who couldn't shop in Israel on the Sabbath except in kibbutzim. These markets were earning the Palestinians an estimated $300 million annually, half as much as they receive in foreign aid and about one-quarter of their GNP.

Keeping the Peace

Eager to lure Jewish buyers, Arab shopkeepers did all they could to keep the peace and promote good relations with their customers. Arab merchants developed a lucrative trade with Israel. Palestinian agriculture, once primitive, became advanced and prosperous. The large surplus of workers this created found employment in Israel as unskilled labor. Gradually they acquired new skills, raising their income or opening new industrial and commercial ventures, many of which became quite prosperous.

Employment in and trade with Israel were major reasons for the dramatic improvement in the Palestinian standard of living. But they also had unintended consequences, some painful. They brought Arab traditionalists into intimate contact with a modern society and acquainted them with the workings of a boisterous democracy. This forced adjustments in Palestinian family and clan structure and authoritarian political frameworks. So did the violent struggle against Israel, which offered lower-class youths adventure and an avenue for rapid upward mobility through accomplishments in terrorist exploits.

> ***"[Palestinians] cared more about feeding their families . . . than grabbing for instant political gratification."***

The prosperity enjoyed by tradesmen stirred resentment among the Arab bureaucratic and intellectual elites. They had earned up to four times as much as workers under Jordanian rule, but now saw unskilled laborers in Israel earning far more than they could. Contact between the Arabs' almost medieval ethos of loyalty to location and clan and the Israelis' super-modern, sometimes brazenly liberal ethos exacerbated the religious and national conflict. Confronting modernity caused deep anxiety—notably among students whose parents could now send them to Israeli universities, where they were indoctrinated by radical leftist Israeli academics promoting Palestinian statehood with greater fervor than most Arabs. Soon, the newly established colleges and universities in the disputed territories were hotbeds of radicalism, first Marxist, then Islamic fundamentalist.

Concurrently, among the older, more settled Palestinians, a more moderate middle class was gradually developing. It held out the hope that some accommodation could evolve in time, as Arabs and Jews found it mutually advantageous to work and trade with each other.

All this, Oslo ruined by focusing primarily on politics. Conceived in the utopian hope that peace could be bought from a reformed Arafat and his Tunisian cohorts in exchange for territory, Oslo postulated that Arafat would turn his proven brutality against his more radical allies, terrorist groups Hamas and Islamic Jihad. Under the guidance of a messianic Israeli prime minister Shimon Peres captivated by a vision of a New Middle East where factories and hotels rather than armies would keep borders peaceful, the Israeli peace camp made a bargain with the devil, totally ignoring the realities of Israeli and Arab society. It was bound to backfire. Arafat fashioned his "Authority" after the only model he knew, repressive Arab regimes. He dedicated his regime not to civil order and economic development but to the waging of war. He oppressed not Hamas and Islamic Jihad, but the majority of Palestinians who for years had been quietly working out an uneasy but pragmatic modus vivendi with Israel, a real if informal peace.

> ***"Arabs and Jews found it mutually advantageous to work and trade with each other."***

Arafat's 12 security services and 50,000 soldiers engaged in summary executions, kidnapping, rape, and extortion, spreading corruption and poverty wherever they went. Some of the funds donated by the United States and Europe for economic reconstruction, especially among the refugees, were simply stolen; most were used to build a war machine, paying for weapons and soldiers, as well as for the Palestinian Authority's 140,000 bureaucrats. It did not matter to Arafat and his comrades if the war they waged—the second intifada, which began in September 2000—resulted in the almost total destruction of the Palestinian economy. The Palestinian standard of living fell by more than half, and unemployment soared to 60 percent, up from almost full employment before Oslo. The more miserable the Palestinians became, the easier it was for Arafat's relentless propaganda broadcasts to rechannel public rage against the Israelis.

Even as it grew evident that Arafat had no interest in peace, the international Peace Now camp, whose adherents dominate the State Department and many European chancelleries, plunged ahead, promising ever more international meetings at which ever more concessions would be made to terrorism, encouraging Arafat's regime to attempt further blackmail of Israel by the use of violence. It is reported that the United States may reward Arafat with a Palestinian state.

True, there is talk about the need to reform the Palestinian Authority. But reform cannot be only political. If the Palestinians are to have the slightest chance of repairing their system, arrangements must first be worked out to secure law and order. Then a civilian Palestinian leadership, presiding over a demilitarized administration, should be encouraged to employ pro-market economists and political scientists to inventory the institutions still operative in Palestinian society so as to reshape some, shut down others, and establish new ones. Only then will a civilian government be able to tackle the practical problems aggravating the conflict, especially the Palestinians' dismal poverty.

Creating a Law-Abiding Government

The United States and the European Union, which financed Arafat's criminal regime, must now help Palestinian moderates create a law-abiding government that facilitates economic growth. Such moderates will make themselves known once they cease to be terrorized by Arafat and his gangs. Their task is not an easy one, but if Germany and Japan could do it after World War II, there is no reason the Palestinians, a hard-working and intelligent people, can't do it now.

Once a Palestinian entity ceases to pose a threat to Israel, Israel will be able to reduce drastically the number of closures it imposes on Palestinian cities and villages. These closures, designed to prevent terrorist attacks, have punished Arab workers seeking employment, pushing some into the lap of Hamas. With more resources available for peace, Israel could quickly develop and deploy sophisticated detection equipment that would make security precautions, which now can delay the flow of goods by weeks, less onerous. This alone would remove a major impediment to Palestinian economic activity.

While Israel bears no moral responsibility for the refugee problem [thousands of Palestinian refugees of the 1967 war wish to return to Palestine] that resulted from deadly Arab aggression against it, it should do all it can to restore these unfortunates to normal life, as it has for Jewish refugees from Arab lands. Israel should provide housing to displaced Arabs once the stiff opposition of the Palestinian Authority, which nursed and exploited the refugees' plight, is gone. Government-owned land near the "camps" should be provided with infrastructure, and refugee families invited to construct dwellings in their customary cooperative manner. They could also be offered low-interest building loans or compensation for lost property when appropriate.

A massive building program would provide jobs and income for Palestinian construction workers and contractors. It would prime the pump in related trades and services and jump-start a Palestinian economic upturn.

Opening Up Trade

The Palestinian Arabs have a comparative advantage in labor intensive trades. Israel should open its markets to their products. Israeli farmers unable to compete with Arab farmers growing vegetables should be helped to move to the production of upscale products—exotic fruits, vegetables and flowers, speciality cheeses, and wines. Similar arrangements could be worked out in the construction materials, apparel, and footwear industries and other sectors where Arab competition displaced Israeli workers.

> ***"[Israel] should do all it can to restore [Palestinian refugees] to normal life."***

The Israeli government must also cut its high taxes and red tape, which inhibit Israeli and Arab entrepreneurs alike and discourage joint ventures. Israeli policy should facilitate the construction of Palestinian-Israeli industrial parks, like the one built near the Gaza Strip (but unused since the intifada) by the Israeli industrialist Stef Wertheimer. Constructed where Palestinian areas and Israel meet, such parks could alleviate the security and logistical problems involved in busing tens of thousands of Arab workers to Israel daily. They could also provide Arab entrepreneurs a modern infrastructure for manufacturing and other business.

Israel must keep its hands off the informal markets that have sprung up along the edges of Palestinian areas, which have been extremely popular with Israeli bargain-hunters. These markets, in a sort of commercial no man's land, should be encouraged to flourish, as they provide the best environment for peaceful relations.

Prolonged national conflicts are not susceptible to quick fixes. It took Europe centuries to overcome intractable national and religious conflicts. Economic cooperation and growth were essential to resolving them. New interests and benefits created by economic integration helped people transcend the old barriers and made some of them irrelevant. This can happen in the Middle East.

Economic development may be more arduous and less glamorous than peace processing, but it has proved its ability to moderate the Israeli-Palestinian conflict. This is no small accomplishment, considering the violence and mayhem unleashed when leaders have pursued a political settlement first.

Chapter 4

Should the United States Get Involved with Problems in the Middle East?

Chapter Preface

The United States sends Israel about $3 billion in financial and military aid every year. Most Americans—60 to 70 percent—approve of U.S. support of Israel. Others argue that this foreign aid intensifies the tension between the United States and Arab countries, who believe that Israel should withdraw from territories that rightfully belong to Palestinians. Indeed, terrorist Osama bin Laden, who masterminded the September 11, 2001, terrorist attacks on America, cites U.S. support of Israel as a major reason why many Arabs resent the United States. In light of this hostility, many Americans wonder why the United States continues its support of Israel. Stephen Zunes, the Middle East editor of *Foreign Policy in Focus*, contends that the United States supports Israel to further its own interests in the Middle East.

According to Zunes, since its inception in 1948, Israel has proven a useful ally to the United States, especially during the Cold War. For instance, Israel's powerful military, the strongest in the region, keeps potential enemies of the United States—such as Syria, a Soviet ally during the Cold War—under control. In addition, Israel's numerous wars provided battlefield testing of American arms, often against Soviet weapons. Furthermore, Israel's intelligence department has helped U.S. intelligence agencies gather information and plan covert operations in the Middle East. Finally, Israel possesses an enormous nuclear arsenal and has collaborated with the United States on weapons research and manufacture. Zunes states that "U.S. foreign policy is motivated primarily to advance its own perceived strategic interests."

Moreover, Zunes maintains that U.S. support of Israel increased as Israel grew stronger in the Middle East. For example, in the Six Day War in 1967, Israel demonstrated its military superiority in the region when it defeated Egypt, Syria, and Jordan and captured a significant amount of territory. After this victory, U.S. aid to Israel increased by 450 percent. The *New York Times* contends that part of this increase was intended to reward Israel for providing the United States with samples of new Soviet weapons. In 1973, after Israel defeated Arab armies fortified with Soviet aid, U.S. military support increased by another 800 percent. When the United States and Israel conducted their first cooperative naval and air military exercises in 1983 and 1984, Israel received another $1.5 billion in economic assistance. U.S. aid to Israel shot up again after the September 11 terrorist attacks to ensure Israeli cooperation in the war against terrorism. As stated by Zunes, "The correlation is clear: the stronger and more willing to cooperate with U.S. interests that Israel becomes, the stronger the support."

While Israel may be a useful ally, many analysts argue that Israel's friendship is not worth inciting enmity in the rest of the region. To many Arabs, who believe that Israel has oppressed and brutalized Palestinians for more than thirty years, U.S. support of Israel violates the American values of freedom and democracy. According to journalist Chris Toensing, this contradiction proves to many Arabs that the "United States doesn't act on its principles—it acts in its self-interest. Often, those interests collide with the aspirations of Middle Eastern peoples for democracy and prosperity, even dignity." The September 11 terrorist attacks proved that acting in U.S. interests despite Arab opposition may have deadly consequences. To avoid future attacks, many believe that the United States must reevaluate whether an Israeli ally is worth numerous Arab enemies.

The authors in the following chapter debate to what extent the United States should get involved with problems in the Middle East, including whether or not U.S. aid to Israel should continue.

The United States Must Wage a War Against Middle Eastern Terrorism

by David Pryce-Jones

About the author: *David Pryce-Jones is a senior editor of the* National Review *and the author of* The Closed Circle: An Interpretation of the Arabs.

The terrorist attack on the United States in September 2001 will have grave repercussions over the whole world for years to come. The purpose behind the attack was to separate America and its allies from everyone else, and the Muslim world in particular. For the past decade or so, Muslim extremists have been on the march, fighting neighbors of other religions wherever they find them: Hindus in Kashmir, Jews in Israel, Orthodox Russians in Chechnya, animists and Christians in Africa. In the perspective of the suicide bombers, Americans are Westerners but also Christians, therefore the principal legitimate objects of holy war. These Muslim extremists have been trying to open their version of an ideological and armed struggle with global implications: Muslims and as much of the Third World as possible versus democracy. This ambition is now out in the open.

Preferring Appeasement to War

Put in familiar European terms, this attack is the equivalent of the German occupation of the Rhineland in 1936. The failure of Britain and France to rise to that occasion led Hitler to the conclusion that no matter how aggressive he was the democracies would always prefer appeasement to war. A similar failure now to rise to the occasion will place every democratic country in jeopardy. All manner of changes in attitudes towards security, asylum, and human rights have to be envisaged as the open society takes measures to defend itself.

The democracies are not on their own in the coming struggle, but time and intelligence are needed in order to prepare for what lies ahead. The Muslim world

David Pryce-Jones, "We Are Waging a Just War," *New Criterion*, vol. 20, November 2001, pp. 21–26.

does not present a unified bloc. On the contrary, it is split by sectarian and ethnic disputes as well as by internal power struggles. The extremists represent a small—though no doubt growing—minority. Destroying everything before them, they have already provoked civil war in Algeria, Sudan, and Afghanistan, and they have destabilized Egypt, Lebanon, Saudi Arabia, the Palestine Authority, and not least Pakistan. The response of these countries' respective leaders is critical to American success.

The terrorist attack on America serves as a last-minute warning to moderate Muslim leaders to mend their ways and join the extremists. Backed into such a corner, the Pakistani President Pervez Musharraf has instead dropped the Taliban [former ruling body of Afghanistan] and sided outright with America. Egypt, far and away the most influential Arab country, is dancing on a tightrope because it too has long been under continuous threat from its extremists. Muammar Qaddafi in Libya and General Omar Bashir in Sudan have similarly decided that they have more to fear from their extremists than from the United States. About a dozen terror groups have bases in or around Damascus [in Syria] but the young [Syrian] president Bashar Assad may not necessarily protect them. In one of the customary internal power struggles of the Muslim world, Iran is suspicious of the Taliban, and for the first time in years at least some of its leaders are not preaching "Death to America" in the mosques. A wise America will hold a heavy stick behind its back and in its hand as enticing a bunch of carrots as possible, including remission of debt, trade advantages, and political support against extremists. This is, essentially, a hearts and minds operation.

"The Muslim world does not present a unified bloc."

A Fantasy of Islamic Supremacy

A fantasy is loose in the world, the fantasy of an Islamic supremacy that is destined to triumph everywhere. Some of its advocates claim that eventually Christian countries will become Muslim, in what would amount to a reverse colonialism. Like Communism before it, this Islamic extremism aims to impose its vision on others and call it universal peace. Here, in an unexpected form, is another totalitarian movement. Like all such movements, it does not hesitate to use violence. True believers in each and every totalitarianism always take their stand on the specious and murderous grounds that the ends justify the means.

The huge majority of Muslims understand only too clearly that the extremists do not speak in their name but are likely to unleash Armageddon on all, and they view this with horror. The escape of so many millions of refugees from Afghanistan, for instance, is a public vote of no-confidence in the Taliban. For some, even unknown Nauru—the world's smallest independent republic—is evidently preferable to home. Untold millions of Muslims long to emigrate to the West, whose freedom and prosperity are the stuff of their dreams.

Needless to say, this Islamic fantasy has nothing to do with Islam proper, a religion like all other great religions, with a genuine vision of justice and equality at its core. Indeed, the damage that the Islamic triumphalist fantasy does to Islam as well as Muslim countries and peoples is at least as severe and dangerous as the damage it does to democracy. The same was true about other totalitarianisms: Nazism utterly ruined Germany, Communism utterly ruined Russia.

Contrary to Islam

To judge by their reported conduct, the September 11, 2001, suicide bombers were living in an atmosphere that had nothing to do with Islam. According to Islamic teaching, whoever commits suicide is condemned to hell. Their central purpose, then, was contrary to their religion. They had shaved off their beards, they spent time in bars, they became drunk, they frequented strip clubs. They carried rolls of hundred dollar bills and spent them ostentatiously. We may suppose that at some level, consciously or unconsciously, they were enjoying the America they were planning to destroy. For it is here, in a most complex relationship of attraction and repulsion, that we must begin to understand the motivations of the terrorists, and so frame our responses.

> ***"Islam [has] a genuine vision of justice and equality at its core."***

Each man kills the thing he loves, in the famous words of Oscar Wilde. Premeditated killing of unknown people in an act that simultaneously kills oneself requires a life-denying hate so exceptional that it is in a realm of fanaticism all its own. Such hate signifies a total human failure. This corresponds to the turmoil of the Muslim world today. Each and every Muslim country faces intractable problems of demography, lack of resources and skills, ethnic and religious strife, and selfish government; each and every Muslim suffers from this jumble of assorted ills.

As if that were not enough, Muslim extremists and even some moderates have come to believe that everything wrong with their world is the fault of the Jews. This is partly a relic from the tribal past, and partly another mistaken interpretation of the present. They think in a sort of syllogism. Jews are wicked by definition. America helps Jews. Therefore America is wicked. And yet another false syllogism: Saddam Hussein is an Arab, America wishes to remove Saddam Hussein, therefore America persecutes Arabs. Years will have to pass before the extremists grasp that the humane and democratic values that unite Israel and America serve no conspiratorial anti-Islamic purposes. But that is the context in which America must now operate.

The Roots of Muslim Resentment

The causes of today's turmoil go deep into the roots of history. The major intellectual developments of the West—the Renaissance with its concept of humanism and the Age of Enlightenment during which scientific principles by and large replaced religious dogma—passed the Muslim world by. Muslims everywhere were in the grip of the absolute system of one-man despotism that they had inherited from their forebears and that they believed protected their religion and identity. Western energy and creativity of which they were unaware duly overwhelmed them, and they could do nothing about it. There were Muslim rulers who resisted, and their names have entered Muslim and Western lore alike: Emir Abdel Kader in Algeria, Shamyl in the Caucasus, the Mahdi with his Sudanese dervishes, the so-called Mad Mullah of Berbera.

A nineteenth-century Muslim philosopher, Jamal al-Din al-Afghani, spoke for all such. He did not hesitate to stigmatize Muslims as backward. He swung between extreme self-pity about their common plight and ferocious insistence that the remedy lay in violence. Putting his finger on what he thought was the crux of the matter, he wrote, "It is amazing that it was precisely the Christians who invented Krupp's cannons and the machine gun before the Muslims." The analysis was false; stemming from science, improved weaponry carried no religious connotation. But al-Afghani succeeded in imprinting throughout the Muslim world a sense of inferiority to the West. The Muslim masses, otherwise proud people, came to see the West as an entity deliberately out to shame and humiliate them. Today's Islamic fantasy springs from this mindset in which self-pity and revenge go hand in hand.

Two alternatives were open to Muslims in practice. One was to retreat into the fortress of Muslim identity and reject the West. Numberless groups and organizations have chosen that course, from the Muslim Brotherhood to Hamas and Islamic Jihad and Hizballah today, as well as the Taliban and their proxy, Osama bin Laden. They see themselves engaged in a war on two fronts, against the West and against opponents who are fellow Muslims. They live out the triumphalist fantasy.

> ***"Muslim extremists and even some moderates have come to believe that everything wrong with their world is the fault of the Jews."***

The other alternative was to seek to discover the source of European energy and mastery. In every colonized Muslim country leaders believed that nationalism was the great western secret, and accordingly they formed nationalist movements, and ultimately nationalist states. Islamic extremists and nationalists shared a common need to acquire European weapons. Either way, in order for Muslims to recover their pride, a test of strength with the Europeans was built into the future.

The End of Colonialism

After the Second World War, the colonial powers no longer had interests in the Middle East that they deemed worth a real test of strength, and they retreated. The encounter so far between Muslims and the West had been a profound movement of history with pluses and minuses for both sides. But at least the end of colonialism seemed to absolve Muslims, and in particular Arabs, from the sense of shame tormenting them.

For fifty years and more, the Muslim world has been independent, free to organize as it wishes, and, moreover, several Muslim countries are beneficiaries of a petrodollar bonanza, which they can dispose of for any end they like. Throughout this period Muslim and Arab rulers have plumped for the outward signs of Western life, such as high-rise buildings, hospitals, and colleges. They have imported modernity as though it were a commodity like any other. But once again, in an incomplete and misleading analysis of the position, they did not recognize that the true source of Western strength lay in a democratic political system that liberated people's energies and had nothing to do with nationalism.

Instead, the leaders of nationalist movements lost no time in promoting themselves absolute one-man rulers of their own countries. Gamal Abdel Nasser in Egypt was the model for them all. The result has been a present-day mimicry of the historic despotisms of the past. Nothing like democracy exists in the Muslim world, where Turkey alone has ever experienced a change of government through a free and unrigged election, and there only once. Parliaments exist to rubberstamp the ruler's decrees. There is no freedom of speech or of assembly, no civil rights, but only the dreaded secret police, prisons, torture, and execution. The injustice is flagrant. Corruption is everywhere. Excluded from any say, the masses still have no control over their destiny, but they are able to protest only through a riot. Power changes hands by assassination or coup. In the absence of mechanisms for power-sharing and mediation, every national and international conflict of interest degenerates into a test of strength.

"The Muslim masses . . . came to see the West as an entity deliberately out to shame and humiliate them."

Muslims and Arabs have nobody to blame but themselves for so disastrous a social and political failure. There are intellectuals who point this out, but they are few. It is far more comforting to displace the blame on to others. At the very end of 1978, Ayatollah Khomeini carefully staged a coup in Iran and seized power from the shah. In a large and potentially rich country, he was able to bring up-to-date al-Afghani's expressions of self-pity and revenge.

Muslims, the ayatollah held, were weak because the West had deliberately made them so. It was another self-serving falsehood. In reality the West displays a yawning indifference to all manifestations of religion, but the ayatollah crystallized the contemporary Islamic fantasy that the West is actually out to destroy Islam. In response, Muslims had the duty to unite against the West and all its works, especially in its most salient incarnation, America, dubbed the Great Satan. He advised former Soviet leader Mikhail Gorbachev to show the way by converting to Islam. Nationalist rulers, Saddam Hussein for instance, had to be obliged to subscribe to his fantasy, if need be by war to the death.

Grasping at Fantasies

Muslims everywhere, rich and poor, educated men like Osama bin Laden and illiterate youths, have eagerly absorbed Khomeini's prescriptions and formed an archipelago of conspiratorial groups in half the countries of the world, often clandestinely linked in a manner reminiscent of former Communist cells, volunteering to right the wrongs they believe to have been done to them, and to establish an Islamic utopia. Many of them take advantage of Western medicine, technology, and education, depending on these benefits that they are unable to provide for themselves. The contradiction powers the grievance, impotence, and hate of their fantasy.

The suicide bombers have at last engaged the United States in a test of strength according to their standards. Muslim—and especially Arab—one-man rulers will be watching for signs that the United States understands the stakes and has the resolve to act as it should. If they detect weakness in Washington, they will have no choice but to pay lip-service to the Islamic fantasy and at least pretend to join the ideological war against the West. Anything less leaves them at the mercy of assassination or a coup undertaken by extremists. American strength and determination to see this through, however, will encourage them to join the coalition of Western allies. As was exactly the case in forming the earlier coalition to fight the Gulf War against Saddam Hussein, they and others in their position must be sure to end on the winning side.

For the present, we do not know whether the suicide bombers had ultimate sponsorship from a Muslim or Arab state. Any such state must also be brought to account, if necessary by an outright invasion that leads to a change of regime. This is a just war if ever there was one, in defence of life and liberty against an ideological enemy. If the United States and its allies were to retreat from the test of strength imposed on them, or botch it somehow through inadequate preparation or loss of will, then the extremists will conclude that they have the West on the run. They will strive on for victory. Who can guess how far hate and killing will then spread, or how destructive it will prove for mankind.

The United States Should Continue to Support Israel

by Victor Davis Hanson

About the author: *Victor Davis Hanson is the author of* Carnage and Culture: Landmark Battles in the Rise of Western Power.

The Muslim world is mystified as to why Americans support the existence of Israel. Some critics in the Middle East excuse "the American people," while castigating our government. In their eyes, our official policy could not really reflect grassroots opinion. Others misinformed spin elaborate conspiracy theories involving the power of joint Mossad-CIA plots, Old Testament fundamentalists, international bankers, and Jewish control of Hollywood, the media, and the U.S. Congress. But why does an overwhelming majority of Americans (according to most polls between 60 and 70% of the electorate) support Israel—and more rather than less so after [the attacks on] September 11, 2001? The answer is found in values—not in brainwashing or because of innate affinity for a particular race or creed. Israel is a democracy. Its opponents are not. Much misinformation abounds on this issue. Libya, Syria, and Iraq are dictatorships, far more brutal than even those in Egypt or Pakistan. But even "parliaments" in Iran, Morocco, Jordan, and on the West Bank are not truly and freely democratic. In all of them, candidates are either screened, preselected, or under coercion. Daily television and newspapers are subject to restrictions and censorship; "elected" leaders are not open to public audit and censure. There is a reason, after all, why in the last decade Americans have dealt with Israeli prime ministers Benjamin Netanyahu, Ehud Barak, and Ariel Sharon—and no one other than Yasser Arafat, the Husseins in Jordan, the Assads in Syria, Hosni Mubarak, and who knows what in Lebanon, Algeria, and Afghanistan. Death, not voters, brings changes of rule in the Arab world.

The Arab street pronounces that it is the responsibility of the United States—who gives money to Egypt, Palestine, Jordan, Afghanistan and others, has troops stationed in the Gulf, and buys oil from the Muslim world—to use its influence to instill democracies. They forget that sadly these days we rarely have such power to engineer sweeping constitutional reform; that true freedom requires the blood and courage of native patriots—a George Washington, Thomas Jefferson, or Thomas Paine—not outside nations; and that democracy demands some prior traditions of cultural tolerance, widespread literacy, and free markets. Moreover, we give Israel billions as well—but have little control whether they wish to elect a Yitzhak Rabin or an Ariel Sharon.

Israel is also secular. The ultra-Orthodox do not run the government unless they can garner a majority of voters. Americans have always harbored suspicion of anyone who nods violently when reading Holy Scripture—whether in madrassas, near the Wailing Wall, or in the local Church of the Redeemer down the street. In Israel, however, Americans detect that free speech and liberality of custom and religion are more ubiquitous than, say, in Saudi Arabia, Iran, or Palestine—and so surmise that the Jewish state is more the creation of European emigres than of indigenous Middle-Eastern fundamentalists.

Pluralism exists in Israel, rarely so in the Arabic world. We see an Israeli peace party, spirited debate between Left and Right, and both homegrown damnation and advocacy for the settlers outside the 1967 borders. Judaism is fissured by a variety of splinter orthodoxies without gunfights. There are openly agnostic and atheistic Israeli Jews who enjoy influence in Israeli culture and politics. In theory, such parallels exist in the Arab world, but in actuality rarely so. We know that heretical mullahs are heretical more often in London, Paris, or New York—not in Teheran or among the Taliban. No Palestinian politician would go on CNN and call for Mr. Arafat's resignation; his opposition rests among bombers, not in raucous televised debates.

Israeli newspapers and television reflect a diversity of views, from rabid Zionism to almost suicidal pacifism. There are Arab-Israeli legislators—and plenty of Jewish intellectuals—who openly write and broadcast in opposition to the particular government of the day. Is that liberality ever really true in Palestine? Could a Palestinian, Egyptian, or Syrian novelist write something favorable about former Israeli prime minister Golda Meir, hostile to Mr. Assad or Mubarak, or craft a systematic satire about Islam? Past experience suggests such iconoclasts and would-be critics might suffer stones and fatwas rather than mere ripostes in the letters to the editor of the local newspapers. Palestinian spokesmen are quite vocal and unbridled on American television, but most of us—who ourselves instinctively welcome self-criticism and reflection—sense that such garrulousness and freewheeling invective are reserved only for us, rarely for Mr. Arafat's authority.

Israel's Ingenuity

Americans also see ingenuity from Israel, both technological and cultural—achievement that is not reflective of genes, but rather of the culture of freedom. There are thousands of brilliant and highly educated Palestinians. But in the conditions of the Middle East, they have little opportunity for free expression or to open a business without government bribe or tribal payoff. The result is that even American farmers in strange places like central California are always amazed by drip-irrigation products, sophisticated water pumps, and ingenious agricultural appurtenances that are created and produced in Israel. So far we have seen few trademarked in Algeria, Afghanistan, or Qatar.

> ***"Death, not voters, brings changes of rule in the Arab world."***

There is also an affinity between the Israeli and Western militaries that transcends mere official exchanges and arms sales. We do not see goose-stepping soldiers in Haifa as we do in Baghdad. Nor are there in Tel-Aviv hooded troops with plastic bombs strapped to their sides on parade. Nor do Israeli presidents wear plastic sunglasses, carry pistols to the U.N., or have chests full of cheap and tawdry metals. Young rank-and-file Israeli men and women enjoy a familiarity among one another, and their officers are more akin to our own army than to the Islamist groups Republican Guard, Hamas, or Islamic Jihad.

The Israelis also far better reflect the abject lethality of the Western way of war. Here perhaps lies the greatest misunderstanding of military history on the part of the Arab world. The so-called Islamic street believes that sheer numbers and territory—a billion Muslims, a century of oil reserves, and millions of square miles—should mysteriously result in lethal armies. History teaches us that war is rarely that simple. Instead, the degree militaries are westernized—technology that is a fruit of secular research, group discipline arising from consensual societies, logistical efficiency that derives from capitalism, and flexibility that is the dividend from constant public audit and private individualism—determines victory, despite disadvantages in numbers, natural resources, individual genius, or logistics.

Creative Arms

We hear a quite boring refrain from enraged Palestinians of "Apache helicopters" and "F-16s". But in the Lebanese war of the early 1980s we saw what happens in dogfights between advanced Israel and Syrian jets in the same manner Saddam Hussein's sophisticated weapons were rendered junk in days by our counterparts. So Israel's power is more the result of a system, not merely of imported hardware. The Arab world does not have a creative arms industry; Israel does—whether that be ingenious footpads to wear while detecting mines or drone aircraft that fly at night over Mr. Arafat's house. If the Palestinians truly wished military parity, then the Arab world should create their own research programs immune to religious or political censure, and ensure that students are mastering calculus rather than the Koran.

Nor are Americans ignorant of the recent past. The United States was not a colonial power in the Middle East, but developed ties there as a reaction to, not as a catalyst of, its complex history. Israel was instead both created and abandoned by Europeans. The 20th century taught Americans that some Europeans would annihilate millions of Jews—and others prove unwilling or unable to stop such a holocaust. We sensed that the first three wars in the Middle East were not fought to return the West Bank, but to finish off what Hitler could not. And we suspect now that, while hundreds of millions of Arabs would accept a permanent Israel inside its 1967 borders, a few million would not—and those few would not necessarily be restrained by those who did accept the Jewish state.

> ***"Israeli newspapers and television reflect a diversity of views."***

Somehow we in the American heartland sense that Israel—whether its gross national product, free society, or liberal press—is a wound to the psyche, not a threat to the material condition, of the Arab world. Israel did not murder the Kurds or Shiites. It does not butcher Islam's children in Algeria. Nor did it kill over a million on the Iranian-Iraqi border—much less blow apart Afghanistan, erase from the face of the earth entire villages and their living inhabitants in Syria, or turn parts of Cairo into literal sewers. Yet both the victims and the perpetrators of those crimes against Muslims answer "Israel" to every problem. But Americans, more than any people in history, live in the present and future, not the past, loath scapegoating and the cult of victimization, and are tired of those, here and abroad, who increasingly blame others for their own self-induced pathologies.

The Europeans are quite cynical about all this. Tel Aviv, much better than Cairo or Damascus, reflects the liberal values of Paris or London. Yet the Europeans rarely these days do anything that is not calibrated in terms of gaining money or avoiding trouble—and in that sense for them Israel is simply a very bad deal. All the sophisticated op-eds about . . . Islamic liberalism cannot hide the fact that Europe's policy in the Middle East is based on little more than naked self-interest. If Israel were wiped out tomorrow, Europeans would ask for a brief minute of silence, then sigh relief, and without a blink roll up their sleeves to get down to trade and business.

Saying Something About America

Our seemingly idiosyncratic support for Israel, then, also says something about ourselves rather than just our ally. In brutal Realpolitik, the Europeans are right that there is nothing much to gain from aiding Israel. Helping a few million costs us the friendship of nearly a billion. An offended Israel will snub us; but some in an irate Muslim world engineered slaughter in Manhattan. Despite our periodic tiffs, we don't fear that any frenzied Israelis will hijack an American plane or murder Marines in their sleep. No Jews are screaming at us on the evening news that we give billions collectively to Mubarak, the Jordanians, and Mr. Arafat. And Israelis lack the cash reserves of Kuwait and Saudi Arabia, and they do not go on buying sprees in the U.S. or import whole industries from America. So the reason we each support whom we do says something about both Europe and the United States.

Instead of railing at America, Palestinians should instead see in our policy toward Israel their future hope, rather than present despair—since it is based on disinterested values that can evolve, rather than on race, religion, or language that often cannot. If the Palestinians really wished to even the score with the Israelis in American eyes, then regular elections, a free press, an open and honest economy, and religious tolerance alone would do what suicide bombers and a duplicitous terrorist leader could not.

The United States Should Go to War with Iraq

by Frank J. Gaffney

About the author: *Frank J. Gaffney held senior positions in the Ronald Reagan Defense Department and signed the 1998 open letter of the Committee for Peace and Security in the Gulf. He is the president of the Center for Security Policy in Washington.*

In February 1998 a group of distinguished security-policy practitioners addressed an open letter to President Bill Clinton under the banner of the Committee for Peace and Security in the Gulf. The signatories were seized with what was even then a pressing problem: the need to remove Saddam Hussein from power.

These experts—many of whom now hold top positions in the George W. Bush administration (including Secretary of Defense Donald Rumsfeld, Deputy Secretary of Defense Paul Wolfowitz, Deputy Secretary of State Richard Armitage, Undersecretaries of State John Bolton and Paula Dobriansky and Undersecretaries of Defense Douglas Feith and Dov Zakheim)—felt compelled to call for regime change in Iraq for reasons that are, if anything, still more compelling now:

> Despite [Saddam's] defeat in the [Persian] Gulf War, continuing sanctions and the determined effort of U.N. inspectors to fetter out and destroy his weapons of mass destruction, Saddam Hussein has been able to develop biological and chemical munitions. To underscore the threat posed by these deadly devices, [then-secretary of state Madeleine Albright and then-secretary of defense William Cohen] have said that these weapons could be used against our own people. . . .
>
> Iraq's position is unacceptable. While Iraq is not unique in possessing these weapons, it is the only country which has used them—not just against its enemies, but its own people as well. We must assume that Saddam is prepared to use them again. This poses a danger to our friends, our allies and to our nation.

Frank J. Gaffney, "Symposium: Should Iraq Be the Next Target for the U.S. Military in the War on Terror? Yes: Saddam Hussein Is More of a Threat Today than He Was Before or During the Persian Gulf War," *Insight on the News*, vol. 18, May 6, 2002, pp. 40–44.

Saddam's Weapons

Today, years after the last U.N. weapons inspector was compelled to leave Iraq, Saddam not only has active chemical and bio-weapons programs but surely also has resumed the aggressive effort he was making before Operation Desert Storm to acquire atomic and, in due course, thermonuclear arms.

Defectors have revealed that his covert program is so far advanced technologically that the only thing preventing Saddam from having fully functional nuclear weapons is access to sufficient quantities of fissile material. Once he has enriched uranium or plutonium, he would be able at a minimum to build radiological, or "dirty," bombs. It strains credulity that, given his vast oil revenues and the black market that has developed in such material since the collapse of the Soviet empire, this need will go unfulfilled for very long—if it has not already begun to be satisfied.

"Saddam Hussein has been able to develop biological and chemical munitions."

Saddam continues to work as well at building the means of delivering such weapons of mass destruction (WMDs) against targets farther removed than his own people. (The gruesome details of his use of chemical weapons against Kurdish population centers in 1988 has been documented by journalist Jeffrey Goldberg in the *New Yorker* magazine.) Fighter aircraft, cruise missiles and ballistic missiles capable of serving this purpose—at least with small payloads of chemical or biological weapons—are in his inventory today. Given the closed nature of Iraq under Saddam's misrule, it is reasonable to expect that this equipment's capability for WMD applications is being secretly modernized with the assistance of the Russian, Chinese and/or North Korean technicians who busily are proliferating WMDs and relevant delivery systems throughout the Middle East and, indeed, the world.

The danger that such weapons might be used by Saddam against the United States is today even more clear than it was when Rumsfeld et al. addressed the topic in 1998. After all, we now have compelling evidence of Iraq's involvement in international terrorism. Iraq expert and best-selling author Laurie Mylroie has argued convincingly that Iraqi intelligence was implicated in the first World Trade Center bombing in 1993.

And there is more compelling evidence tying Mohammed Atta (the terrorist believed to have led the hijackers on the devastating September 11, 2001, attack on the World Trade Center twin towers) to Saddam than there is to Osama bin Laden. (This includes Atta's meeting with a known Iraqi agent in Prague shortly before the attack and a facility in Iraq, equipped with a jetliner, that defectors report is used to train would-be hijackers.)

Saddam's large biological-weapons program is particularly ominous in light of the interest expressed by Atta and some of his colleagues in the use of crop dusters. At this writing it is unclear whether there is more than coincidence in some of the apparent connections between those associated with the September 11, 2001, attacks and the anthrax used against Florida-based tabloids, other media organizations and top congressional figures. (For example, one of the hijackers received medical treatment shortly before his death for what the attending physician believes may have been symptoms of cutaneous anthrax, and several of the hijackers rented an apartment from a woman married to an executive at one of the anthrax-targeted tabloids).

It is safe to say, however, that had the particular strain of anthrax—of a sophisticated type that Iraq and very few other nations could produce—been delivered to Congress and the other recipients via crop duster instead of the U.S. Postal Service, there likely would have been many thousands of dead.

It would be in keeping with such efforts—in which cutouts appear to have been used by Saddam to inflict lethal blows on the United States while concealing Iraq's true role—if the "Butcher of Baghdad" were to try next to exploit America's complete vulnerability to missile attack. This could be done with catastrophic effect, thanks to the continuing absence of any deployed U.S. missile-defense system, should the Iraqi despot arrange to have one of the Scud missiles he is believed to have hidden from U.S. warplanes and U.N. inspectors launched from a third-country-registered ship operating off our coast.

In short, today even more than in 1998, it is clear that the risk of Saddam engaging, either directly or indirectly, in the use of WMDs no longer safely can be ignored. Similarly, we now know that there is no practical alternative to regime change in Iraq if that threat is to be mitigated, let alone eliminated.

If anything, Saddam has been emboldened by successive U.S. administrations' failures to deal decisively with him and his reign of terror. He successfully has defied U.S. presidents, the United Nations, his treaty commitments and international law. He has worn down inspectors and sanction regimes, diplomats and no-fly zones. He has shown himself to be as resilient to unenforced claims that he is being kept in "his box" as he is to humanitarian appeals to use oil-for-food monies as they were intended—namely, to alleviate the suffering of the Iraqi people. He will make an even greater mockery of any so-called "smart-sanctions" regime, further corrupting and intimidating his neighbors as his wealth and power continue to be restored by Europeans, Russians and Chinese anxious to resume doing business with him.

> ***"[The United States has] compelling evidence of Iraq's involvement in international terrorism."***

End Saddam's Misrule

For these reasons, we have no choice but to do what Rumsfeld, Wolfowitz and their colleagues recommended in 1998: Take at once whatever steps are necessary to end Saddam's misrule and liberate the Iraqi people. Unfortunately, we cannot be sure that such steps will result in the elimination of all Iraqi WMD programs. If we pursue the sort of strategy for accomplishing Saddam's downfall that was laid out by the Coalition for Peace and Security in the Gulf, however, it should end the threat they pose.

> ***"The risk of Saddam engaging . . . in the use of WMDs no longer safely can be ignored."***

That means ruling out the notion of pursuing Saddam's downfall via a coup d'etat that very well could wind up merely replacing one dangerous Iraqi dictator with another, possibly equally odious, despot. The latter, however, could be freed from the constraints under which the Butcher of Baghdad currently operates simply because he is not Saddam. As the signatories of the coalition's open letter put it in 1998:

> For years, the United States has tried to remove Saddam by encouraging coups and internal conspiracies. These attempts have all failed. Saddam is more wily, brutal and conspiratorial than any likely conspiracy the United States might mobilize against him. Saddam must be overpowered; he will not be brought down by a coup d'etat. But Saddam has an Achilles' heel: lacking popular support, he rules by terror. The same brutality which makes it unlikely that any coups or conspiracies can succeed makes him hated by his own people and the rank and file of his military. Iraq today is ripe for a broad-based insurrection. We must exploit this opportunity.

Instead, the Committee for Peace and Security in the Gulf recommended "a comprehensive political and military strategy for bringing down Saddam and his regime." Specifically, it proposed that the United States: a) "recognize a provisional government of Iraq based on the principles and leaders of the Iraqi National Congress that is representative of all the peoples of Iraq"; b) "restore and enhance the safe haven in northern Iraq to allow the provisional government to extend its authority there and establish a zone in southern Iraq from which Saddam's ground forces would also be excluded"; and c) "lift sanctions in liberated areas."

Relief for the Iraqi People

The last of these is particularly noteworthy. As the committee's signatories observed: "Sanctions are instruments of war against Saddam's regime, but they should be quickly lifted on those who have freed themselves from it." Also, the oil resources and products of the liberated areas should help fund the provisional government's insurrection and humanitarian relief for the people of liberated Iraq, as should unfrozen "Iraqi assets—which amount to $1.6 billion in the United States and Britain alone" that can help "the provisional government to fund its insurrection."

Importantly, the committee acknowledged that the United States had a responsibility to "help expand liberated areas of Iraq by assisting the provisional government's offensive against Saddam Hussein's regime logistically and through other means." The signatories counseled that "a systematic air campaign [be launched] against the pillars of [Saddam's] power—the Republican Guard divisions which prop him up and the military infrastructure that sustains him." They also recommended that "U.S. ground-force equipment [be positioned] in the region so that, as a last resort, we have the capacity to protect and assist the anti-Saddam forces in the northern and southern parts of Iraq."

This prescription for effecting regime change in Iraq would have the advantage of empowering the Iraqi people to help liberate themselves with a minimum of U.S. military involvement and risk. It is past time it be given a chance to work. Indeed, we no longer can afford to do otherwise.

The United States Should Promote Democracy in the Middle East

by Richard W. Murphy and F. Gregory Gause

About the authors: *Richard W. Murphy is a senior fellow at the Council on Foreign Relations, and F. Gregory Gause is an assistant professor at the University of Vermont.*

Is democracy a policy goal of the United States in the Middle East? Officials are reticent to use the word democracy in their statements on the Muslim Middle East. However, they do not explicitly exclude the region from their general foreign policy goals of expanding the number of democracies and market economies throughout the world. In speeches and policy statements to Congress, administration officials put democracy on the list of good things Washington wants in the region, along with peace, "moderation," "stability," economic development and the isolation of "rogue states" (Iraq, Iran and Libya). For example, former Assistant Secretary of State for Near East Affairs Robert Pelletreau listed "promoting more open political and economic systems, and respect for human rights and the rule of law" as one of seven American objectives in the Middle East. When elections (whose results are in accord with American interests) occur in the region, administration officials point to them as evidence that America's global policy of "democratic enlargement" can bear fruit "even" in the Muslim Middle East. The United States Agency for International Development (USAID) has funded a multimillion-dollar project on "governance" in the region, so taxpayer money is being put where officials' mouths are.

Stark Choices

Perhaps more importantly, the United States is seen in the region as being on record, at least rhetorically, as supporting democracy. Human rights and prodemocracy movements in Middle Eastern countries look to Washington for

Richard W. Murphy and F. Gregory Gause, "Democracy and U.S. Policy in the Muslim Middle East," *Middle East Policy*, vol. 5, January 1997, pp. 58–68.

support, despite American unwillingness to criticize the many undemocratic U.S. allies in the region. Yet when real elections do occur, American policy goals can be set back. Islamist parties that do not hide their opposition to American political and cultural influence in the region frequently do well. The results even of Israeli elections can complicate U.S. diplomatic initiatives. Nowhere in the world do the cross-pressures of America's interests and America's ideals present starker choices.

> ***"Human rights and prodemocracy movements in Middle Eastern countries look to Washington for support."***

Persian Gulf security and progress on the Arab-Israeli peace process rank far ahead of promoting participatory politics in the list of America's real goals in the Muslim Middle East, and that is as it should be. However, there are an increasing number of elections, of more or less legitimate provenance, occurring in Muslim countries to which the United States has to respond. Since November 1995 Algeria has held a presidential election; Egypt, Turkey, Iran, Lebanon and Kuwait have had parliamentary elections; and Palestinians elected a legislative authority. American officials have been called upon, and will be called upon, to pronounce upon the fairness and openness of such elections. In a number of cases, the United States faces the difficult task of balancing between its principles—support for free and fair elections—and its particular interests in supporting some incumbent regimes and delegitimizing others.

When elections stand in the way of securing American security and economic goals, Washington drops its normal rhetoric of "democratic enlargement." When countries that oppose the United States on these issues, such as Iran, have elections, those elections are ipso facto seen as undemocratic. When countries that support the United States on these issues have sham elections, or ignore their own constitutions in prohibiting or postponing elections, Washington remains silent. There is a pervasive sense in the Middle East that the United States does not support democracy in the region, but rather supports what is in its strategic interest and calls it democratic.

What is widely seen as blatant U.S. hypocrisy on the democracy issue has a corrosive effect on America's standing in the region. It is particularly harmful among groups that are disposed to look favorably toward the United States—those who want their governments to be more open and responsive to the sentiments of the people. In this case, talk is not cheap. There is an easy solution to this problem, which we discuss in more detail below. It can be summarized simply: U.S. policy makers should talk much less about democracy in the Muslim Middle East, and do a little bit more to promote it.

The Democracy Conundrum in the Middle East

In most of the world, U.S. advocacy of democracy represents a happy marriage of American values and American interests. Elections in Latin America,

Eastern Europe and East Asia have brought to power, for the most part up to now, leaders who are favorably disposed toward the United States and who support the market-oriented economic policies that Washington urges. In many cases, these new leaders have supplanted communists (Eastern Europe) or economic nationalists (Latin America) with whom the United States had difficulty doing business, both politically and economically. Even where communists in Eastern Europe have resumed to power through the ballot box, they do so much transformed. In such circumstances, American support for democracy is cost-free. Publicly promoting our values serves our interests.

Such is not the case in the Muslim Middle East. The United States has no problem dealing with most incumbent regimes in the Middle East (with the exceptions of Libya, Iran and Iraq). American interests are intimately tied up with the ruling elites in Turkey, Egypt, Jordan, Saudi Arabia and the smaller Gulf states. Washington even has a promising relationship with Syrian President Hafiz al-Asad, a prickly leader who hardly shares American democratic values. Former mayor of New York Rudolph Guiliani might have declared Yasir Arafat persona non grata at Lincoln Center, but the head of the Palestine Liberation Organization (PLO) is certainly now Washington's favorite Palestinian. The status quo in the Middle East serves American interests very well. Domestic political change, be it democratic or otherwise, would probably bring to power people less likely to follow Washington's lead.

"U.S. policy makers should talk much less about democracy in the Muslim Middle East, and do a little bit more to promote it."

Moves toward greater democracy in any of these Middle Eastern countries (including the Palestinian Authority) would undoubtedly increase the power of Islamist political groups, as recent elections demonstrate. For the first time in the history of the Turkish Republic, a party with an explicitly Islamist platform received a plurality of votes in a legislative election. The Welfare party polled over 21 percent of the vote and received 158 seats (nearly 30 percent of the total) in the Turkish elections of December 1995. The Islamic Action Front, the political face of the Islamist political group the Muslim Brotherhood, is the largest group in the Jordanian parliament. The arrest and military trial of about 100 Muslim Brotherhood leaders in Egypt, on the eve of the November 1995 elections to the Egyptian parliament, is a signal of where the Hosni Mubarak government sees its most threatening challenger. While Hamas [a Muslim terrorist organization] boycotted the recent legislative elections to the Palestinian Authority, it is clear that this Islamist group is Yasir Arafat's major opposition in Palestinian politics. Eighteen of the 40 Kuwaiti parliamentarians elected in October 1992 were members of the three Islamist groups that fielded candidates or independents endorsed by one of those groups. Islamists held on to about that number of seats in the 1996 elections. Moreover, newly emerging Islamist opposition groups are presenting the Saudi regime with its most serious domestic challenge since the heyday of Egypt's Gamal Abdel Nasser's Pan-Arabism [the notion of uniting all Arab countries under a single government] in the 1960s.

Thus, for the foreseeable future more open politics in the Middle East likely mean more "Islamic" politics. That is something that unnerves Washington, and with good reason. Islamist groups uniformly oppose the Arab-Israeli peace process that is at the heart of American policy in the Middle East; some (Hezbollah, Hamas) actively confront Israel. They criticize the close relations their governments have with the United States, seeing in such ties a veiled form of political domination. Most centrally, they see the American consumer culture as the biggest threat to the "re-Islamization" of the social values of their societies. In short any American administration would find it more difficult to do business with Islamic regimes than with the current incumbents in almost all Middle Eastern states.

The democracy conundrum for the United States in the Muslim Middle East is straightforward. American interests are tied up with incumbent regimes; American values, if pursued vigorously, could weaken those regimes. The problem is not that Muslims are not "ready" for democracy, as some have condescendingly argued. It is that Washington is not ready for the choices that they would probably make.

Serving American Interests

Two recent elections in the Arab world highlight the democracy conundrum for the United States. In one, it appeared that American principles and American interests were served. In the January 1996 voting for the legislature of the new Palestinian Authority in the West Bank and Gaza, candidates of Yasir Arafat's Fatah group and affiliated independents took 68 out of 88 seats. Candidates close to Hamas received only 5 seats. Arafat himself was elected president of the authority with well over 80 percent of the vote against token opposition. Turnout was high—according to some estimates over 70 percent of registered voters—as Palestinians enthusiastically voted in their first national elections. USAID provided logistical support to the election organizers and held seminars for Palestinians on voting procedures. International monitors pronounced the vote free and fair, and the United States officially congratulated Arafat on his victory and complimented the Palestinians for a successful exercise in democracy.

> ***"Egyptian liberals . . . were genuinely puzzled and hurt that the United States would not even provide verbal support [for free elections]."***

But what if the results had been different? A hypothetical question, to be sure, but not an outlandish one. Both Hamas and Arafat's leftist opposition urged a boycott of the elections. It is doubtful they will do so on the next round, if there is a next round. After some years of rule by Arafat, Palestinian voters might find themselves in the mood for a change, particularly if final-status negotiations with Israel have stalled and real Palestinian independence seems unlikely. . . . Arafat might have to rely on less democratic methods to turn out a convincing majority to support him in a future election. What would Washington's response be? We have an example in another recent election in the Arab world.

"Encouraging our friends to open up their political systems . . . is the best way Washington can help to assure their long-term stability."

In late November and early December 1995 Egyptians went to the polls to elect a new parliament in two rounds of voting. During the campaign the government arrested a number of leading figures in the Muslim Brotherhood who were running for election. In a pre-election security round-up, hundreds of campaign workers and poll watchers for Brotherhood candidates were detained by the police. President Mubarak's National Democratic party won a crushing victory, with party members and affiliated independents taking 444 out of 458 seats. Only one candidate affiliated with the Muslim Brotherhood won a seat.

The head of the Egyptian Organization for Human Rights, a local non-governmental organization which monitored the voting, called the elections "a real insult to democracy." The group reported widespread ballot rigging, fraud, harassment of candidates and voters, and arrests. The Egyptian government contended that the poll was free and fair. . . .

The balloting placed the United States Embassy in Cairo in a very difficult position. Called upon for a comment, the Embassy simply said that it took cognizance of the fact that there were reports of fraud in the voting. This response pleased no one. The Egyptian government was enraged, with government newspapers rejecting what they termed American interference in the domestic affairs of Egypt. Advocates of democracy and human rights questioned why Washington would keep silent in the face of such massive fraud. Egyptian liberals with whom we spoke were genuinely puzzled and hurt that the United States would not even provide verbal support to a cause—free elections—that Washington actively encourages elsewhere. Egyptian Islamists did not have to be told why: the United States prefers the increasingly autocratic Mubarak regime to any democratic alternative, because that alternative would inevitably be more "Islamic." Thus the American waffle on "democracy" in Egypt irritated a pivotal Middle East ally without gaining the United States any friends in Egyptian society. Far from settling issues, the Egyptian elections have only raised tensions and increased the political polarization in the country. . . .

Is the clash between American values and American interests in the Muslim Middle East insoluble? No. The United States in fact has an interest in dealing with stable, broadly based regimes in the region. Encouraging our friends to open up their political systems, in an evolutionary way, is the best way Washington can help to assure their long-term stability. We should be clear that, while near-term democratic transitions in key Middle East allies are not in America's interest, gradual steps toward more participatory politics are. The leverage the United States can use in this direction is limited, because of the immediate and important American interests at stake in our relations with a number of Middle East regimes. But such leverage does exist.

The first step Washington should take is to confront America's own hypocrisy on the democracy question. American policymakers should make clear that our tangible interests in the Middle East are more important than the immediate promotion of democracy. They should not be afraid to say that, while not opposed to democratic transitions, the United States is not particularly pressing for them, either. Our policy will be based on our interests, not on pious statements about our values. Middle Easterners believe this anyway; stating it publicly can only gain Washington credit for honesty, a commodity in preciously short supply in Middle Eastern politics.

It is also important that the United States not exaggerate the Islamist "bogeyman." The further away a country is from the core American interests in the Middle East—Arab-Israeli peace and Gulf oil—the more comfortable Washington should be about dealing with Islamist forces. . . . Where Islamist groups oppose regimes that Washington also opposes, as in Libya and Iraq, we should not be dissuaded from dealing with those groups by questionable theoretical arguments about a "clash of civilizations" between Islam and the West. Islamist governments, even revolutionary ones like Iran, have to sell their products on world markets. We should remember that the United States is boycotting Iranian commerce, not the other way around. The rational basis for American fears of "Islamic" political change in the Middle East rests upon specific differences of opinion on Arab Israeli issues and on the strong American ties with a number of incumbent regimes challenged by Islamist opposition. Washington must be at pains, in both word and in deed, to make clear that its policy is governed by those specific interests, not by a general opposition to political forces that call themselves "Islamic."

"Turkey demonstrates that an open and institutionalized political system can accommodate Islamists' political activity."

In stating its policy, Washington should also be clear that it favors efforts to allow more wide-ranging public discussion and more freedom to publicly organize for political purposes in the Muslim Middle East. One of the reasons that Islamist groups dominate the political field is that they do not need "civic space" to organize politically. The protected space, both metaphorically and physically, provided by mosques, religious schools and other religious institutions allows Islamist groups to build social bases of support. Non-Islamist political organizations lack such space. They are caught between nervous governments intent on dominating all aspects of public life and Islamist groups intent on monopolizing opposition discourse and activity. The United States should use what leverage it has to help open up the space for other political groups to emerge, groups that could ameliorate the growing polarization of Arab politics between American-supported regimes and Islamist oppositions.

Turkey: An Example

The results of the December 1995 parliamentary elections in Turkey are a good indication of how a political system can develop when the opportunities for political organizing are not limited to ruling parties and underground Islamic oppositions. The Welfare party, Turkey's Islamic party, won the poll with 21.3 percent of the vote. However, two right-center secular parties, the True Path party of Prime Minister Tansu Ciller and the Motherland party, founded by the late Turgut Ozal, former prime minister and former president of Turkey, each received nearly 20 percent of the vote. The Democratic Left and Republican People's parties, successors to Kemal Ataturk's Republican People's party, together polled 25 percent. Secular parties with a history of support for Turkey's membership in NATO won the support of an overwhelming majority of Turks, and control 392 of the 550 seats in parliament. When Welfare party leader Necmettin Erbekan was called upon to form a government in June 1996 (as a result of the collapse of the Motherland-True Path coalition government), he had to accept the True Path as a governing partner with Ciller as foreign minister. It remains impossible for the Welfare party to form a government on its own.

In Turkey, decades of democratic practice have allowed the development of strong political parties across the electoral spectrum. Those parties serve as a check on each other, and a guarantee against a single political movement, supported by a minority of Turks, coming to dominate the government as a result of one election. The Turkish road to democracy has had plenty of bumps, with military coups in 1960 and 1980, a Latin American–style military pronunciamento in 1971 and severe political polarization and civil violence in the 1970s. However, Turkey demonstrates that an open and institutionalized political system can accommodate Islamists' political activity and avoid the dangerous polarization of politics into an autocratic secular government and a violent, under-ground Islamist opposition so characteristic of many Arab states. The United States has nothing to fear from the Turkish model, and much to admire in it.

> ***"If one of our allies stages an electoral farce, the United States should not try to give it a democratic cover."***

A modest American policy toward encouraging our Arab allies to emulate, in a gradual and evolutionary way, the Turkish model would consist of the following elements:

• Support for freedom of expression. While Islamic groups would be the immediate beneficiaries of such liberalization, it would encourage other political tendencies to enter the public arena. Logistical support for independent publishers of books and newspapers would be a good use of some small part of American and international organization aid to the states of the region.

• Dealing seriously with participatory institutions in Middle Eastern states, even if the governments themselves do not. The USAID "governance" project has taken some useful steps in this direction, providing technical assistance to legislatures in Arab states. American diplomats should consult with and take seriously the views of members of appointed consultative assemblies in the Gulf countries and the elected legislatures in Egypt, Jordan and Kuwait. Washington should urge that its important agreements with Arab governments be debated and approved by such assemblies, even if at the outset such approval would be a foregone conclusion. It is interesting to note that the United States signed a defense agreement with Kuwait, after Desert Storm, that was never submitted to the Kuwaiti parliament. The evolution of these institutions into freer and more representative institutions is the best hope for stable political transitions in these countries.

• Provide opportunities for political activists, including Islamist activists, to meet with American politicians and analysts, even if such meetings displease ruling regimes. That kind of networking, particularly in the countries with smaller populations, can be very useful in establishing personal links that could be important in times of crisis and transition. It is disheartening to note that, despite the importance of Saudi Arabia and the smaller Gulf monarchies to U.S. interests in the Middle East, very few American resources are available for exchange programs with these countries. Such exchange programs are not going to convert every Middle Eastern activist into a Jeffersonian democrat. But they could help Washington establish lines of communication with important political and social figures in Middle Eastern countries. When Ayatollah Khomeini came to power in Iran, he was an unknown figure to Washington. That kind of thing should not happen again.

• Notice and take seriously important social groups that already exist in the Muslim Middle East. A largely ignored but enormously important group in all these states is the chamber of commerce. In many countries the chamber is the only existing social organization that has some independence from both the government and Islamist groups. The chambers generally support the American goal of more open economies. With the general trend toward privatization, the political and economic clout of the chambers will only increase in the future.

• When democratic transitions and real elections do occur, support them, even if their direction at the outset is uncertain. The mealy-mouthed American response to the Algerian military intervention halting the electoral process in 1991 did more to damage Washington's image among devoted democrats in the Arab world than any recent U.S. policy.

• Be honest about sham elections. If one of our allies stages an electoral farce, the United States should not try to give it a democratic cover. Washington should make clear to our allies that we are not pushing them to have elections, but, if they do, Washington will evaluate those elections on their merits. Relations will not be cut off nor aid stopped because of sham elections, but the United States will not lie about the nature of those elections simply to avoid hurting the feelings of autocratic rulers. . . .

A Realistic Approach

The steps outlined for a realistic American approach to its Middle Eastern "democracy conundrum" are hardly a panacea. They will not dramatically change the nature of politics in the Muslim Middle East. But they will help to remove the odor of insincerity that characterizes much official American discourse about democracy in the region. They will signal that the United States, within the limits of its interests, is serious about encouraging participatory institutions and broader based politics in its Middle Eastern allies. They might even, at the margins, improve the chances for gradual and evolutionary political change in the area, the best guarantee of stability and American interests there. A little less empty talk and a little more modest action could go some distance to decreasing the extent to which Muslim Middle Easterners see American policy toward political change in their countries as nothing but hypocrisy.

The U.S. War on Terrorism Is Unethical

by Rahul Mahajan

About the author: *Rahul Mahajan is a graduate student in physics at the University of Texas at Austin and an antiwar activist, serving on the National Boards of Peace Action and the Education for Peace in Iraq Center.*

The world changed on September 11, 2001. That's not just media hype. The way some historians refer to 1914–1991 as the "short twentieth century," many are now calling September 11, 2001, the real beginning of the twenty-first century. It's too early to know whether that assessment will be borne out, but it cannot simply be dismissed.

The terrorist attacks of September 11, 2001, forever ended the idea that the United States could somehow float above the rest of the earth, of it and not of it at the same time. Americans can no longer foster the illusion that what happens to the rest of the world doesn't affect them. It is more crucial than ever that we understand what kind of world we are living in, and what the United States has done to make it what it is.

It is not enough to say that the attacks were crimes against humanity, though they were, and that terrorism like that must be stopped, though it must. It's also not enough to say that the hijackers were religious extremists, though they were. One must also understand the role the United States has played in promoting religious extremism, directly, as in the Afghan jihad, and indirectly, by destroying all alternatives through its ceaseless attacks on the left and by pursuing policies that foster resentment and anger.

Myths of the War on Terrorism

It is of particular importance to understand its newest policies, the so-called "war on terrorism." Of the many ways to approach it, perhaps the most straightforward is to examine the official view of the war on terrorism that has emerged and is being pushed on the public, and refuting it point by point.

Rahul Mahajan, "The New Crusade: America's War on Terrorism," *Monthly Review*, vol. 53, February 2002, pp. 15–24.

These are some of the main myths about that war:

The attack was like Pearl Harbor, and therefore, as in the Second World War, we had to declare war or risk destruction. The truth is that Pearl Harbor was an attack by a powerful, expansionist state that had the capacity to subjugate all of East Asia. The attacks of September 11, 2001, were committed by nineteen men, part of a series of networks that has a few thousand hard-core militants, with access to modest financial resources. Since they were hardly an immediate, all-encompassing threat, options other than war could have been explored.

> ***"One must . . . understand the role the United States has played in promoting religious extremism."***

This was an attack on freedom. Whatever considerations exist in the mind of Osama bin Laden [the terrorist who masterminded the attacks on September 11, 2001,] or members of his network [al-Qaeda], his recently broadcast statements contain no mention of any resentment of American democracy, freedom, or the role of women. They mention specific grievances regarding U.S. policy in the Middle East: the sanctions on Iraq, maintained largely by the United States, which have killed over one million civilians; material and political support for Israel's military occupation of Palestine and its frequent military attacks, carried out with American weapons, on practically unarmed Palestinians; and U.S. military occupation of the Gulf and support for corrupt regimes that serve the interests of U.S. corporations before those of the people. The terrorists' own vision for the states of the Middle East is, if imaginable, even more horrific than the current reality, and would presumably involve even greater limits on freedom than are already in place. Their recruiting points, however, the issues that make them potentially relevant as a political force, have to do with U.S. domination of the region, not with the internal organization of American society.

You're with us or you're with the terrorists. This polarization, foisted on the world to frighten possible dissenters from America's course of action, is the logic of tyranny, even of extermination. Anti-war protesters who condemn the terrorist attacks of September 11, 2001, along with the criminal acts of the United States in Afghanistan, and countries that do the same, don't fit into this scheme, and certainly don't deserve to be tarred with the same brush as the terrorists.

Fighting Afghanistan

The war on Afghanistan was self-defense. In fact, people in Afghanistan at the time of the attack had no way of menacing the United States from afar since they have no ICBMs [intercontinental ballistic missiles] or long-range bombers. Someone in Afghanistan intending to attack the United States had to get there first. If there was an imminent threat, it was from terrorists already in the United States or in Europe. Thus, there was enough time to seek Security Council authorization, which is required unless one is attacking the source of an imminent threat. Instead, the U.S. deliberately chose not to seek it. The four weeks between the attack and the war that passed virtually without incident are proof that there was no immediate, overwhelming need for military action, a fundamental requirement of any claim to act in self-defense.

The Bush administration turned away from its emerging unilateralism . . . to a new multilateralism. This assumes that "multilateralism" means first predetermining one's agenda, then attempting to browbeat or bribe other countries into agreement or acquiescence. True multilateralism would involve setting up international structures that are democratic, transparent, and accountable to the people, institutions, and governments of the world and abiding by the decisions of these authorities whether favorable or not. The United States has consistently set itself against any such path. In this case, the United States refused even to seek the authority from the appropriate body in this case, the Security Council. This even though the United States could likely have gained its acquiescence by use of its standard methods of threats and bribery. It seems that the United States wishes very firmly and deliberately to claim the right of unilateral aggression.

There were four weeks of restraint as the Bush administration tried a diplomatic solution to the problem. Much of the "restraint" was simply to find time to move troops and materiel into place and to browbeat reluctant countries like Pakistan, Uzbekistan, and Tajikistan into providing staging areas and overflight rights. Also, there was real concern about destabilizing many allied governments in the Islamic world. No diplomatic solution was tried; the administration line was consistently "no negotiations." They made demands no sovereign country could accept; free access of the U.S. military to sensitive sites, plus the right arbitrarily to demand that an unspecified group of people be "turned over." They also refused to present the Taliban with evidence. In spite of all this, the Taliban was willing to negotiate delivery to a neutral third party. In fact, a deal had been worked out to have bin Laden tried in Pakistan by a tribunal which would then decide whether or not to turn him over to the United States. The U.S. government didn't even want that. Its "diplomacy" was deliberately designed to lead to war.

"The United States wishes very firmly and deliberately to claim the right of unilateral aggression."

Imperial Credibility and Leverage

Revenge was the motive for the war. Although many people felt an emotional desire for revenge, the two principal reasons for war cannot be described in these terms. The first reason is that of imperial credibility. The United States is an empire, of a different kind from the Roman or the British, but still one that holds sway over much of the world through a combination of economic and military domination. In order to remain in power, an empire must show no weakness; it must crush any threat to its control. The last half of the Vietnam War, after the U.S. government realized there would be no political victory, was fought for credibility to show other countries the price of defiance. The need was all the greater with such a devastating attack in the center of imperial power. The second reason is leverage over the oil and natural gas of Central Asia. Afghanistan is the one country that the United States could control through which a pipeline can be run from those reserves to the Indian Ocean, for the rapidly growing Asian market. The war would provide an opportunity for that, as well as a chance to set up military bases in the former Soviet republics of the region.

The war was a humanitarian intervention as well as an attempt to get the terrorists. The food drops were mere military propaganda—enough food for 37,500 people a day, if it was distributed, which it couldn't be—and they accompanied bombing that disrupted aid programs designed to feed millions. The lack of humanitarian intent was shown later by the U.S. government's ignoring a call by aid agencies and U.N. officials for a bombing halt so enough food could be trucked in. UNICEF estimated that because of the disruption of aid caused by the bombing and earlier the threat of bombing, as many as 100,000 more children might die in the winter. After the withdrawal of the Taliban, as much of the country collapsed into chaos and bandits started looting aid stores, the United States held up for almost a month proposals for a peacekeeping force, and didn't even pressure the Northern Alliance to restore order and facilitate aid, as aid workers were unable to reach at least one million people in desperate need.

The war was conducted by surgical strikes, minimizing collateral damage. There's no such thing as a surgical strike—the most precise weapons miss 20–30 percent of the time, and only 60 percent of the ordnance dropped on Afghanistan has been precision-guided. The United States has also used such devastating weapons as cluster bombs and daisy cutters, which by their nature are indiscriminate, so "collateral damage" cannot be controlled. Also, U.S. bombing campaigns generally deliberately target civilian infrastructure. In this case, there are reports of power stations, telephone exchanges, and even a major dam being destroyed, with potentially catastrophic effects. Totaling up all reports, including those from the foreign press, Professor Marc Herold of the University of New Hampshire estimated the number of civilians killed directly by bombs and bullets as of December 6, 2001, to be 3,767, a number he feels is, if anything, an underestimation. This is already greater than the number of innocents who died in the attacks on September 11, and it doesn't include the likely greater number who have died of indirect effects.

"The food drops [in Afghanistan] were mere military propaganda."

It was a war of civilization against barbarism. As if the above weren't enough, at the siege of Kunduz, Afghanistan, where thousands of foreign fighters were trapped along with many thousands of Afghan Taliban fighters, Defense Secretary Donald Rumsfeld did everything short of calling for the foreigners to be killed. Later, a group of foreigners imprisoned in a fort and convinced they were going to be killed staged a rebellion. The fort was bombed and strafed by U.S. planes, even though later reports indicate that perhaps hundreds of the prisoners had their hands bound—this is almost certainly a war crime. At the same time, government officials and media pundits began calling for Osama bin Laden to be killed even if he surrendered.

"The United States harbors many terrorists."

Fighting Terrorism with Terrorism

It was a war against terrorism. The Northern Alliance, which the United States has put in power over most of Afghanistan, is a bunch of terrorists, known for torture, killing civilians, and raping women. The United States harbors many terrorists, like Emanuel Constant of Haiti, a number of Cubans, and Henry Kissinger. It still runs its own terrorist training camp, the School of the Americas/Western Hemisphere Institute for Security Cooperation. It still supports Israeli state terrorism against the Palestinians. And it is committing state terrorism itself, by recklessly endangering civilians for its political goals.

The administration's primary motive has been to ensure the security of Americans. The war has greatly increased the risks to Americans. By creating a tremendous pool of anger in the Muslim world, it is the ultimate recruiting vehicle for bin Laden, who is seen as a hero by many now, though he was ignored before. It was not even the best way to catch bin Laden, as pointed out above. Other measures decrease security as well. Calls to increase the scope of CIA operations and involve them more with criminals and terrorists seem to ignore the fact that it was just such CIA meddling that helped create the international Islamic extremist movement. Bush administration calls to sell weapons to countries that violate human rights destabilize the world. And missile defense, which would not have helped at all with an attack like this even if it was technically feasible, threatens to set off a new arms race. On the home-front, corporate profits and the ideology of free enterprise were more important to the administration than increasing security through the nationalization of airport security personnel, even though corporations have been found to be using convicted felons and paying barely over minimum wage, thus ensuring low motivation and incompetence. The profits of Bayer, the maker of Cipro, used to treat anthrax, were more important than ensuring a reasonably-priced supply of Cipro for people in case of a large-scale anthrax attack.

The attacks of September 11, 2001, united us together in a noble enterprise.

Although many people did come together, the Bush administration tried to use that idea of unity to subvert democracy, even calling for Congress to give the president trade promotion authority (the right to present trade agreements "as is," so Congress can approve or disapprove but not amend) as part of the "war on terrorism." In the end, there was no unity; airline corporations were bailed out, while laid-off airline employees got nothing; the Republicans tried to give corporations a huge tax break in their economic stimulus package, while no provision was made to counter surging unemployment; and legislative aides on Capitol Hill got vastly better treatment during the anthrax scare than did postal workers.

American Self-Delusion

This whole enterprise has also shed light on some longer-standing myths we hold about ourselves:

All sectors of society have an abiding commitment to civil liberties and due process of law. The 2001 USA PATRIOT Act allows law enforcement far greater power, including the right to search your house without notification. It can effectively deprive noncitizens of basic rights like habeas corpus. Attorney-client privilege has been breached in some cases. Many people have been held incommunicado for months in the ongoing investigation. Bush has even authorized the use of military tribunals, which can use secret evidence, convict on very low standards of evidence, and deny a defendant the right to choose a lawyer. The FBI has even considered sending detainees to other countries to be tortured. Although there is significant opposition to these threats to civil liberties and due process, it is not as yet very widespread.

> ***"A majority of Americans now approve of racial profiling."***

We've made tremendous progress on racism. A majority of Americans now approve of racial profiling. There was a huge upsurge in hate crimes after September 11, 2001. And many people have openly expressed appallingly racist and even genocidal sentiments. Calls to nuke entire countries have been made. Although there is now a small group of (mostly younger) people largely free of racist sentiments, for the majority, the progress has mainly been in learning how to hide their racism.

We honor dissent and the right to free speech. Public discourse was characterized by an extreme overreaction to the small number of people who spoke against war. Several journalists have been fired, and many people subjected to death threats and other harassment. A rightwing foundation has brought out a report criticizing academia for not rallying round the flag even though the number of dissenters in academia were few and far between. With the constant demonization of dissent and misrepresentation of dissenters by elite institutions, it's not surprising that much of the populace has gone the same way—a recent

CBS/NYT poll found 38 percent saying anti-war "marches and rallies" should not be allowed.

Calling for Blood

We have the freest and most independent media in the world. From the first hours, the mass media outdid any other sector of society in calling for blood. They showed, as they always do in wartime, a tremendous subservience to the government, with almost no dissenting points of view expressed. When they did criticize government officials, it was almost always for not bombing enough. Most seriously, there was tremendous self-censorship. Numerous critical issues were covered hardly at all: the fact that a deal for extradition of bin Laden had been worked out; the fact that the United States had planned war against Afghanistan since before the attacks; the connection of oil with the war; and more. Worst was the persistent lack of attention to civilian casualties. Only a few incidents were even reported, and those were dismissed by constant repetition of Pentagon claims that they were "propaganda." As a result, many think that a handful of civilians were killed, whereas the truth is that thousands were. The government, not satisfied with this level of subservience, imposed unprecedented restrictions, not allowing any press pools until the end of November 2001, allowing virtually no interviews with soldiers, and keeping the press from reporting even well known information. Some of the foreign press, whose reportage could not be controlled by such means, was treated more harshly. The U.S. government asked Qatar to censor al-Jazeera and later bombed its office in Kabul, as well as bombing civilian Afghan radio repeatedly, a war crime. The U.S. press also ridiculed and misrepresented the anti-war movement, insinuating that it had only slogans, not analysis; that it did not condemn the terrorist attacks; and, worst, that its solution was to "do nothing."

In fact, that was perhaps the biggest myth of the whole enterprise—that there was no other alternative, so we must either wreak destruction on Afghanistan or do nothing. Repeated efforts by the anti-war movement to indicate the foundations of a real solution—a genuine international investigation based on cooperation with not just governments but people, based on a dramatic change in U.S. policy in the Middle East to win over the "hearts and minds" of people there—were to little avail.

> ***"The main practitioner of [terrorism] attacks that . . . target civilians . . . is . . . [the U.S.] government."***

These myths made a real difference. Although the majority of Americans have supported the supposed war on terrorism, their support has been based on a misunderstanding of how the war was being conducted, how much "collateral damage" there was, and what alternatives were possible.

To have any chance of dealing with the problem of international terrorism, we must change the role of the United States in the world. In an essay entitled "The War Comes Home," published on the Web the day after the attacks, I wrote, "The main practitioner of attacks that either deliberately target civilians, or are so indiscriminate that it makes no difference, is no shadowy Middle Eastern terrorist, but our own government." These attacks run the gamut from direct bombing, as the United States has done in Iraq (on numerous occasions), Serbia, Sudan, Afghanistan, and other countries in the past ten years alone, to denying people access to the basic necessities of life. From the sanctions on Iraq, which have for years involved denying basic medical care to millions, to efforts to keep South Africa from providing affordable AIDS drugs to its citizens, the United States has killed countless civilians.

There is always a justification, as there is for any killing anywhere; for the sanctions on Iraq, it is the security of Iraq's neighbors, and for denying AIDS drugs, it is the need to maintain corporate profits. For the terrorists who attacked on September 11, 2001, it was the need to oppose U.S.-sanctioned murder and oppression in their part of the world. If "terrorism" is to be given an unbiased definition, it must involve the killing of noncombatants for political purposes, no matter who does it or what noble goals they proclaim.

The Philosophy of Terrorism

When Madeleine Albright, then Secretary of State, went on *60 Minutes* on May 12, 1996, Lesley Stahl said, referring to the sanctions on Iraq, "We have heard that a half million children have died. I mean, that's more children than died in Hiroshima. And, you know, is the price worth it?" Albright, not contesting the figure, replied, "I think this is a very hard choice, but the price—we think the price is worth it." That is the philosophy of terrorism. The people who crashed planes into the World Trade Center killed almost four thousand people because they resented U.S. domination of the Middle East. The U.S. government helped to kill a half million children in Iraq in order to preserve that domination.

It is the common fashion to dismiss such juxtapositions as claims of "moral equivalence." In fact, that concept is irrelevant. Whether or not the U.S. government is "morally equivalent" to the terrorists, whatever that might mean, the point is that citizens of the United States have an obligation to oppose its crimes even before they would oppose the crimes of others over whom they have less control.

This does not mean efforts should not be made to stop terrorists of the ilk of Osama bin Laden. It simply means that terrorist efforts to stop them should not be made. The war on Afghanistan has been even worse—terrorist in its methods and designed primarily to project U.S. imperial power, not to stop the terrorists.

If Albright appears on *60 Minutes* again, this time she should be asked whether she thinks U.S. policy goals in the Middle East were also worth the deaths of thousands of Americans.

The United States Should Stop Supporting Israel

by Matt Bowles

About the author: *Matt Bowles heads the Washington, D.C., chapter of SUSTAIN (Stop U.S. Tax-Funded Aid to Israel Now), a nonprofit organization opposed to U.S. aid to Israel.*

Israel has maintained an illegal occupation of the West Bank and Gaza Strip (Palestinian territories) for 35 years, entrenching an apartheid regime that looks remarkably like the former South African regime—hemming the Palestinians into small, noncontiguous bantustans, imposing 'closures' and 'curfews' to control where they go and when, while maintaining control over the natural resources, exploiting Palestinian labor, and prohibiting indigenous economic development.

The Israeli military (IDF)—the third or fourth most powerful military in the world—routinely uses tanks, Apache helicopter gunships, and F-16 fighter jets (all subsidized by the U.S.) against a population that has no military and none of the protective institutions of a modern state.

All of this, Israel tells its citizens and the international community, is for 'Israeli security'. The reality, not surprisingly, is that these policies have resulted in a drastic increase in attacks on Israel. These attacks are then used as a pretext for further Israeli incursions into Palestinian areas and more violations of Palestinian human rights—none of which makes Israeli civilians more secure; all of which further entrenches Israel's colonial apartheid regime. Most Americans do not realize the extent to which this is all funded by U.S. aid, nor do they understand the specific economic relationship the U.S. has with Israel and how that differs from other countries.

The Aid Pipeline

There are at least three ways in which aid to Israel is different from that of any other country. First, since 1982, U.S. aid to Israel has been transferred in one lump sum at the beginning of each fiscal year, which immediately begins to

Matt Bowles, "U.S. Aid—Lifeblood of the Occupation," *Left Turn*, March/April 2002, pp. 19–22.

collect interest in U.S. banks. Aid that goes to other countries is disbursed throughout the year in quarterly installments.

Second, Israel is not required to account for specific purchases. Most countries receive aid for very specific purposes and must account for how it is spent. Israel is allowed to place U.S. aid into its general fund, effectively eliminating any distinctions between types of aid. Therefore, U.S. tax-payers are helping to fund an illegal occupation, the expansion of colonial-settlement projects, and gross human rights violations against the Palestinian civilian population.

A third difference is the sheer amount of aid the U.S. gives to Israel, unparalleled in the history of U.S. foreign policy. Israel usually receives roughly one third of the entire foreign aid budget, despite the fact that Israel comprises less than .001 of the world's population and already has one of the world's higher per capita incomes. In other words, Israel, a country of approximately 6 million people, is currently receiving more U.S. aid than all of Africa, Latin America and the Caribbean combined when you take out Egypt and Colombia.

In 2002, the U.S. Congress approved $2.76 billion in its annual aid package for Israel. The total amount of direct U.S. aid to Israel has been constant, at around $3 billion (usually 60% military and 40% economic) per year for the last quarter century. A plan was implemented to phase out all economic aid and provide corresponding increases in military aid by 2008. In 2002 Israel received $2.04 billion in military aid and $720 million in economic aid—these numbers will get more disproportionate each year until there is only military aid.

Indirect Aid

In addition to nearly $3 billion in direct aid, Israel usually gets another $3 billion or so in indirect aid: military support from the defense budget, forgiven loans, and special grants. While some of the indirect aid is difficult to measure precisely, it is safe to say that Israel's total aid (direct and indirect) amounts to at least five billion dollars annually. . . .

According to the American-Israeli Cooperative Enterprise (AICE), from 1949–2001 the U.S. gave Israel a total of $94,966,300,000. The direct and indirect aid from 2002 should put the total U.S. aid to Israel from 1949 to 2002 at over one hundred billion dollars. What is not widely known, however, is that most of this aid violates American laws. The Arms Export Control Act stipulates that U.S.-supplied weapons be used only "for legitimate self-defense."

> ***"[Israel's] policies have resulted in a drastic increase in attacks on Israel."***

Moreover, the U.S. Foreign Assistance Act prohibits military assistance to any country "which engages in a consistent pattern of gross violations of internationally recognized human rights." The Proxmire amendment bans military assistance to any government that refuses to sign the Nuclear Non-Proliferation

Treaty and to allow inspection of its nuclear facilities, which Israel refuses to do. To understand why the U.S. spends this much money funding the brutal repression of a colonized people, it is necessary to examine the benefits for weapons manufacturers and, particularly, the role that Israel plays in the expansion and maintenance of U.S. imperialism.

A Very Special Relationship

In the fall of 1993, when many were supporting what they hoped would become a viable peace process, 78 senators wrote to former President Bill Clinton insisting that aid to Israel remain at current levels. Their reasons were the "massive procurement of sophisticated arms by Arab states." Yet the letter neglected to mention that 80% of those arms to Arab countries came from the U.S. itself.

Politics professor Stephen Zunes has argued that the Aerospace Industry Association (AIA), which promotes these massive arms shipments, is even more influential in determining U.S. policy towards Israel than the notorious AIPAC (American Israel Public Affairs Committee) lobby. AIA has given two times more money to campaigns than all of the pro-Israel groups combined. Zunes asserts that the general thrust of U.S. policy would be pretty much the same even if AIPAC didn't exist: "We didn't need a pro-Indonesia lobby to support Indonesia in its savage repression of East Timor all these years."

> ***"The primary U.S. interest in the Middle East is . . . to maintain control of the oil in the region."***

The 'special relationship' between the U.S. and Israel must be understood within the overall American imperialist project and the quest for global hegemony, beginning in the late 1960s and early 1970s. For example, 99% of all U.S. aid to Israel came after 1967, despite the fact that Israel was relatively more vulnerable in earlier years (from 1948–1967). Not coincidentally, it was in 1967 that Israel won the Six-Day War against several Arab countries, establishing itself as a regional superpower. Also, in the late 1960s and particularly in the early 1970s . . . the U.S. was looking to establish 'spheres of influence'—regional superpowers in each significant area of the world to help the U.S. police them.

The primary U.S. interest in the Middle East is, and has always been, to maintain control of the oil in the region, primarily because this is the source of energy that supplies the industrial economies of Europe and Japan. The U.S. goal has been to insure that there is no indigenous threat to their domination of these energy resources. In the late 1960s and early 1970s, the U.S. made the strategic decision to ally itself with Israel and Iran, which were referred to as 'our two eyes in the middle east' and the 'guardians of the gulf.' It was at this point that aid increased drastically, from $24 million in 1967 (before the war), to $634 million in 1971, to a staggering $2.6 billion in 1974, where it has remained relatively consistent ever since.

A Military Stronghold

Israel was to be a military stronghold, a client state, and a proxy army, protecting U.S. interests in the Middle East and throughout the world. Subsidized by the CIA, Israel served U.S. interests well beyond the immediate region, setting up dependable client regimes (usually military-based dictatorships) to control local societies. Political critic Noam Chomsky has documented this extensively: Israel was the main force that established the Mobutu dictatorship in Zaire, for example. They also supported Idi Amin in Uganda, early on, as well as Haile Selasse in Ethopia, and Emperor Bokassa in the Central African Republic.

"[The United States] has turned Israel into a military outpost . . . that is economically dependent on the U.S."

Israel became especially useful when the U.S. came under popular human rights pressure in the 1970s to stop supporting death squads and dictatorships in Latin America. The U.S. began to use Israel as a surrogate to continue its support. Chomsky documents how Israel established close relations with the neo-Nazi and military regimes of Argentina and Chile. Israel also supported genocidal attacks on the indigenous population of Guatemala, and sent arms to El Salvador and Honduras to support the contras. This was all a secondary role, however.

The primary role for Israel was to be the Sparta of the Middle East. During the Cold War, the U.S. especially needed Israel as a proxy army because direct intervention in the region was too dangerous, as the Soviets were allied with neighboring states. Over the last thirty years, the U.S. has pursued a two-track approach to dominating the region and its resources: It has turned Israel into a military outpost (now probably the most militarized society in the world) that is economically dependent on the U.S. while propping up corrupt Arab dictatorships such as those in Egypt, Jordan and Saudi Arabia. These regimes are afraid of their own people and, thus, are very insecure. Therefore, they are inclined to collaborate with the U.S. at any cost.

Prospects for Activism

Since the end of the Cold War, the nuclear threat associated with direct intervention in the Middle East has disappeared and the U.S. has started a gradual and direct militarization of the region. This began with the Gulf War—putting U.S. military bases in Saudi Arabia (the primary source of oil), among other places—and has continued through the 'war on terrorism.' This direct U.S. militarization has lessened the importance of Israel for U.S. domination of the region.

Although U.S. aid has not decreased yet, there have been other observable shifts. The first obvious one is the mainstream media reporting on the conflict. Although there is still, of course, an anti-Palestinian bias, the coverage has shifted significantly in comparison to ten years ago. This has been noticeable in both journalistic accounts of Israeli human rights abuses and the publication of pro-Palestinian op-eds in major papers such as the *Washington Post* and the *Boston Globe*.

There are also some stirrings in the U.S. Congress. Representative John Conyers (D-MI) requested that President George W. Bush investigate whether Israel's use of American F-16s is violating the Arms Export Control Act. Further, Senator Robert Byrd (D-WV) recently complained about giving aid without conditions: "There are no strings on the money. There is no requirement that the bloodshed abate before the funding is released." Other elected representatives are slowly starting to open up to the issue as well, but there is a long way to go on Capitol Hill.

The most important development, however, has been the rising tide of concern and activism around the Palestinian issue in the U.S. left. The desperate plight of the Palestinians is gaining increasing prominence in the movement against Bush's 'war on terrorism,' and it is gradually entering into the movement against corporate globalization.

For years the Palestinian cause was marginalized by the left in America. Since this intifada broke out [in 2000], that began to shift significantly and has moved even further since the terrorist attacks on September 11, 2001. With the new 'anti-war' movement, there has come a deeper understanding of U.S. policy in the Middle East and how the question of Palestine fits into progressive organizing.

> ***"For years the Palestinian cause was marginalized by the left in America."***

Israeli Apartheid

In Durban, South Africa in September 2001, at the UN Global Conference Against Racism, one of the most pressing issues on the global agenda was the Palestinian struggle against Israel's racist policies. 30,000 people from South Africa and around the world demonstrated against Zionism, branding it as a form of apartheid no different than the system that blacks suffered through in South Africa. Shortly after, the U.S. and Israel stormed out of the conference.

In Europe and America, a range of organizations have risen in opposition to Israeli apartheid and in support of Palestinian human rights and self-determination. Just over the last year or two, organizations such as Students for Justice in Palestine, based at the University of California at Berkeley, have begun organizing a divestment campaign, modeled after the campaign that helped bring down South African apartheid. SUSTAIN (Stop U.S. Tax-funded Aid to Israel Now!) chapters in a number of cities have focused their efforts on stopping U.S. aid to Israel, which is the lifeblood of Israeli occupation and continued abuses of Palestinian rights.

Many Jewish organizations have emerged as well, such as Not in My Name, which counters the popular media assertion that all Jewish people blindly support the policies of the state of Israel. Jews Against the Occupation is another organization, which has taken a stand not only against the occupation, but also in support of the right of Palestinian refugees to return. These movements, and particularly their newfound connection with the larger anti-war, anti-imperialist, and anti-corporate globalization movements, are where the possibilities lie to advance the Palestinian struggle.

The hope for Palestine is in the internationalization of the struggle. The building of a massive, international movement against Israeli apartheid seems to be the most effective and promising form of resistance at this time. The demands must be that Israel comply with international law and implement the relevant UN resolutions. Specifically, it must recognize that all Palestinian refugees have the right to return, immediately end the occupation, and give all citizens of Israel equal treatment under the law.

We must demand that all U.S. aid to Israel be stopped until Israel complies with these demands. Only when the Palestinians are afforded their rights under international law, and are respected as human beings, can a genuine process of conflict resolution and healing begin. For all the hype over peace camps and dialogue initiatives, until the structural inequalities are dealt with, there will be no justice for Palestinians and, thus, no peace for Israel.

The United States Should Not Go to War with Iraq

by Brent Scowcroft

About the author: *Brent Scowcroft has served on the President's Advisory Committee on Arms Control, the Commission on Strategic Forces, and the President's Special Review Board. He is considered one of the country's leading experts on national security, defense, and foreign policy.*

Our nation is presently engaged in a debate about whether to launch a war against Iraq. Leaks of various strategies for an attack on Iraq appear with regularity. The Bush administration vows regime change, but states that no decision has been made whether, much less when, to launch an invasion.

It is beyond dispute that Saddam Hussein is a menace. He terrorizes and brutalizes his own people. He has launched war on two of his neighbors. He devotes enormous effort to rebuilding his military forces and equipping them with weapons of mass destruction. We will all be better off when he is gone.

That said, we need to think through this issue very carefully. We need to analyze the relationship between Iraq and our other pressing priorities—notably the war on terrorism—as well as the best strategy and tactics available were we to move to change the regime in Baghdad.

Saddam's strategic objective appears to be to dominate the Persian Gulf, to control oil from the region, or both.

That clearly poses a real threat to key U.S. interests. But there is scant evidence to tie Saddam to terrorist organizations, and even less to the Sept. 11 attacks. Indeed Saddam's goals have little in common with the terrorists who threaten us, and there is little incentive for him to make common cause with them.

He is unlikely to risk his investment in weapons of mass destruction, much less his country, by handing such weapons to terrorists who would use them for their own purposes and leave Baghdad as the return address. Threatening to use these weapons for blackmail—much less their actual use—would open him and his entire regime to a devastating response by the U.S. While Saddam is thoroughly evil, he is above all a power-hungry survivor.

Saddam is a familiar dictatorial aggressor, with traditional goals for his aggression. There is little evidence to indicate that the United States itself is an object of his aggression. Rather, Saddam's problem with the U.S. appears to be that we stand in the way of his ambitions. He seeks weapons of mass destruction not to arm terrorists, but to deter us from intervening to block his aggressive designs.

> ***"Saddam Hussein is a menace."***

Given Saddam's aggressive regional ambitions, as well as his ruthlessness and unpredictability, it may at some point be wise to remove him from power. Whether and when that point should come ought to depend on overall U.S. national security priorities. Our pre-eminent security priority—underscored repeatedly by the president—is the war on terrorism. An attack on Iraq at this time would seriously jeopardize, if not destroy, the global counterterrorist campaign we have undertaken.

The United States could certainly defeat the Iraqi military and destroy Saddam's regime. But it would not be a cakewalk. On the contrary, it undoubtedly would be very expensive—with serious consequences for the U.S. and global economy—and could as well be bloody. In fact, Saddam would be likely to conclude he had nothing left to lose, leading him to unleash whatever weapons of mass destruction he possesses.

Israel would have to expect to be the first casualty, as in 1991 when Saddam sought to bring Israel into the Gulf conflict. This time, using weapons of mass destruction, he might succeed, provoking Israel to respond, perhaps with nuclear weapons, unleashing an Armageddon in the Middle East. Finally, if we are to achieve our strategic objectives in Iraq, a military campaign very likely would have to be followed by a large-scale, long-term military occupation.

But the central point is that any campaign against Iraq, whatever the strategy, cost and risks, is certain to divert us for some indefinite period from our war on terrorism. Worse, there is a virtual consensus in the world against an attack on Iraq at this time. So long as that sentiment persists, it would require the U.S. to pursue a virtual go-it-alone strategy against Iraq, making any military operations correspondingly more difficult and expensive. The most serious cost, however, would be to the war on terrorism. Ignoring that clear sentiment would result in a serious degradation in international cooperation with us against terrorism. And make no mistake, we simply cannot win that war without enthusiastic international cooperation, especially on intelligence.

Possibly the most dire consequences would be the effect in the region. The shared view in the region is that Iraq is principally an obsession of the U.S. The obsession of the region, however, is the Israeli-Palestinian conflict. If we were seen to be turning our backs on that bitter conflict—which the region, rightly or wrongly, perceives to be clearly within our power to resolve—in order to go after Iraq, there would be an explosion of outrage against us. We would be seen as ignoring a key interest of the Muslim world in order to satisfy what is seen to be a narrow American interest.

Even without Israeli involvement, the results could well destabilize Arab regimes in the region, ironically facilitating one of Saddam's strategic objectives. At a minimum, it would stifle any cooperation on terrorism, and could even swell the ranks of the terrorists. Conversely, the more progress we make in the war on terrorism, and the more we are seen to be committed to resolving the Israel-Palestinian issue, the greater will be the international support for going after Saddam.

If we are truly serious about the war on terrorism, it must remain our top priority. However, should Saddam Hussein be found to be clearly implicated in the events of Sept. 11, that could make him a key counterterrorist target, rather than a competing priority, and significantly shift world opinion toward support for regime change.

In any event, we should be pressing the United Nations Security Council to insist on an effective no-notice inspection regime for Iraq—any time, anywhere, no permission required. On this point, senior administration officials have opined that Saddam Hussein would never agree to such an inspection regime. But if he did, inspections would serve to keep him off balance and under close observation, even if all his weapons of mass destruction capabilities were not uncovered. And if he refused, his rejection could provide the persuasive casus belli which many claim we do not now have. Compelling evidence that Saddam had acquired nuclear-weapons capability could have a similar effect.

> ***"An attack on Iraq . . . would seriously jeopardize . . . the global counterterrorist campaign."***

In sum, if we will act in full awareness of the intimate interrelationship of the key issues in the region, keeping counterterrorism as our foremost priority, there is much potential for success across the entire range of our security interests—including Iraq. If we reject a comprehensive perspective, however, we put at risk our campaign against terrorism as well as stability and security in a vital region of the world.

Mr. Scowcroft, national security adviser under President Gerald Ford and George H.W. Bush, is founder and president of the Forum for International Policy.

Organizations to Contact

The editors have compiled the following list of organizations concerned with the issues debated in this book. The descriptions are derived from materials provided by the organizations. All have publications or information available for interested readers. The list was compiled on the date of publication of the present volume; the information provided here may change. Be aware that many organizations take several weeks or longer to respond to inquiries, so allow as much time as possible.

American Jewish Congress
15 E. 84th St., New York, NY 10028
(212) 879-4500 • fax: (212) 249-3672
e-mail: pr@ajcongress.org • website: www.ajcongress.org

The congress is dedicated to combating bigotry by lobbying for improved laws and legislation. It also supports the Middle East peace process through education and political activism. Its publications include the magazine *Congress Monthly* and the newsletter *Radical Islamic Fundamentalism Update.*

Americans for Middle East Understanding (AMEU)
475 Riverside Dr., Room 245, New York, NY 10115-0245
(212) 870-2053 • fax: (212) 870-2050
e-mail: ameu@aol.com • website: http://members.aol.com/ameulink

AMEU's purpose is to foster a better understanding in America of the history, goals, and values of Middle Eastern cultures and peoples, the rights of Palestinians, and the forces shaping U.S. policy in the Middle East. AMEU publishes the *Link*, a bimonthly newsletter, as well as books and pamphlets on the Middle East.

Anti-Defamation League (ADL)
823 United Nations Plaza, New York, NY 10017
(212) 885-7700 • fax: (212) 867-0779
website: www.adl.org

The Anti-Defamation League is a human relations organization dedicated to combating all forms of prejudice and bigotry. It publishes a wide range of materials on Israel, the Middle East, and the Arab-Israeli peace process, including the *Israel Accord* and *Towards Final Status: Pending Issues in Israeli-Palestinian Negotiations.* The ADL also maintains a bimonthly online newsletter, *Frontline.*

Center for Middle Eastern Studies
University of Texas, Austin, TX 78712
(512) 471-3881 • fax: (512) 471-7834
e-mail: cmes@menic.texas.edu • website: http://menic.utexas.edu/menic/cmes

The center was established by the U.S. Department of Education to promote a better understanding of the Middle East. It provides research and instructional materials, and publishes three series of books on the Middle East: the Modern Middle East Series, the Middle East Monograph Series, and the Modern Middle East Literatures in Translation Series.

Foundation for Middle East Peace
1763 N St. NW, Washington, DC 20036
(202) 835-3650 • fax: (202) 835-3651
website: www.fmep.org

The foundation assists the peaceful resolution of the Israeli-Palestinian conflict by making financial grants available within the Arab and Jewish communities. It publishes the bimonthly *Report on Israeli Settlements in the Occupied Territories* and additional books and papers.

Institute for Palestine Studies (IPS)
3501 M St. NW, Washington, DC 20007
(202) 342-3990 • fax: (202) 342-3927
website: www.ipsjps.org

The Institute for Palestine Studies is a private, nonprofit, pro-Arab institute unaffiliated with any political organization or government. Established in 1963 in Beirut, the institute promotes research, analysis, and documentation of the Arab-Israeli conflict and its resolution. IPS publishes quarterlies in three languages and maintains offices all over the world. In addition to editing the *Journal of Palestine Studies*, the institute's U.S. branch publishes books and documents on the Arab-Israeli conflict and Palestinian affairs.

Jordan Information Bureau
2319 Wyoming Ave. NW, Washington, DC 20008
(202) 265-1606 • fax: (202) 667-0777
website: www.jordanembassyus.org

The bureau provides political, cultural, and economic information on Jordan. It publishes fact sheets, speeches by Jordanian officials, government documents, and the bimonthly *Jordan Issues and Perspectives.*

Middle East Policy Council
1730 M St. NW, Suite 512, Washington, DC 20036-4505
(202) 296-6767 • fax: (202) 296-5791
e-mail: general@mepc.org • website: www.mepc.org

The Middle East Policy Council was founded in 1981 to expand public discussion and understanding of issues affecting U.S. policy in the Middle East. The council is a nonprofit educational organization that operates nationwide. It publishes the quarterly *Middle East Policy Journal* and offers workshops for secondary-level educators on how to teach students about the Arab world and Islam.

Middle East Research and Information Project (MERIP)
1500 Massachusetts Ave. NW, Washington, DC 20005
(202) 223-3677 • fax: (202) 223-3604
website: www.merip.org

MERIP is a nonprofit, nongovernmental organization with no links to any religious, educational, or political organizations in the United States or elsewhere. MERIP feels that understanding of the Middle East in the United States and Europe is limited and plagued by stereotypes and misconceptions. The project strives to end these limitations by addressing a broad range of social, political, and cultural issues and by soliciting writings and views from authors from the Middle East that are not often read in the West. Its newsletter, *Middle East Report,* is published four times a year, and MERIP offers an extensive list of other Middle East Internet resources.

United Nations Commission on Human Rights (UNCHR)
United Nations, New York, NY 10017
website: www.unhchr.ch

UNCHR works with the international community and promotes human rights as the foundation of freedom, justice, and peace in the world. Its many resources include fact sheets about human rights, a searchable Middle East database on its website, and a human rights study series.

Washington Institute for Near East Policy
1828 L St. NW, Suite 1050, Washington, DC 20036
(202) 452-0650 • fax: (202) 223-5364
e-mail: info@washingtoninstitute.org • website: www.washingtoninstitute.org

The institute is an independent organization that produces research and analysis on the Middle East and on U.S. policy in the region. It publishes numerous position papers and reports on Arab and Israeli politics and social developments. It also publishes position papers on Middle Eastern military issues and U.S. policy, including "The Future of Iraq" and "Building for Peace: An American Strategy for the Middle East."

Bibliography

Books

M.J. Akbar — *The Shade of Swords: Jihad and the Conflict Between Islam and Christianity.* New York: Routledge, 2002.

Anonymous — *Through Our Enemies' Eyes: Osama bin Laden, Radical Islam, and the Future of America.* London: Brasseys, 2002.

Said K. Arburish — *A Brutal Friendship: The West and the Arab Elite.* New York: St. Martin's, 1997.

Karen Armstrong — *Holy War: The Crusades and Their Impact on Today's World.* New York: Anchor, 2001.

Henry T. Azzam — *The Arab World Facing the Challenge of the New Millennium.* London: IB Tauris, 2002.

Mitchell Geoffrey Bard — *Myths and Facts: A Guide to the Arab-Israeli Conflict.* Chevy Chase, MD: American-Israeli Cooperative Enterprise, 2001.

Berch Berberoglu — *Turmoil in the Middle East: Imperialism, War, and Political Instability.* New York: State University of New York Press, 1999.

Yossef Bodansky — *The High Cost of Peace: How Washington's Middle East Policy Left America Vulnerable to Terrorism.* Roseville, CA: Prima, 2002.

Colin Gilbert Chapman — *Whose Promised Land? The Continuing Crisis over Israel and Palestine.* Grand Rapids, MI: Baker, 2002.

Youssef M. Choueiri — *Arab Nationalism: A History: Nation and State in the Arab World.* Malden, MA: Blackwell, 2001.

Mark Downes — *Iran's Unresolved Revolution.* Hampshire, UK: Ashgate, 2002.

Steven Duncan — *The Rants, Raves, and Thoughts of Yasser Arafat: The Leader in His Own Words and Those of Others.* Brooklyn, NY: On Your Own, 2002.

Marc H. Ellis — *Israel and Palestine: Out of the Ashes.* London: Pluto, 2002.

Elizabeth Warnock Fernea, ed. — *Remembering Childhood in the Middle East: Memoirs from a Century of Change.* Austin: University of Texas Press, 2002.

Gershom Gorenberg *The End of Days: Fundamentalism and the Struggle for the Temple Mount.* New York: Free Press, 2000.

Fred Halliday *Islam and the Myth of Confrontation: Religion and Politics in the Middle East.* London: IB Tauris, 2002.

R. Stephen Humphreys *Between Memory and Desire: The Middle East in a Troubled Age.* Berkeley: University of California Press, 1999.

Sayyid H. Hurreiz *Folklore and Folklife in the United Arab Emirates: Culture and Civilization in the Middle East.* Melbourne, Australia: Melbourne University Press, 2002.

Joe Laredo *Living and Working in the Middle East.* London: Survival, 2002.

Bernard Lewis *What Went Wrong: Western Impact and Middle Eastern Response.* Oxford: Oxford University Press, 2001.

Sandra Mackey *The Reckoning: Iraq and the Legacy of Saddam Hussein.* New York: W.W. Norton, 2002.

David McDowall *A Modern History of the Kurds.* London: IB Tauris, 2001.

Beverley Milton-Edwards and Peter Hinchcliffe *Conflicts in the Middle East Since 1945.* New York: Routledge, 2001.

Tim Niblock *"Pariah States" and Sanctions in the Middle East: Iraq, Libya, Sudan.* Boulder, CO: Lynne Rienner, 2002.

Michael B. Oren *Six Days of War: June 1967 and the Making of the Modern Middle East.* Oxford: Oxford University Press, 2002.

Daniel Pipes *In the Path of God: Islam and Political Power.* Somerset, NJ: Transaction, 2002.

Madawi Al-Rasheed *A History of Saudi Arabia.* Cambridge: Cambridge University Press, 2002.

Hazim Saghie *The Predicament of the Individual in the Middle East.* London: Saqi, 2001.

Avi Shlaim *The Iron Wall: Israel and the Arab World.* New York: W.W. Norton, 2001.

Lester Sumrall and Stephen Sumrall *Jihad—The Holy War: Time Bomb in the Middle East.* South Bend, IN: Sumrall, 2002.

Periodicals

Yossi Beilin "A Plan For Peace: The Solution for the Israeli-Palestinian Conflict—Once the Two Sides Decide That They Want a Solution—Is Clear," *American Prospect*, March 11, 2002.

James Emery "The Muslim World's Take on Terrorism," *World & I*, January 2002.

Robert Fisk "We Get the Arab Leaders We Deserve," *New Statesman,* October 16, 2000.

Bibliography

Graham E. Fuller — "Longing for a 'Reasonable Arab World,'" *Middle East Quarterly*, December 2000.

Gary C. Gambill — "The Balance of Terror: War by Other Means in the Contemporary Middle East," *Journal of Palestine Studies,* Autumn 1998.

Reuel Marc Gerecht — "Losing the Middle East? When It Comes to Peacemaking, Don't Trust the Saudis and Egyptians," *Weekly Standard*, March 18, 2002.

Farhad Kazemi — "Gender, Islam, and Politics," *Social Research,* Summer 2000.

As'ad Abu Khalil — "Problems with Current U.S. Policy," *Foreign Policy in Focus*, February 2000.

Charles A. Kimball — "Roots of Rancor: Examining Islamic Militancy," *Christian Century*, October 24, 2001.

Aharon Klieman — "Shifting Power in the Middle East," *World & I,* September 1999.

Michael G. Knapp — "Distortion of Islam by Muslim Extremists," *Military Intelligence Professional Bulletin*, July–September 2002.

Benjamin Netanyahu — "The Root Cause of Terrorism: It's Tyranny," *Wall Street Journal*, April 19, 2002.

Nawaf Obaid — "A Defense of the Saudis," *National Review*, May 10, 2002.

Ralph Peters — "A Remedy for Radical Islam," *Wall Street Journal*, April 29, 2002.

Daniel Pipes — "The Real 'New Middle East,'" *Commentary,* November 1998.

Allan Ramsay — "Saddam—'Father of Victories?'" *Contemporary Review*, August 2000.

Claudia Rosett — "Free Arabia," *Wall Street Journal*, August 14, 2002.

Mustafa Al Sayyid — "Mixed Message: The Arab and Muslim Response to 'Terrorism,'" *Washington Quarterly*, Spring 2002.

Lance Selfa — "Zionism: False Messiah," *International Socialist Review*, Spring 1998.

Dov Waxman — "Turkey and Israel: A New Balance of Power in the Middle East," *Washington Quarterly*, Winter 1999.

Index

Dayan, Moshe, 46
Declaration of Principles on Interim Self-Government Arrangements. *See* Oslo peace accord
democracy
  Arab media charades of, 63
  efforts at, in the Middle East, 29, 30, 173–74, 176–78
  fear of, 60–61
  ignorance of, 59–60
  Islam as incompatible with, 25–26
  Islamist political groups and, 172–73
  lack of, 21–22
    blaming the West for problems associated with, 61–62
    need for self-criticism on, 62–63
  legitimizing right to rule and, 21
  as U.S. policy goal in the Middle East, 170–71, 174–76
  U.S. support to Israel and, 160–61
  see also politics
Doron, Daniel, 145
Drake, Christine, 74
Dubai, 71

East Jerusalem, 43
economic growth, 145–46, 147
Economist (newspaper), 107
education system, 17–18
Egypt
  arrests for Satan worship in, 19–20
  democratic process in, 174
  Pan-Arabism and, 34
  water and, 78–79
  weapons of mass destruction and, 101–102, 104
Egyptian Organization for Human Rights, 174
elections, 172
  in Egypt, 174
  Palestinian issue and, 173–74
  in Turkey, 176–78
Emerson, Steven, 94
Esman, Milton, 21
Ethiopia, 78

Faruqi, Ismail, 87
Fatah, 141, 173
Faysal I (king of Syria), 33–34
Fergany, Nader, 19
France
  colonial rule by, 41
  Suez conflict and, 45
Freeman, Charles, 113
Free Officer Movement, 44
Friedman, Thomas, 113–14
Fukuyama, Francis, 20

Gaffney, Frank J., 165
Gargash, Anwar, 70
Gause, F. Gregory, 170
Gaza Strip
  Ariel Sharon's policy goals on, 51
  Six-Day War and, 46
  after war of 1948, 43
Gemayel, Bashir, 52
Golan Heights
  annexed by Israel, 47
  Six-Day War and, 46
Gold, Dore, 51, 53
Gorenberg, Gershom, 50
government. *See* democracy; politics
Great Britain
  colonial rule by, 41
  oil and, 70, 71
  Persian Gulf control by, 69
  Suez conflict and, 44, 45
Greater Syria, 33–34
Gulf War
  nuclear weapons and, 105–106

Hamas, 139–40, 172
Hanson, Victor Davis, 59, 160
Hashemite family, 33–34, 36, 44
Herold, Marc, 182
Hezbollah, 41
Hilali, A.Z., 28
Hinchcliffe, Peter, 40
Hogarth, David, 36
Hunter, Shireen, 22
Huntington, Samuel, 28, 94
Hussein, Saddam
  goals of, 193–94
  as a menace, 193
  U.S. call to remove from power, 165, 167–69
  U.S. dealings with, 167
  see also Iraq

ibn Saud, Abdul Aziz, 23
illiteracy, 17
immigration, 66–67, 75–76
International Atomic Energy Agency (IAEA), 99
International Institute of Islamic Thought, 87
Iran
  conflict with Iraq, 38–39
  oil and, 69, 71
  Pan-Arabism and, 37–38

Sudan, 25
Suez Canal Company, 44
Suez War (1956), 44–45
suicide attacks, 140, 141–42, 143
suicide bombings, 138–39
Sullivan, Antony T., 94
SUSTAIN (Stop U.S. Tax-funded Aid to Israel Now!), 191
Suter, Keith, 28
Syria
 Pan-Arabism and, 33–34
 water shortage and, 80
 weapons of mass destruction and, 100–101, 104

Tenet, George, 55
terrorism
 change in leadership and, 54
 history of Palestinian, 122–23
 Islam denounces, 95–97
 Palestinian campaigns against Israel, 138–40
 Palestinian legitimization of, 140–41
 permanent Israeli occupation could end, 124–25
 Saudi Arabia as fostering, 113–15
 U.S. philosophy on, 186
 Yasser Arafat and, 55–56, 57, 123–24, 126, 127–28
 see also September 11th terrorist attack; war on terrorism
Tigris-Euphrates Valley, 75, 77–78
Tracinski, Robert, 122
True Path Party, 176
Turkey
 democratic process in, 176–78
 water shortage and, 77, 78

Umayyads, the, 22
UN Global Conference Against Racism (2001), 191
United Nations (UN), 42–43, 46, 117
United Nations Special Commission (UNSCOM), 99
United States
 aid and support to Israel
  arms shipments and, 189
  as different than aid to other countries, 187–88
  indirect aid and, 188–89
  Israeli role as military stronghold and, 190
  reasons for, 160–62, 163–64
  as self-serving, 152–53
 Arab immigration to, 66–67
 Ariel Sharon's policies and, 53
 call for regime change in Iraq, 165, 167–69
 Gulf oil production and, 70, 71
 Islamist groups on, 173
 Middle East foreign policy
  Arab misunderstanding on, 64–65
  need for change in, 185–86
  not going to war with Iraq and, 193–95
  promoting democracy, 170–71, 174–76
  as self-serving, 171–72
 Muslims in. *See* Muslim Americans
 risk of weapons of mass destruction to, 104–105
 self-delusion by, 184–85
 television program on Israel in, 132
 see also war on terrorism; West, the
United States Agency for International Development (USAID), 170
USA Patriot Act (2001), 184
U.S. Foreign Assistance Act, 188

violence. *See* terrorism

Wahhabism, 23–24, 113
Wahaj, Siraj, 86
War of 1948, 43–44
war on terrorism
 changing international role of United States and, 185–86
 civilians killed in, 182
 media on, 185
 myths of, 179–84
 need for, 159
 war with Iraq diverting U.S. from, 194
Wassil, Nasr Farid, 19
water shortage
 causes of conflict over, 75–76
 future of conflicts over, 80–81
 Jordan-Yarmuk basin and, 79–80
 Middle East geography and, 74–75
 in the Nile Basin, 78–79
 political tensions from, 76–77
 in the Tigris-Euphrates Valley, 77–78
weapons of mass destruction
 Arab defiance on, 102–103
 Egypt and, 101–102
 Gulf War and, 105–106
 Iraq and, 99, 166–67, 193–95
 Israel and, 98–99, 105
 Libya and, 101
 risks to U.S. interests and, 104–105
 Syria and, 100–101
 U.S. inspections of Iraq and, 195
Weaver, Mary Ann, 89